FREE VIDEO   FREE   FREE VIDEO

Essential Test Tips Video from Trivium Test Prep

Dear Customer,

Thank you for purchasing from Trivium Test Prep! We're honored to help you prepare for your Praxis exam.

To show our appreciation, we're offering a **FREE *Praxis Essential Test Tips* Video by Trivium Test Prep**.* Our video includes 35 test preparation strategies that will make you successful on the Praxis. All we ask is that you email us your feedback and describe your experience with our product. Amazing, awful, or just so-so: we want to hear what you have to say!

To receive your **FREE *Praxis Essential Test Tips* Video**, please email us at 5star@ triviumtestprep.com. Include "Free 5 Star" in the subject line and the following information in your email:

1. The title of the product you purchased.
2. Your rating from 1 – 5 (with 5 being the best).
3. Your feedback about the product, including how our materials helped you meet your goals and ways in which we can improve our products.
4. Your full name and shipping address so we can send your **FREE *Praxis Essential Test Tips* Video**.

If you have any questions or concerns please feel free to contact us directly at 5star@triviumtestprep.com.

Thank you!

- Trivium Test Prep Team

*To get access to the free video please email us at 5star@triviumtestprep.com, and please follow the instructions above.

Praxis II English Language Arts Content Knowledge (5038) Study Guide

Review Book with Practice Test Questions for the Praxis ELA Exam

About the Authors

Dr. Judith R. Coats has twenty-two years of experience teaching English in higher education and at the high school level. Specializing in grammar and writing, she has taught Advanced Grammar, Fundamentals of Composition, Composition and Research, and Research Writing. She has also taught directed study courses online including Short Story and Young Adult Literature.

Dr. Coats earned her MA in English/Writing from Northern Michigan University in 2002 and her EdD in 2012 at Regent University in Virginia. There, her research focused on the Reed and Kellogg System of sentence diagramming and implementing the system in higher education with adult learners. She has taught in Haiti and Canada and is the author of several published articles and works of fiction.

Pamela VanderVeen has thirty-one years of classroom experience in reading and high school English. She began her career as a Title 1 Reading teacher and went on to teach fourth grade for three years and high school English for twenty-six years. Currently, she is Coordinator of Curriculum, Instruction, and Assessment at the Forbush School in Baltimore, Maryland, where she supports teachers with curriculum materials, familiarizes teachers with the Common Core Standards, helps them implement related curricula, monitors classroom instruction, and provides progress assessments.

Ms. VanderVeen was awarded her MA in Education from the University of Delaware in 1995. She has written and published educational materials for twenty-four years, including instructional units, activities, and practice assessments. She has written ancillary materials for many texts, conducted editorial work, and correlated materials to state standards.

Table of Contents

Online Resources i

Introduction iii

ONE: Reading 1
  LITERATURE 2
  INFORMATIONAL TEXTS AND RHETORIC 45

TWO: Language Use and Vocabulary 65
  GRAMMAR 65
  VOCABULARY 97
  DIVERSITY 102
  RESEARCH-BASED ACQUISITION 104

THREE: Writing, Speaking, and Listening 111
  WRITING 111
  SPEAKING AND LISTENING 125
  TEACHING AND ASSESSING COMMUNICATION 133

FOUR: Practice Test 141
  ANSWER KEY 177

Online Resources

To help you fully prepare for your Praxis English Language Arts: Content Knowledge (5038) exam, Cirrus includes online resources with the purchase of this study guide.

PRACTICE TEST

In addition to the practice test included in this book, we also offer an online exam. Since many exams today are computer based, getting to practice your test-taking skills on the computer is a great way to prepare.

FLASH CARDS

A convenient supplement to this study guide, Cirrus's flash cards enable you to review important terms easily on your computer or smartphone.

CHEAT SHEETS

Review the core skills you need to master the exam with easy-to-read Cheat Sheets.

FROM STRESS TO SUCCESS

Watch From Stress to Success, a brief but insightful YouTube video that offers the tips, tricks, and secrets experts use to score higher on the exam.

REVIEWS

Leave a review, send us helpful feedback, or sign up for Cirrus promotions—including free books!

Access these materials at:

www.cirrustestprep.com/praxis-5038-online-resources

Introduction

Congratulations on choosing to take the Praxis English Language Arts (ELA): Content Knowledge (5038) exam! By purchasing this book, you've taken the first step toward becoming an English language arts teacher.

This guide will provide you with a detailed overview of the Praxis, so you know exactly what to expect on test day. We'll take you through all the concepts covered on the test and give you the opportunity to test your knowledge with practice questions. Even if it's been a while since you last took a major test, don't worry; we'll make sure you're more than ready!

WHAT IS THE PRAXIS?

Praxis Series tests are a part of teaching licensure in approximately forty states. Each state uses the tests and scores in different ways, so be sure to check the certification requirements in your state by going to www.ets.org/praxis/states. There, you will find information detailing the role of the Praxis tests in determining teaching certification in your state, what scores are required, and how to transfer Praxis scores from one state to another.

WHAT'S ON THE PRAXIS?

The content in this guide will prepare you for the Praxis English Language Arts: Content Knowledge (5038) exam. This multiple-choice test assesses whether you possess the knowledge and skills necessary to become a secondary school English language arts teacher. You have a maximum of 150 minutes to complete the entire test. The test always has a total of 130 multiple-choice questions; however, the number of questions specific to each subject is approximate (see the following table).

Praxis ELA: Content Knowledge (5038) Content

Concepts	Approximate Number of Questions	Percentage
Reading	49	38 percent
Language Use and Vocabulary	33	25 percent
Writing, Speaking, and Listening	48	37 percent
Total	**always 130**	**150 minutes**

You will answer approximately forty-nine multiple-choice questions (38 percent of the test) related to reading. The reading section focuses on two types of reading sources: literature and informational texts. The former will require knowledge of major works and authors from around the world as well as historical movements in literature. Questions will explore literary genres and their major forms; literary elements, poetic devices, and their contributions to a text; and reading and research strategies. The latter requires an understanding of how authors develop a written argument through textual evidence, diction, structure, appeals, and other rhetorical strategies.

You will answer approximately thirty-three multiple-choice questions (25 percent of the test) related to language use and vocabulary. Generally, this section assesses your ability to follow the conventions of standard American English, including grammar, mechanics, and syntax. You should also be able to use various techniques, such as context clues and syntactical knowledge, to determine the meaning of words. Be aware of how various references, such as the dictionary, thesaurus, or encyclopedia, promote language use. Questions will also explore teaching strategies that reinforce vocabulary and language development and how those strategies can be implemented in a classroom.

You will answer approximately forty-eight multiple-choice questions (37 percent of the test) related to writing, speaking, and listening. The test will cover different types of writing, their distinctions, and their purposes. You should understand the characteristics of effective writing, research, speech delivery, and oral communication. Be aware of strategies for instructing students in effective communication, conducting research appropriately, and integrating the components of coherent writing into their work.

HOW IS THE PRAXIS SCORED?

The multiple-choice questions are equally weighted. Keep in mind that some multiple-choice questions are experimental questions for the purpose of the Praxis test writers and will not count toward your overall score. However, since those questions are not indicated on the test, you must respond to every question. There is no penalty for guessing on Praxis tests, so be sure to eliminate answer choices and answer every question. If you still do not know the answer, guess; you may get it right!

Your score report will be available on your Praxis account for one year, but you can also opt for a paper report. The score report includes your score and the passing score for the states you identified as score recipients. Your score will be available immediately after the test.

HOW IS THE PRAXIS ADMINISTERED?

The Praxis Series tests are administered as computerized tests and are offered at testing centers across the nation. To find a testing center near you, go to http://www.ets.org/praxis/register. At this site, you can create a Praxis account, check testing dates, register for a test, or find instructions for registering via mail or phone. The Praxis website allows you to take a practice test to acclimate yourself to the computerized format.

On the day of your test, be sure to bring your admission ticket (which is provided when you register) and photo ID. The testing facility will provide pencils and erasers and an area outside of the testing room to store your personal belongings. You are allowed no personal effects in the testing area. Cell phones and other electronic, photographic, recording, or listening devices are not permitted in the testing center at all, and bringing those items may be cause for dismissal, forfeiture of your testing fees, and cancellation of your scores. For details on what is and is not permitted at your testing center, refer to http://www.ets.org/praxis/test_day/bring.

ABOUT CIRRUS TEST PREP

Cirrus Test Prep study guides are designed by current and former educators and are tailored to meet your needs as an incoming educator. Our guides offer all of the resources necessary to help you pass teacher certification tests across the nation.

Cirrus clouds are graceful, wispy clouds characterized by their high altitude. Just like cirrus clouds, Cirrus Test Prep's goal is to help educators "aim high" when it comes to obtaining their teacher certification and entering the classroom.

ABOUT THIS GUIDE

This guide will help you master the most important test topics and also develop critical test-taking skills. We have built features into our books to prepare you for your tests and increase your score. Along with a detailed summary of the test's format, content, and scoring, we offer an in-depth overview of the content knowledge required to pass the test. Our sidebars provide interesting information, highlight key concepts, and review content so that you can solidify your understanding of the exam's concepts. Test your knowledge with sample questions and detailed answer explanations in the text that help you think through the problems on the exam, and with two full-length practice tests that reflect the content and format of the Praxis. We're pleased you've chosen Cirrus to be a part of your professional journey.

Reading

In today's English classrooms, teachers are equipping their students for success by devoting the bulk of their time to reading and discussing a variety of texts. This interactive approach to reading instruction (as opposed to a lecture-based approach, for example) is based on the theory of **constructivism**: as readers become involved with a text, they construct meaning through an active process of integrating what they are reading with their own reactions, knowledge, beliefs, and ideas.

The constructivist perspective is linked to studies in cognition; constructivists are interested in the thinking processes readers use to comprehend and interpret text. Many variables affect how a reader understands what he or she is reading including prior knowledge of the subject of the text, mental schemas and assumptions, and motivation levels. For example, the extent of a reader's experience with narrative structures might determine how effectively he or she can follow the events of a new story; readers who are familiar with the logical structures of an argument may be better able to process the reasoning of persuasive text; the reader who takes time to understand, revisit, and reflect on the piece of writing will likely have a deeper understanding of it than a more casual reader.

> **DID YOU KNOW?**
>
> **Cognition** is thinking; it encompasses the mental processes of understanding, reasoning, and knowing.

Constructivism also places emphasis on how the social and cultural backgrounds of readers influence how they understand and experience a text. For example, when reading the introduction to Alice Walker's short story "Everyday Use," white, middle class students who have grown up in the urban areas of northern states may struggle to relate to a mom who wears overalls and kills hogs. Generally, students who have experiences that, in some way, mirror the details of the text are better able to make meaningful personal connections with it.

In addition, constructivists emphasize that most learning and understanding occurs in a social context: that is, readers are better able to construct interpretations of and find meaning in a text when they have opportunities to engage in dialogue with others about that text. In an English classroom, for instance, a teacher might initiate a discussion with an open-ended, text-based question. Student A may answer with an assertion and a simple explanation. Then, Student B might disagree and explain her reasoning. Student A can then respond by elaborating on his original idea. Other students listening to this collision of thought can begin to examine the merits of each position and perhaps, after a prompt from the teacher, return to the text to look for textual evidence to contribute to the discussion. Students might even revise their original interpretations when they are confronted by the ideas of others. During such open discussions, students not only deepen their understandings of the text but also get to practice thinking critically and communicating effectively.

> **DID YOU KNOW?**
>
> **Schemas** are cognitive connections that are molded in an individual's mind over time and shape a person's worldview. Knowledge is stored as a complex web of schemas; learning occurs when new information links to existing schematic networks.

The main implication of constructivist theory for reading instruction is that teachers should design lessons that require students both to respond to and interact with text as they read and to interact with each other through authentic discussion and debate. Activities that provide opportunities for students to process, share, and examine their thoughts about texts are essential.

LITERATURE

Not all texts can be classified as literature. In vague terms, creative writers write to entertain; however, the goal of authors, poets, and playwrights is rarely that simple. Literary texts, especially when written well, have the capacity to create an experience for the reader by reflecting through language some universal aspect of life or human nature. The power of language—in the form of literature—to elicit interpretive responses in readers has given rise to the field of **literary criticism**, the formal study, analysis, and evaluation of literary texts.

LITERARY TRADITIONS

The field of literary criticism continually shapes English literature courses. A critical approach to literature—which takes into account historical, philosophical, cultural, and social traditions—lends itself easily to valuable interdisciplinary instruction. Effective teachers set a clear purpose, some guiding questions, and a logical structure for their course. They also select course texts purposefully, taking into account each text's origin, relevance, and canonicity.

American literature is usually studied chronologically or thematically, beginning with texts from the early colonists, who wrote about exploration, Native American relations, and life in the New World. This early Colonial Period (1620 – 1750) was followed by the Age of Revolution (1750 – 1815) with texts centered on the colonies' quest for independence. Following the revolution, Romantic/Transcendental Period (1800 – 1865) writers placed an emphasis on the power of imagination, the celebration of individualism, and a love of nature in an effort to break away from British literary tradition. Authors of the Realistic Period (1855 – 1910) sought to portray American life as it truly was and emphasized verisimilitude (likeness to life). The Realistic Period included Civil War writers, Regionalists, and Naturalists. Next, in the Modern Period (1900 – 1950) writers wrote about the World Wars, alienation, the Roaring Twenties, the Depression, and the changing world. Writers of the Harlem Renaissance were also considered part of the Modernist Period. Writers of the Postmodern Period (1950 – present) have challenged traditional values and structures and shown heightened concern for social issues. Across the centuries, the prevailing themes of American literature include individualism, the American dream/reality, cultural diversity, tolerance, and the search for identity.

> **DID YOU KNOW?**
>
> A **canon** in literature is a group of works that are considered to be culturally, artistically, or historically significant. *Canonicity*, therefore, refers to whether the work is considered important enough to be a part of the broad literature canon.

Table 1.1. is a list of authors and literary periods. Please keep in mind that this list is an approximation; it is not exhaustive, nor is it fixed. Scholars are not necessarily in agreement on which author belongs to which period.

Table 1.1. Noteworthy American Authors and Titles

Period	Author	Titles
The Colonial Period (1620 – 1750)	William Bradford	*Of Plymouth Plantation*
	Anne Bradstreet	*The Tenth Muse Lately Sprung Up in America...* and other various poetry
	Olaudah Equiano	*The Interesting Narrative of the Life of Olaudah Equiano*
	Jonathan Edwards	"Sinners in the Hands of an Angry God"
The Age of Revolution (1750 – 1815)	Thomas Paine	*Common Sense* and various essays
	Thomas Jefferson	various essays and speeches
	Benjamin Franklin	*Poor Richard's Almanack*

Table 1.1. Noteworthy American Authors and Titles (continued)

Period	Author	Titles
The Romantic Period (1800 – 1865)	Edgar Allan Poe	"The Raven," "The Tell-Tale Heart," other various short stories and poetry
	James Fenimore Cooper	*The Last of the Mohicans*
	Sojourner Truth	"Ain't I a Woman"
	Washington Irving	"The Devil and Tom Walker"
	Emily Dickinson	"I'm Nobody! Who Are You?" and other various poetry
	Nathaniel Hawthorne	*The Scarlet Letter*
	Herman Melville	*Moby Dick*
Transcendentalism (1830 – 1865)	Walt Whitman	"Song of Myself" and "Oh Captain! My Captain!"
	Ralph Waldo Emerson	*Self-Reliance* and *The American Scholar*
	Henry David Thoreau	*Walden* and *Civil Disobedience*
Realism (1855 – 1900)	William Dean Howells	editor of *Atlantic Monthly* and *Harper's Magazine*
	Mark Twain	*The Adventures of Huckleberry Finn* and various essays
Civil War Period (1855 – 1870)	Mary Chesnut	*Diary of Mary Chesnut*
	Abraham Lincoln	"The Gettysburg Address"
	Frederick Douglass	*My Bondage and My Freedom*
Regionalism (1865 – 1920)	Willa Cather	*My Antonia*
	William Faulkner	*Absalom! Absalom!*
Naturalism (1880 – 1915)	Jack London	*The Call of the Wild*
	Kate Chopin	*The Awakening*
	John Steinbeck	*The Grapes of Wrath*
The Modern Period (1910 – 1945)	Robert Frost	*A Boy's Will, North of Boston*
	E.E. Cummings	various poetry
	Sinclair Lewis	*Babbit, Main Street*
	Edith Wharton	*The Age of Innocence*
	Flannery O'Connor	*Wise Blood*, various short stories
	Katherine Porter	*Ship of Fools*, various short stories
	Ezra Pound	*Ripostes, Hugh Selwyn Mauberley*

Period	Author	Titles
The Modern Period (1910 – 1945)	Eudora Welty	*The Optimist's Daughter*
	Tennessee Williams	"A Streetcar Named Desire," "The Glass Menagerie," other plays
	Margaret Mitchell	*Gone with the Wind*
Harlem Renaissance (1920 – 1930)	Langston Hughes	various poems
	Countee Cullen	various poems
	Zora Neale Hurston	*Their Eyes Were Watching God*
Lost Generation (1920 – 1950)	Gertrude Stein	*The Autobiography of Alice B. Toklas, Tender Buttons*, and other works
	Ernest Hemingway	*The Old Man and the Sea, A Farewell to Arms*, and *For Whom the Bell Tolls*
	T.S. Eliot	"The Love Song of J. Alfred Prufrock" and other poetry and plays
	F. Scott Fitzgerald	*The Great Gatsby, Tender is the Night*
Contemporary Literature (1950 – present)	J.D. Salinger	*The Catcher in the Rye*
	Alice Walker	*The Color Purple*
	Cormac McCarthy	*The Road, No Country for Old Men*
	Martin Luther King	various speeches and letters
	Sandra Cisneros	*The House on Mango Street*
	Joseph Heller	*Catch-22*
	Don DiLillo	*White Noise*
	Richard Wright	*Black Boy*
	John Updike	*Rabbit, Run*
	Amy Tan	*The Joy Luck Club*
	Kurt Vonnegut	*Slaughterhouse-Five, Cat's Cradle*
	Nikki Giovanni	*Black Feeling, Black Talk, Black Judgement*; other works
	August Wilson	*The Pittsburgh Cycle*
	Ursula K. Le Guin	*The Left Hand of Darkness*

British literature includes the literary texts of the British Isles. Generally, the literature of Great Britain reflects changes in culture and thinking over time and is, therefore, usually studied chronologically by period. The first period of recorded texts is the Anglo-Saxon Period (449 – 1066). People of this era shared epic poems about courageous heroes; their concern was morality and goodness.

The Medieval Period (1066 – 1485) followed with a focus on religion, romance, diversity, and chivalry. Morality plays and folk ballads were popular during this time. Next was the Renaissance Period (1485 – 1660), which included the Elizabethan Age of great English drama and public theatres. People were interested in love and in the nature of human beings. During the Restoration Period (1660 – 1798), comedies of manners, essays, and satires were popular; this period included the Age of Sensibility and is also referred to as the Enlightenment, a title that reflects the cultural emphasis on logic, reason, and rules. As a reaction to this emphasis on rational thought, the Romantic Period (1785 – 1830) began. People believed truth was found in nature and unrestrained imaginative experience. Many poems and lyrical ballads were written, as well as imaginative gothic horror novels. The Victorian Period (1832 – 1900) was a time of social, religious, and economic turmoil. The growing middle class enjoyed the benefits of mass printing in the form of novels and magazines. Elegies were also popular. Writers of the Modern Era (1900 – 1945) preferred novels related to social issues in which characters experienced epiphanies. Some novelists played with style by writing in a stream of consciousness. By the late twentieth century, novelists became interested in psychology and close observation of human behaviors and relationships.

Table 1.2. Noteworthy British Authors and Titles

Period	Author	Titles
The Anglo-Saxon Period (449 – 1066): [Old English Period]		*Beowulf*
The Medieval Period (1066 – 1485): [Middle English Period]	Chaucer	*The Canterbury Tales*
	Sir Thomas Mallory	*Le Morte d'Arthur*
		Everyman
The Renaissance Period (1485 – 1660): [Neoclassical Period]	Christopher Marlow	various poems
	Edmund Spenser	various poems
	William Shakespeare	various plays
Elizabethan Age Writers	John Donne	various poems
	Ben Johnson	various poems
	John Milton	*Paradise Lost*
The Restoration Period (1660 – 1798)	Samuel Pepys	diaries
	Alexander Pope	various poems
	Samuel Johnson	various poems
	Jonathan Swift	*Gulliver's Travels*
The Age of Sensibility	various authors	gothic novels

Period	Author	Titles
The Enlightenment	Francis Bacon	various essays
	John Locke	various essays
	Jean Jacques Rosseau	various essays
Metaphysical Poets	John Donne	various poems
	Andrew Marvell	various poems
	George Herbert	various poems
The Romantic Period (1785 – 1830)	William Wordsworth	various poems
	John Keats	various poems
	Lord Byron	various poems
	Percy Bysshe Shelley	various poems
	Samuel Taylor Coleridge	"The Rime of the Ancient Mariner"
	Mary Shelley	*Frankenstein*
The Victorian Period (1832 – 1900)	Alfred Tennyson	various poems
	Robert Browning	various poems
	Elizabeth Browning	various poems
	Rudyard Kipling	various poems
	Charles Dickens	*A Tale of Two Cities*
	Thomas Hardy	*Return of the Native*
The Modern Era (1900 – 1945)	Joseph Conrad	*Lord Jim* and *The Heart of Darkness*
	D. H. Lawrence	*Women in Love*
	George Orwell	*Shooting an Elephant*
	Bernard Shaw	*Pygmalion*
	Virginia Woolf	*Mrs. Dalloway* and various stories
	Katherine Mansfield	various stories
	Doris Lessing	various stories
	William Yeats	various poems
	T. S. Eliot	various poems
	Dylan Thomas	various poems

World literature can refer to all national literatures, but the term usually refers to a group of important representative literary works that are circulated and studied around the globe. These works come from a variety of areas including France,

Africa, India, China, Japan, ancient Greece and Rome, and the ancient Middle East. Such works include *The Epic of Gilgamesh* (the Fertile Crescent), *The Odyssey*, Greek tragedies, *The Tale of Genji* (Japan), *Journey to the West* (China), and *Things Fall Apart* (Africa). The emphasis of study in a world literature course or unit is usually the cultural, philosophical, and historical context of the literary works. Sometimes, the works are grouped by commonalities, as in the study of lyrical poetry, creation myths, or hero tales; other times selections are chosen to highlight how certain literary ideas have moved across cultures.

Non-Western literature is from any country other than the United States, Western Europe, and ancient Greece and Rome. Some examples of authors from non-Western countries are Isabel Allende and Gabriel Garcia Marquez from Latin America, Bessie Head and Ngugi WaThiong'o from Africa, and Rumi of Persia. Usually studies of non-Western literature focus on the contrasts between Western and non-Western perspectives with the goal of achieving familiarity with the rich histories, intellectual traditions, and cultural beliefs represented in the works. Often, studies emphasize both the interconnectedness and the diversity of cultures.

Young adult literature includes texts written for adolescent readers, youth up to age twenty-five. Usually, the texts are fictional, problem novels, and romances; however nonfiction, poetry, graphic novels, and comics are popular as well. Young adult literature aims to be relevant to young people, to address their needs and interests, and to allow them to see themselves in the stories. Typical themes involve dealing with social issues, answering moral and ethical questions, relating to others, finding acceptance while maintaining uniqueness, and discovering one's individual identity.

SAMPLE QUESTIONS

Select the appropriate answer choice based on the following description of a text.

1) This text provides a factually accurate account of the Civil War; in writing it, the author observed and recorded descriptions of and reactions to events of the war. The text is subjective, told from the first person point of view, and filled with the details that impressed the writer. As it reveals the personal responses of a person in the midst of turmoil, it offers insights into the occurrences and effects of the Civil War.

   What text does the passage describe?

   A.   "Oh Captain! My Captain!"

   B.   *The Diary of Mary Chestnut*

   C.   *The Gettysburg Address*

   D.   *My Bondage and My Freedom*

   Answers

   A.   Incorrect. "Oh Captain! My Captain!" is a poem by Walt Whitman about the loss of President Lincoln; it is not really about the Civil War itself.

B.   **Correct.** *The Diary of Mary Chestnut* is Mary Chestnut's diary; during the Civil War, she recorded her observations and thoughts about the war in it.

C.   Incorrect. *The Gettysburg Address* is a speech given by President Lincoln during the Civil War.

D.   Incorrect. *My Bondage and My Freedom* is Frederick Douglass' autobiography. Douglass describes his life as a slave, his journey to freedom, and his early work as an Abolitionist.

2)   **When planning lessons on a given literary text, an English teacher often includes information about the type of text. For example, when teaching Thomas Gray's "Elegy Written in a Country Churchyard," she introduces the definition and characteristics of elegies. In addition, she will often engage students in discussions or activities that explore how people respond to loss and grief. By applying these best practices, the teacher hopes to improve the comprehension levels of her students.**

The author of the preceding passage is pointing out that

A.   teachers who provide background information recognize that having prior knowledge about the text structure and topic improves student comprehension.

B.   teachers who follow the curriculum in addition to having students answer the questions in the teacher's manual are able to increase student knowledge about literature and individual texts.

C.   instruction in different kinds of poetry, including Romantic poetry and the poetry of the ancient Greeks, increases student literacy.

D.   instruction that spends inordinate amounts of time on background information detracts from the effect of the text and does not give students sufficient time to examine their responses or to discuss their interpretations.

Answers

A.   **Correct.** Constructivism is based on the belief that readers use their prior knowledge to construct meanings. Teachers, therefore, must provide students with the background information necessary for them to understand the text.

B.   Incorrect. The purpose of teaching background information is not to gain knowledge for knowledge's sake but to help students more effectively construct meaning.

C.   Incorrect. In this choice, the teacher is giving students the information they will need to comprehend poetry in general, not the specific poem identified.

D.   Incorrect. Without an understanding of the text structures and subject matter, students will not know the purpose of the text and most likely will struggle to grasp the speaker's meaning.

3) **What kind of literature is represented in an English class that studies "Sonnet 29," "Sonnet 73," *Hamlet*, *Pygmalion*, and *A Modest Proposal*, among other selections?**

A. American literature

B. British literature

C. World literature

D. Non-Western literature

Answers

A. Incorrect. The selections are written by William Shakespeare, George Bernard Shaw, and Jonathan Swift, none of whom were American.

B. Correct. Shakespeare, Bernard Shaw, and Jonathan Swift were British writers.

C. Incorrect. While some of these texts might be included in a world literature class, the list of texts for such a course would also be much more diverse, including authors from several different countries or cultures.

D. Incorrect. None of these texts are non-Western.

4) **Which of the following is NOT a way that class discussions support the constructivist theory of reading instruction?**

A. They offer students a chance to hear the ideas of their fellow students and to increase their knowledge of diverse viewpoints.

B. They provide students practice with social interaction by forcing them to listen to others and respect alternative opinions.

C. They challenge students to use concrete evidence, which enhances their knowledge and memory of the text.

D. They give students the opportunity to express their interpretations, to consider any alternative viewpoints, and to examine their ideas in terms of the evidence that is mentioned.

Answers

A. Incorrect. Constructivists argue that an individual's social and cultural perspective influences his or her interpretation of literary texts.

B. Incorrect. Constructivists argue that learning most effectively occurs in a social environment.

C. Correct. A strong familiarity with the exact details of the text, while important, is less important to constructivists than the individual's personal understanding of the text.

D. Incorrect. During discussions, students learn to articulate their interpretations, consider alternative viewpoints, and examine their ideas in terms of the logic and evidence that is mentioned.

CONTEXTS

Context refers to both the historical and cultural time a text was written. The critical emphasis on context is based on the theory of situated cognition, which suggests that human activity is socially situated, unavoidably influenced by its social and cultural surroundings. Therefore, the choices humans make—including the choices an author makes about his or her work—must be understood in light of the circumstances that frame them. To truly understand a text, then, students must be aware of the social and cultural influences that were acting on the author as he or she wrote.

Cultural context refers to the literary, artistic, and musical movements that were going on at the time a work was written. *Civil Disobedience* by Henry David Thoreau exemplifies this point that an author's purposes are, at least to some degree, culturally responsive. Thoreau was a Romantic Transcendentalist influenced by Ralph Waldo Emerson's idea of self-reliance; he was profoundly disturbed by the concepts of majority rule and mandatory conformity to unjust laws. Thus, his purpose in writing *Civil Disobedience* was to persuade his readers to be self-reliant by following their own sense of right and wrong, even when that meant disregarding the law.

Historical context refers to the time the author was writing, which students must be able to distinguish from the setting of the story itself. The setting of Nathanial Hawthorne's *The Scarlet Letter*, for example, is seventeenth century Boston, a Puritan village of the Massachusetts Bay Colony in which conformity is expected as a way of preventing sin. However, to truly understand the author's work, students must know that Hawthorne actually wrote his novel in 1849. Like Thoreau, he was reacting to the ideas of Emerson and the Romantic Transcendentalists; he was interested in the early Women's Rights Movement, which asserted that women can be self-reliant, must have individual rights, and must not conform to practices that subjugated them. However, unlike Thoreau, Hawthorne was a Romantic *Anti*-Transcendentalist: he recognized the human capacity for individuality but also its capacity for darkness, sin, and evil. Hawthorne created a story that explored the admirable but lonely lifestyle of self-reliance, non-conformity, and individualism.

In planning reading instruction, teachers can implement a few context-related best practices in order to ensure students are getting as much as they can from their studies. First, effective teachers frame the study of a literary work with information about its context. Second, they integrate into this study some essential or life question that would make the study of the text more personally meaningful to students. (If the text is *Civil Disobedience*, for example, then the essential question of the unit of study could be the following: *When is non-conformity the right alternative?*) They may also include some additional guiding questions related to context: *How have the cultural-historical issues of the author's time influenced his or her artistic choices? How are the characters responding to and forming relationships within the social situation of the text, and how does this reflect the author's perspective on his or her own society?*

Effective teachers also incorporate a number of different techniques for teaching context. They may begin a context-based lesson by first having students activate prior knowledge, revisiting any previous English or history lessons that might contribute to their understanding of the text. Next, if time permits, they might assign a short research activity about the historical, cultural, and geographical context of a literary text to help students form the habit of making their own inquiries about background information. Alternatively, if pressed for time, the didactic approach of giving a short lecture on the context of a text can also be time well spent. Finally, they will return to discussions of context as their studies progress: students look for familiar historical or cultural ideas as well as any intertextual references that may help them gain a deeper understanding of the work.

SAMPLE QUESTIONS

The questions below refer to the first stanza of "The Sun Rising" by John Donne, 1572 – 1631.

> Busy old fool, unruly Sun,
> Why dost thou thus,
> Through windows, and through curtains, call on us?
> Must to thy motions lovers' seasons run?
> Saucy pedantic wretch, go chide
> Late school-boys and sour prentices,
> Go tell court-huntsmen that the king will ride,
> Call country ants to harvest offices;
> Love, all alike, no season knows nor clime,
> Nor hours, days, months, which are the rags of time.

5) **The conceit in the initial lines of the poem structures the rest of it. What is the best explanation of this conceit?**

   A. The couple wants to stay in bed rather than getting up because they are arrogant and think work is for common people, the "country ants."

   B. The couple is deeply offended by the intrusive sun's chiding remarks.

   C. The central argument of the first lines is that the light of day exposes people who are only interested in having fun at night.

   D. The sun is like a busy old fool because it forces people to get up and deal with everyday responsibilities as opposed to the eternal, significant aspects of life such as romantic love, which cannot be controlled by time.

Answers

   A. Incorrect. Conceits have nothing to do with status or social position; a conceit is an extended metaphor that reveals similarities between two things that, when shown together, seem to make an unusual comparison.

B. Incorrect. Although the speaker does describe the sun as intrusive and annoying, there is little evidence that the couple is deeply offended.

C. Incorrect. There is little evidence that the couple prefers to have fun at night, only that they do not like to behave according to the sun's changing status.

D. **Correct.** A conceit is a figure of speech that creates a parallel between two dissimilar things; in this case the parallel is drawn between the sun and a busy old fool, who annoys people by forcing them to get up in the morning.

6) **How would knowing that the "The Sun Rising" is a metaphysical poem enhance the reader's understanding of it?**

A. The reader will infer that the poem is about philosophical questions.

B. The reader will recognize that the figures of speech being used were common in the time the poem was written.

C. The reader will infer that the poem reflects the realistic concerns of twentieth century society.

D. The reader will interpret the poem as mocking religion and faith.

Answers

A. **Correct.** Philosophical concerns are often the subject of metaphysical poetry.

B. Incorrect. Figures of speech in metaphysical poetry, referred to as *conceits*, are not familiar; they are unusual and intended to be thought-provoking.

C. Incorrect. Metaphysical poetry was written in the seventeenth century.

D. Incorrect. Metaphysical poetry does deal with religious and spiritual matters; however, it does so in a serious, not mocking, way.

The following questions refer to the excerpt below from chapter one, "The Prison Door," of The Scarlet Letter *by Nathaniel Hawthorne.*

A throng of bearded men, in sad-colored garments and gray, steeple-crowned hats, intermixed with women, some wearing hoods, and others bareheaded, was assembled in front of a wooden edifice, the door of which was heavily timbered with oak, and studded with iron spikes.

The founders of a new colony, whatever Utopia of human virtue and happiness they might originally project, have invariably recognized it among their earliest practical necessities to allot a portion of the virgin soil as a cemetery, and another portion as the site of a prison.

7)   **What do the first two sentences of *The Scarlet Letter* reveal?**

   A.   the historical context of the text

   B.   the text is literary nonfiction

   C.   the author's purpose

   D.   the text is satirical prose

   Answers

   A.   Correct. The setting of the novel, the Massachusetts Bay Colony, seventeenth century Boston, is revealed by the way the people are dressed and mention of the new colony.

   B.   Incorrect. Although the description is vivid and poetic, the text is fictional; the characters are inventions of the author.

   C.   Incorrect. There isn't enough text to reveal the author's purpose in writing the novel.

   D.   Incorrect. The mocking tone in the second paragraph highlights the obvious fact that the new colony is not a "Utopia of human virtue" if its founders see the need for a prison. However, the mocking tone in itself does not make the text satirical. A satire points out the faults of a person or group in an effort to bring about change; the narrator in this case does not seek change but is, instead, simply commenting on the ironic state of the colony.

8)   **Why would an English teacher take time to explain Hawthorne's mention of a "Utopia of human virtue"?**

   A.   The teacher would be providing an explicit definition in order to avoid differences of opinion about what constitutes human virtue.

   B.   The English teacher would recognize that most students are unfamiliar with literary theory and require an explanation.

   C.   Students would have a better understanding of the setting of the novel if they knew that the Puritans wanted to establish a colony based on biblical principles, which they argued would constitute a perfect society.

   D.   The English teacher would be increasing the rigor of instruction by requiring students to think critically about the vocabulary and terminology.

   Answers

   A.   Incorrect. During discussions, teachers often seek to instigate healthy conflict about such things as human nature and virtue in order to illustrate the many broad perspectives that can influence literary interpretation.

   B.   Incorrect. The phrase "Utopia of human virtue" is not related to literary theory; it references an idea in the novel.

C. **Correct.** Students may not have prior knowledge about the intentions and views of Puritans in the New World, so elaborating on this idea will allow them to build background knowledge.

D. Incorrect. Critical thinking involves the examination of ideas and would require more than a simple introduction to the terminology.

LITERARY GENRES

Literature can be classified into genres and subgenres, categories of works that are similar in format, content, tone, or length. Most works fall into one of four broad genres: nonfiction, fiction, drama, and poetry. As students experience each genre throughout a school year, they should receive instruction that integrates all aspects of literacy. That is, students should experience not only reading practice in the genre, but also receive plentiful writing practice and numerous discussion opportunities to deepen their knowledge of the genre they are studying. Objectives for genre-studies lessons should integrate all levels of Bloom's taxonomy with the goal of equipping students to understand, interpret, discuss, and create works in various genres.

Bloom's taxonomy is a framework for understanding how humans learn. The first level of the taxonomy is **remembering**, the most basic skill a student can be asked to practice. Once they have mastered basic recall, students can be pushed toward **understanding** and **applying** new information and eventually to **analyzing**, **evaluating**, and **creating** texts using their knowledge.

NONFICTION

Nonfiction is a genre of prose writing that is defined by the use of information that is, to the best of the author's knowledge, true and accurate. This quality, though, should not be taken to mean that nonfiction is dry or uninspiring; in fact, nonfiction writing comes in many forms, most of which lend themselves to a degree of creativity and originality in terms of the presentation of the factual information. **Literary nonfiction** or **creative nonfiction**, for example, is a mix of expressive and informative writing that tells a true, verifiable, or documented story in a compelling, artistic way.

Nonfiction texts are written to inform, to reflect, and to entertain. They may take any of the following forms: an **essay** is a short work about a particular topic or idea; a **speech** is a short work with a specific purpose, intended to be presented orally in front of an audience; a **news article** is a short recounting of a particular story; a **biography** is a detailed, creative textual representation of a person's life; and an **autobiography** is an account of an individual's life, told by the individual him- or herself.

Students should be given opportunities to respond to nonfiction texts both in writing, perhaps in the form of a research report, and with interactive activities, like debates and discussions. When working with nonfiction texts, students should pay particular attention to voice and tone, text structures, and thoughts and ideas; students should discover through guided readings, group discussions, and independent reflection that these elements, when taken together with context, can reveal the author's purpose. The author's purpose is a guiding question in successful English classrooms, where the study of nonfiction is dedicated, at least in part, to helping students recognize and understand bias in literature.

Direct instruction should include the following:

▶ identifying the rhetorical strategies used in a nonfiction text

▶ summarizing a nonfiction text by stating the format, the author's purpose, the intended audience, and the central idea or argument

▶ evaluating the writer's assumptions, claims, appeals, and evidence

As students gain familiarity with the nonfiction genre, they should begin writing their own nonfiction pieces, applying their understanding of the author's purpose and using published texts as models for effective voice, tone, and organization.

FICTION

Fiction is a prose genre, made up of narratives whose details are not based in truth but are instead the creation of the author. Fiction is typically written in the form of novels and short stories. Many subgenres fall under the category of fiction.

Folklore is a set of beliefs and stories of a particular people, which are passed down through the generations. Folklore comes in many forms including **fables** (short stories intended to teach moral lessons), **fairy tales** (stories that involve magical creatures such as elves and fairies), **myths** (stories, often involving gods or demigods, that attempt to explain certain practices or phenomena), and **legends** (unverifiable stories that seem to have a degree of realism about them).

Science fiction is a category of fiction in which writers tell imaginative stories that are grounded in scientific and technological theories or realities. Often, science fiction writing explores ideas involving the future of humanity and its relationship with the universe or with technology. A subcategory of science fiction is **dystopian fiction**, in which authors explore social, cultural, and political structures in the context of a futuristic world.

Horror fiction is intended to impact the reader via the experiences of fear, paranoia, or disgust. Often, horror fiction involves paranormal or psychological content. **Mysteries and thrillers**, which may also arouse fear or paranoia, tend to be fast-paced and outcome-driven; they also tend to focus on human behaviors or relationships and not on paranormal activity.

Realistic fiction includes stories that are meant to be relatable for readers. Authors of realistic fiction strive to create a degree of verisimilitude in their writing, especially in the dialogue between characters. **Historical fiction** relies on realistic settings and characters from an earlier time to tell new stories.

Satire is any literary text that uses critical humor to reveal vice and foolishness in individuals and institutions. The purpose of satire is to improve the individual or institution being ridiculed. The literary or rhetorical devices that create satire include the use of sarcasm, irony, mockery, exaggeration, understatement, as well as an honest narrative/speaking voice that is dismayed or appalled by the object of the satire. Satire shows a subject to be ludicrous or wrong; at the same time, satire is an appeal to the reader's reason and sense of virtue.

In planning and facilitating fiction studies, teachers should place emphasis on important literary elements like plot, character, setting, and figurative language. In studying **plot**, students should focus on cause and effect relationships in order to understand why the events unfold as they do. When considering **setting**, students should identify the time and place where the story occurs as well as the cultural and social norms of the society that is being represented. Examination of **character** should involve discussion of how the characters' actions and motivations are influenced by their traits and values. **Figurative language**, discussed in more detail later, should be evaluated in order to uncover deeper meanings suggested by the author.

Teachers should engage students with fiction in a variety of ways. To encourage metacognition, effective teachers might have their students record personal responses to a text in a journal. They may have students compare plot development across a few different texts to illustrate the importance of various plot elements. A speaking and listening activity might require students to present interviews with the characters: one student may interview another (who is acting as one of the characters) and ask about his or her perspectives and motivations. Finally, in teaching fiction, teachers should also make time for students to write fiction. A meaningful assignment might parallel a class text; for example, if a class reads a story about a character maturing, students can write a narrative about one of their own experiences that left them more mature.

DRAMA

Drama is expressive writing that tells a story to an audience through the actions and dialogue of characters, which are brought to life by actors who play the roles onstage. Dramatic works, called **plays**, can be written in poetic or lyrical verse or in regular prose. Along with the **dialogue** between the characters, authors rely on **stage directions** to describe the sets and to give directions to the actors about what they are to do. In some plays, actors perform long speeches in which the characters explain their thinking about philosophical ideas or social issues. These **monologues** can be directed toward another character; if they are delivered as if there were nobody listening, they are called soliloquies (as in Shakespeare's famous "To be or not to be" **soliloquy** from *Hamlet*).

While studying a play, it is important to have students think about how both the stage directions and the dialogue contribute to the play's meaning. To jog their interest, especially in linguistically complex dramas like those of Shakespeare, effective teachers might have students watch video clips of actual performances.

Comparing specific scenes performed by different actors stimulates interest and can be used to introduce discussion about the multiple ways a scene can be interpreted. Additionally, students may benefit from having opportunities to act out scenes or speeches themselves, giving them a medium through which to express their own interpretations of the characters or action. To engage students in writing activities, a teacher may have students write their own scripts or write a research reports on the play's context, author, characters, or subject matter.

POETRY

Poetry is imaginative, expressive verse writing characterized by rhythm, unified and concentrated thought, concrete images, specialized language, and use of patterns. Different poetic forms utilize techniques and structures in unique ways.

A **line** is a unit of poetry. The lines of a poem can be separated by some sort of punctuation, meter, and/or rhyme. Although a line may be a unit of attention, it is usually not a unit of meaning.

A **stanza** is a group of lines followed by a space. Each stanza of a poem may have a specific number of lines; the lines are sometimes arranged in a pattern created by meter and/or a rhyme scheme. The pattern is often repeated in each stanza of the poem, although the pattern can be varied for effect. A stanza with two lines is a couplet; three lines, a tercet; four lines, a quatrain; five lines, a cinquain; and so on. Modern poems may have stanzas with varying lengths or no stanzas at all.

A **ballad** is a short narrative song about an event that is considered important; ballads are intended to be recited. They are characterized by a dramatic immediacy, focusing on one crucial situation or action that often leads to a catastrophe. Ballads are frequently about courage, love, political disputes, or military battles. The narrator in a ballad tends to be the public voice, speaking without personal judgment until it is interrupted by dialogue. Often, repetition is used to express emotion and reinforce the facts. Though the language of folk ballads is plain, usually without descriptive and figurative qualities, the emotional effect of the forceful language is nevertheless impactful. Literary ballads, like "The Rime of the Ancient Mariner" by Samuel Taylor Coleridge, are distinguished by rhythmic, poetic language and stanzas.

A **sonnet** is a lyrical poem composed of fourteen lines, usually written in iambic pentameter (for more information on iambic pentameter and meter, see section "Poetic Devices and Structure"). There are two main structural patterns that sonnets follow. The first is the Italian or Petrarchan pattern, which has eight lines (an **octave**) that follow an *abba abba* rhyme scheme, followed by six lines (a **seste**) that follow either a *cde cde* or a *cd cd cd* rhyme scheme. Usually, the octave in an Italian sonnet poses a question, describes a problem, or tells a story; the seste, then, answers the question, solves the problem, or comments

QUICK REVIEW

Consider what ideas about poetry Aristotle emphasizes when he says, "Poetry is finer and more philosophical than history; for poetry expresses the universal, and history only the particular."

on the story. The second pattern followed in sonnets is the English or Shakespearean pattern, which has three groups of four lines (called **quatrains**) ending with a rhyming **couplet**. The rhyme scheme of the English sonnet is *abab cdcd efef gg*. The quatrains present variations on a single theme, and the couplet is a concluding remark.

A **haiku** is a short poem format, created in Japan, that consists of three lines and seventeen syllables (divided into five, seven, and five between the lines).

Finally, a **villanelle** is usually nineteen lines long; it has five stanzas, each with three lines, and a final stanza of four lines. It includes a refrain—two lines that repeat throughout the poem following a specific pattern. Dylan Thomas' "Do Not Go Gentle into That Good Night" is a common example of a villanelle.

Teachers should incorporate into poetry lessons opportunities for students to respond both to the effect the poem had on them personally, as well as to the aesthetics of the poem itself. To introduce poetry and build interest for a poetry unit, an effective teacher might select an especially forceful poem, read it dramatically, and invite students to share their responses in a discussion forum.

When having students analyze poetry, it is best to promote multiple readings, model with a think-aloud of an analytical reading, provide copies of poems that students can annotate, and perhaps establish a process to follow for collaborative and independent reading of poems. Steps of the process might include:

1. an initial reading to experience the mood of the poem and the musicality of the language

2. a second reading to delineate the pauses and thought units and to identify the speaker

3. a third close reading to take marginal notes on the structure of the poem, the denotation and connotations of unfamiliar words, the impact of imagery and figurative language, and the meaning of confusing lines or phrases

4. a final reading to formulate some thematic ideas, drawn from the details

In conjunction with analyzing poems, students should have opportunity to present their original poetry in classroom "coffee houses." Depending on the literature course, students might also be taught the different poetic forms like sonnets and ballads, in addition to the characteristics of the different types of poetry, including metaphysical poetry or Romantic poetry.

SAMPLE QUESTIONS

The following questions refer to the poem "The Harlem Dancer" by Claude McKay.

Applauding youths laughed with young prostitutes
And watched her perfect, half-clothed body sway,

Her voice was like the sound of blended flutes

Blown by black players upon a picnic day.

She sang and danced on gracefully and calm,

The light gauze hanging loose about her form;

To me she seemed a proudly swaying palm

Grown lovelier for passing through a storm.

Upon her swarthy neck black, shiny curls

Profusely fell; and, tossing coins in praise,

The wine-flushed, bold-eyed boys, and even the girls,

Devoured her with their eager, passionate gaze;

But, looking at her falsely-smiling face

I knew her self was not in that strange place.

9) **What kind of poem is "The Harlem Dancer"?**

  A. a ballad

  B. a villanelle

  C. a sonnet

  D. a satire

  Answers

  A. Incorrect. A ballad tells a dramatic story about a specific situation; this poem describes a dancer, the people watching her, and what her smile suggests to the speaker.

  B. Incorrect. A villanelle is usually nineteen lines, has five stanzas, each with three lines, and a final stanza of four lines. It includes a refrain— two lines that repeat throughout the poem following a specific pattern.

  C. **Correct.** The poem develops a theme about the dancer, contains fourteen lines (three quatrains with an *abab*, *cdcd*, and *efef* rhyme scheme), and ends with a rhyming couplet that concludes the poem.

  D. Incorrect. A satire is a witty text that is written to improve some aspect of society or human behavior by showing it to be ineffective or foolish.

10) **Which statement best explains the conclusion of "The Harlem Dancer"?**

  A. The dancer may appear to be at ease as she dances and smiles, but in actuality, she feels contempt for the men who watch her dance.

  B. The men who watch the dancer have degraded her with their mockery.

  C. The men realize that the dancer is hiding her discomfort by smiling at them.

  D. The dancer maintains her dignity by playing a role and staying emotionally detached from the image she projects.

Answers

A.   Incorrect. The speaker of the poem makes no mention of how the dancer feels about the men.

B.   Incorrect. The speaker indicates that the men desire the dancer and express their appreciation of her by giving her money.

C.   Incorrect. The focus of the men is not on the feelings of the dancer, only on how she makes them feel.

D.   Correct. The speaker describes the dancer as "a proudly-swaying palm" and seems to realize that her smile is false, meant to conceal her lack of investment in what is going on around her.

CLOSE READING AND TEXTUAL EVIDENCE

At the high school level, the goal of reading instruction is to equip students to engage with texts critically and meaningfully. In order to achieve this goal, teachers must place emphasis on the close reading and text analysis skills that make this kind of authentic inquiry possible. Students should be encouraged to seek deeper meanings in a text by paying careful attention to the author's choices and by incorporating their own knowledge in order to draw inferences about the author's purpose and theme.

As students transition to the high school English classroom, they may be taking their first steps beyond comprehension and into analysis. Therefore, they may not be accustomed to reading beyond a surface level. As such, teachers must provide explicit instruction—most effectively via the practice of modelling (discussed later in this chapter)—about how to access the more complex ideas in a text. This involves instructing students in how to identify, analyze, and evaluate the author's broad and narrow choices, often referred to collectively as **author's craft**.

> **QUICK REVIEW**
>
> In *Walden*, Thoreau said, "No way of thinking or doing, however ancient, can be trusted without proof. What everybody echoes or in silence passes by as true today may turn out to be falsehood tomorrow, mere smoke of opinion, which some had trusted for a cloud that would sprinkle fertilizing rain on their fields." Consider how his statement relates to the concept of textual evidence.

When analyzing or evaluating author's craft, students will likely need to make **inferences**. Readers make inferences by using the information from the text in combination with their own experiential knowledge to fill in explanations for what is not stated explicitly in the text. As with close reading, students must receive instruction in making inferences in order to ensure that they are able to draw accurate conclusions about the text based on the evidence contained therein. Teachers should recognize that close reading and analysis skills are not natural abilities and therefore must be instilled through rigorous practice and meaningful discussions. While students may be tempted to reflect only on their own experiences of a text, an effective teacher will push them to constantly return to that text for evidence to support their claims.

SAMPLE QUESTION

The following question refers to this excerpt from "Criticisms and Interpretations" by T. Edgar Pemberton.

Bret Harte has himself told the story of how while occupied with his secretarial duties at the San Francisco Mint—and his literary work religiously carried on outside mint hours—George Barnes, a brother journalist, introduced him to a young man whose appearance was decidedly interesting. "His head" he writes, "was striking. He had the curly hair, the aquiline nose, and even the aquiline eye—an eye so eagle-like that a second lid would not have surprised me—of an unusual and dominant nature. His eyebrows were very thick and bushy. His dress was careless, and his general manner one of supreme indifference to surroundings and circumstances. Barnes introduced him as Mr. Sam Clemens, and remarked that he had shown a very unusual talent in a number of newspaper articles contributed over the signature of 'Mark Twain.'

11) **Which of the following can be inferred about Mark Twain based on supporting evidence?**

    A.   Mark Twain was arrogant. He was "striking" and had "an unusual and dominant nature."

    B.   Mark Twain did not try to impress others. "His dress was careless" and "his general manner [was] one of supreme indifference to surroundings and circumstances."

    C.   Mark Twain knew he would become a famous writer. He told others that "he had shown a very unusual talent in a number of newspaper articles…"

    D.   As a young writer, Mark Twain needed the help of other journalists. "George Barnes, a brother journalist …introduced him as Mr. Sam Clemens…"

Answers

    A.   Incorrect. An inference that Twain is arrogant cannot be made based on his dominant nature alone.

    B.   **Correct.** Mark Twain's careless dress and indifferent attitude support the inference that he was not trying to impress others. To make this inference, readers would use both the details of Twain's behavior and their knowledge of how people act when they want to make a good impression on others.

    C.   Incorrect. The person introducing Mark Twain said that Twain had shown unusual talent.

D.   Incorrect. Although Twain was introduced to Bret Hart, a writer, by the journalist George Barnes, the reader cannot necessarily infer that Twain needed help.

THEMES

Literary texts give concrete form to abstract, thematic ideas. Through a process of carefully examining the concrete details of a text, making evidence-based inferences, and thinking broadly about what these things suggest, readers can come to understand the theme of a literary work—the universal message that the author hopes to communicate through his or her artistic choices. By tracing themes across time, location, and culture, students of literature can begin to recognize some of the common experiences that define humanity such as love, loss, power, betrayal, growing old, and coming of age.

DID YOU KNOW?

A theme is an idea about some aspect of life or human nature.

To guide students through the process of determining a theme, effective teachers begin by providing instruction in how authors craft their ideas using the literary tools of plot, setting, character, figurative language, and point of view. Through close reading and analysis of author's choice, students then infer what the author could be suggesting about life or human nature.

To direct student attention to the thematic ideas of a text, effective teachers might:

- ▶ use two-column response journals to have students record interesting or memorable quotes and their reactions to them
- ▶ use focus questions that push students to make connections with the text, like *how did the author's use of _____ affect your reaction to the story? Why would the author want you to react that way? What about this story can you relate to your own life?*
- ▶ facilitate a discussion about the relationship between elements of the text including the plot and character development, tone, and setting
- ▶ have students record in their journals words or images that are repeated and elements and ideas that are paired or contrasted
- ▶ take the time not only to explain figurative language to students but also to provide instruction in the thought processes that make analysis possible
- ▶ explicitly identify signal words like "as a result" and discuss their meaning with students

By asking students to analyze the author's purpose using specific details, effective teachers push students to make connections, read closely, and improve their critical reading and thinking skills.

SAMPLE QUESTIONS

The following questions refer to sections of the introduction of "The Minister's Black Veil, A Parable," by Nathaniel Hawthorne.

The sexton stood in the porch of Milford meeting-house, pulling busily at the bell-rope. ...The first glimpse of the clergyman's figure was the signal for the bell to cease its summons. "But what has good Parson Hooper got upon his face?" cried the sexton in astonishment...

The cause of so much amazement may appear sufficiently slight. Mr. Hooper, a gentlemanly person, of about thirty, though still a bachelor, was dressed with due clerical neatness...

There was but one thing remarkable in his appearance. Swathed about his forehead, and hanging down over his face, so low as to be shaken by his breath, Mr. Hooper had on a black veil. On a nearer view it seemed to consist of two folds of crape, which entirely concealed his features, except the mouth and chin, but probably did not intercept his sight, further than to give a darkened aspect to all living and inanimate things. With this gloomy shade before him, good Mr. Hooper walked onward, at a slow and quiet pace, stooping somewhat, and looking on the ground, as is customary with abstracted men, yet nodding kindly to those of his parishioners who still waited on the meeting-house steps. But so wonder-struck were they that his greeting hardly met with a return. "I can't really feel as if good Mr. Hooper's face was behind that piece of crape," said the sexton.

"I don't like it," muttered an old woman, as she hobbled into the meeting-house. "He has changed himself into something awful, only by hiding his face."...

That mysterious emblem was never once withdrawn. It shook with his measured breath, as he gave out the psalm; it threw its obscurity between him and the holy page, as he read the Scriptures; and while he prayed the veil lay heavily on his uplifted countenance. Did he seek to hide it from the dread Being whom he was addressing? ...

Mr. Hooper had the reputation of a good preacher, but not an energetic one: he strove to win his people heavenward by mild, persuasive influences, rather than to drive them thither by the thunders of the Word...

The sermon which he now delivered...The subject had reference to secret sin, and those sad mysteries which we hide from our nearest and dearest, and would fain conceal from our own consciousness, even forgetting that the Omniscient can detect them. A subtle power was breathed into his words...

12) **What literary device is present in Hawthorne's introduction of "The Minister's Black Veil"?**

   A. allusion

   B. illusion

   C. symbolism

   D. cliché

Answers

A. Incorrect. An allusion is a reference to history, art, religion, or literature; the characters and events described in this passage are fictional, and there are no references to characters or events in other texts.

B. Incorrect. An illusion is a false perception or idea, neither of which are mentioned in the passage.

C. Correct. The black veil that the minister wears is a symbol. The veil stands out; it is the subject of the introduction, the focus of attention. Readers, like the parishioners described in the text, should be thinking about why the minister is wearing the veil as well as what Hawthorne might be suggesting with such an unusual scene.

D. Incorrect. A cliché is a statement that is obvious and overused. No clichés are used in the passage.

13) **Which cliché best describes the behavior of the minister?**

A. "What goes around comes around."

B. "Actions speak louder than words."

C. "No pain, no gain."

D. "There is nothing new under the sun."

Answers

A. Incorrect. Although the parishioners have a negative view of the veil, the minister doesn't seem bothered by their shock, and there is no mention of repayment or retribution for wrongs.

B. Correct. The minister's action of wearing the veil seems to have a greater effect than the minister's sermons.

C. Incorrect. The parishioners are shocked by the minister but are not in pain. At this point in the story, there is no evidence that the minister is in pain or that anything is being gained.

D. Incorrect. By wearing the veil, the minister is doing something new; he is behaving in an unfamiliar and strange way.

LITERARY ELEMENTS

Just as artists have the tools of color and shape to communicate ideas, so have writers their literary tools. These tools include point of view, plot, setting, character, tone, and figurative language. Each of these elements contributes to the overall idea that is developed in the text and, as such, can provide valuable insight into the theme of the work. **Point of view** is the perspective from which the action in a story is told. By carefully selecting a particular point of view, writers are able to control what their readers know. Most literature is written in either **first person** or **third person** point of view. With the first person or "I" point of view, the action is narrated by a character within the story, which can make it feel more believable and authentic to the reader. However, as a result of the first person point of view, the reader's knowledge and understanding are constrained by what the narrator notices and influenced by what the narrator thinks and values.

An author may, on the other hand, choose to tell the story from the third person point of view. A third person narrator is a voice outside the action of the story, an observer who shares what he or she knows, sees, or hears with the reader. A third person narrator might be fully omniscient (able to see into the minds of the characters and share what they are thinking and feeling), partially omniscient (able to see into the minds of just one or a few characters), or limited (unable to see into the minds of any of the characters and only able to share what can be seen and heard).

Plot structure is the way the author arranges the events of a narrative. In a conventional plot line, the story is structured around a **central conflict**, a struggle between two opposing forces. Conflicts in literature can be categorized in general terms as either internal or external, though most stories have a combination of both. Internal conflicts take place inside the main character's mind; he or she might be making a difficult decision, struggling with change, or sorting out priorities. External conflicts, on the other hand, occur when a character is in conflict with something or someone in the external world—the elements of nature, another character, supernatural forces, destiny, or society.

In a traditional plot structure, the author begins by introducing the **exposition**, important background information about the setting, the characters, and the current state of the world. Following the exposition, an **inciting incident** introduces the antagonist and establishes the conflict. As the story progresses, the conflict becomes more complicated and tension increases, moving the story toward a **climax** or turning point, in which the conflict reaches a crisis point. Finally, there is a **resolution** to the conflict, followed by **falling actions**, events that move the characters away from the conflict and into a new life.

In studying plot, students should be encouraged to focus on cause and effect relationships between events in the story and on the conflict and its resolution. By analyzing how the author chooses to resolve the conflict, the reader can gain a better understanding of the story's theme.

Setting is the geographical and chronological location of events in a story. When considering setting, students should examine how characters interact with their surroundings, how they are influenced by the societal expectations of that time and place, and how the location and time period impact the development of the story. Often, setting can seem inseparable from plot; therefore, a helpful question for beginning the discussion of setting is, *How would this story change if it were set in a different time or place?*

Character development is the process an author uses to create characters that are complex and, to some degree, believable. One way authors develop their characters is directly: they tell the reader explicitly what the character is like by describing traits and assigning values. Sometimes, authors might include the thoughts and feelings of the characters themselves, offering readers even more insight. Authors can also develop their characters indirectly by revealing their actions and interactions with others, sometimes including what one character says or thinks about another and allowing the reader to draw his or her own conclusions. Most authors use a combination of direct and indirect characterization; this ensures that readers know what they need to know while also providing opportunities for reflection and interpretation.

The **tone** of a literary work is created by the author's attitude toward the reader and toward the subject of the text. In a sense, it is the tone of voice he or she uses to speak to the reader. Depending on word choice, an author's tone can range anywhere from playful, familiar, or sincere to detached, sarcastic, or indifferent; it can be alarmed and forceful or philosophical and serious; it might be concerned or careless, saddened or overjoyed, triumphant or defeated. In any case, students should be encouraged to consider how the author uses language to communicate tone and what he or she is suggesting through language choice. Often, this line of questioning will reveal the author's attitude and, ultimately, the theme of the work.

Students should also be able to distinguish the author's tone from **mood**, the emotional atmosphere of a literary work, which shapes the reader's experience of the text. Mood is created through an interplay of the literary elements of plot, character, setting, point of view, tone, and figurative language. By examining the emotional effect of the author's choices, readers can further develop their understanding of the text's larger meaning.

SAMPLE QUESTIONS

14) **What is the difference between the mood of a literary text and the author's tone?**

A. Readers experience the mood of a text; while reading, readers respond emotionally to the text and feel the mood. On the other hand, readers simply recognize the author's tone or attitude toward his or her subject as something that exists apart from them.

B. Readers develop an understanding of how the characters feel, their moods, as well as the attitudes they express, their tone.

C. The mood of a text is fluid; it changes as the characters develop. The tone of a text is stable; it is created by the words and symbols of the text.

D. The mood of a text is understood at the end of a story and is created by how the conflict of the story is resolved. On the other hand, the reader recognizes the tone of a text right from the beginning.

Answers

A. **Correct.** The mood of a text is felt by readers as they interact with the text. The tone is more a reflection of how the author feels, usually communicated through specific diction.

B. Incorrect. The moods and attitudes of the characters of a text are separate from the mood and the tone of the text.

C. Incorrect. The mood may be fluid in the sense that the readers' feelings may fluctuate as they read, but the mood of the story is influenced by more than the characters.

D. Incorrect. The mood of a story can be felt throughout; the way a story ends is only one factor that contributes to the mood.

15) **Which passage below from "A Mystery of Heroism" by Stephen Crane best exemplifies the third person omniscient point of view?**

A. "In the midst of it all Smith and Ferguson, two privates of A Company, were engaged in a heated discussion, which involved the greatest questions of the national existence."

B. "An officer screamed out an order so violently that his voice broke and ended the sentence in a falsetto shriek."

C. "The officer's face was grimy and perspiring, and his uniform was tousled as if he had been in direct grapple with an enemy. He smiled grimly when the men stared at him."

D. "No, it could not be true. He was not a hero. Heroes had no shames in their lives, and, as for him, he remembered borrowing fifteen dollars from a friend and promising to pay it back the next day, and then avoiding that friend for ten months."

Answers

A. Incorrect. In this section of text, two privates are arguing; no information about their thoughts is included in the description.

B. Incorrect. This quotation is a description of the officer as he screams orders; again, no information about the character's thoughts is included.

C. Incorrect. This section of text is a description of an officer; yet again, none of his thoughts are being revealed by the narrator.

D. **Correct.** The narrator is reporting the thoughts of the character, as the character's memory about not acting heroic in the past is revealed.

FIGURATIVE LANGUAGE

Figures of speech are expressions that are understood to have a nonliteral meaning. Rather than stating their ideas directly, authors use figurative language to suggest meaning by speaking of a subject as if it were something else. For example, when Shakespeare says, "All the world's a stage,/ And all men and women merely players," he is speaking of the world as if it is a stage. Since the world is not literally a stage, the reader has to ask how the two are similar and what Shakespeare might be implying about the world through this comparison. Figures of speech extend the meaning of words by engaging the reader's imagination and adding emphasis to different aspects of their subject.

A **metaphor** is a type of figurative language that describes something that may be unfamiliar to the reader (the topic) by referring to it as though it were something else that is more familiar to the reader (the vehicle). A metaphor stands in as a synonym, interchangeable with its corresponding topic. As the reader reflects on the similarities between the topic and the vehicle, he or she forms a clearer understanding of the topic. For example, in Shakespeare's *Romeo and Juliet*, Romeo says that "Juliet is the sun." By making this comparison, Romeo is comparing Juliet's energy to the brightness of the sun, which is familiar to readers.

A **simile** is a type of figurative language that directly points to similarities between two things. As with a metaphor, the author uses a familiar vehicle to express an idea about a less familiar topic. Unlike a metaphor, however, a simile does not replace the object with a figurative description; it compares the vehicle and topic using "like," "as," or similar words. For example, in his poem "The Rime of the Ancient Mariner,"

> **DID YOU KNOW?**
>
> Aristotle claimed that "the greatest thing by far is to have a command of metaphor. This alone cannot be imparted by another; it is the mark of genius, for to make good metaphors implies an eye for resemblances."

Coleridge describes his ship as "idle as a painted ship/ Upon a painted ocean." He speaks about the boat *as if* it were painted (unlike Romeo above, who says explicitly that Juliet *is* the sun itself). The reader understands that paintings do not move, so Coleridge uses this comparison to show the reader that the ship in the poem is completely motionless.

Imagery is vivid description that appeals to the reader's sense of sight, sound, smell, taste, or touch. This type of figurative language allows readers to experience through their senses what is being described; as readers use their imaginations to visualize or recall sensory experience, they are drawn into the scene of the story or poem.

Hyperbole is an overstatement, an exaggeration intended to achieve a particular effect. Hyperbole can create humor or add emphasis to a text by drawing the reader's attention to a particular idea. For example, a character might say he or she is "so hungry, [he or she] could eat a horse." Though the character probably cannot literally eat a horse, the reader understands that he or she is extremely hungry.

Personification is a type of figurative language in which human characteristics are attributed to objects, abstract ideas, natural forces, or animals. For example, if a writer refers to "murmuring pine trees," he or she is attributing to the pine trees the human ability of murmuring. The writer is using the familiar vehicle of the sound of murmuring to help the reader understand the sound pine trees make in the wind.

Symbolism is a literary device in which the author uses a concrete object, action, or character to represent an abstract idea. The significance of the symbol reaches beyond the object's ordinary meaning. Familiar symbols are roses representing beauty, light representing truth, and darkness representing evil. As readers notice an author's use of symbolism, they begin to make connections and to formulate ideas about what the author is suggesting.

An **allusion**, not to be confused with *illusion*, is a reference to a historical person or event, a fictional character or event, a mythological or religious character or event, or an artist or artistic work. When a reader recognizes an allusion, he or she may make associations that contribute to his or her understanding of the text. For example, if a character is described as having a "Mona Lisa smile," an instant image will arise in the minds of most readers. Because allusions can be difficult to recognize, especially for young readers whose experiences are limited, teachers must provide instruction in how to recognize, research, and interpret unfamiliar references.

Clichés are common sayings that lack originality but are familiar and relatable to an audience. Though clichés are not necessarily beneficial to the author who is trying to write a wholly original work, they can be helpful for a writer who is attempting to show that he or she can relate to the audience.

Dialect and **slang** are linguistic qualities that an author might incorporate into his or her writing in order to develop characters or setting. A character's dialect may reveal where he or she is from, while the slang he or she uses may be an indication of social, economic, and educational status.

Authors use **foreshadowing** to hint at the events that are going to unfold in a story. Typically, foreshadowing is intended to create a sense of anticipation and suspense in the reader.

Irony comes in different forms. **Verbal irony** is used when a character or narrator says something that is the opposite of what he or she means. **Situational irony** occurs when something happens that contradicts what the audience expected to happen. **Dramatic irony** occurs when the audience knows about something of which a character or characters are not aware.

SAMPLE QUESTIONS

The following questions refer to a poem by Emily Dickinson.

I'm nobody! Who are you?
Are you nobody, too?
Then there's a pair of us—don't tell!
They'd banish us, you know.

How dreary to be somebody!
How public, like a frog!
To tell your name the livelong day
To an admiring bog!

16) **What best describes the tone of the poem?**

    A.   sorrowful

    B.   regretful

    C.   contemptuous

    D.   suspicious

Answers

    A.   Incorrect. Although the speaker states that she's a "nobody," her lighthearted tone gives no indication that she's sad.

    B.   Incorrect. Though the speaker acknowledges that it may not be advisable to say "I'm nothing," she doesn't seem to regret saying so herself.

    C.   **Correct.** Dickinson seems to have contempt for people who are forever seeking the admiration of others, describing them as "frog[s]" who "tell [their] name[s] the livelong day" to whoever will listen.

    D.   Incorrect. The speaker's tone about being "banished, you know" is nonchalant.

17) **What kind of figurative language is NOT used?**

    A.   simile

    B.   personification

    C.   hyperbole

    D.   metaphor

Answers

    A.   Incorrect. The line, "How public, like a frog" is a simile.

    B.   Incorrect. The frog who can tell his name is personified.

    C.   Incorrect. The line, "To tell your name the livelong day" is hyperbole.

    D.   **Correct.** There is no metaphor in this poem.

The following questions refer to the poem "The Wayfarer" by Stephen Crane.

Perceiving the pathway to truth,
Was struck with astonishment.
It was thickly grown with weeds.
"Ha," he said,
"I see that none has passed here
In a long time."
Later he saw that each weed
Was a singular knife.
"Well," he mumbled at last,
"Doubtless there are other roads."

18) **Which of the following is NOT an example of how Crane develops his theme that the truth is painful?**

A. the symbol of the journey

B. the metaphor that the weeds are knives

C. Crane's melancholic tone

D. the wayfarer's decision to go a different way

Answers

A. **Correct.** The symbol of the journey, in itself, does not suggest a relationship between truth and pain.

B. Incorrect. This metaphor makes a comparison between the narrator's apprehension in the journey toward truth and the fear of physical pain.

C. Incorrect. The narrator's tone suggests that the threat of pain in the pursuit of truth is damaging.

D. Incorrect. The decision of the wayfarer to choose a different path highlights his desire to avoid the pain that he knows he will experience when he encounters the truth.

19) **In the poem above, the description of the road that "was thickly grown with weeds" is an example of** _____

A. an image.

B. a metaphor.

C. a theme.

D. a simile.

Answers

A. **Correct.** The reader can visualize this weedy pathway.

B. Incorrect. A metaphor is figurative language. The pathway is described in concrete terms.

C. Incorrect. A theme is a general idea, an observation about life and people, which is not present in the description of the weeds.

D. Incorrect. A simile, like a metaphor, is figurative language.

POETIC DEVICES AND STRUCTURE

Poets employ poetic devices to create aesthetic effects that impact readers and emphasize meaning. Most poetic devices—including rhyme, rhythm, meter, and repetition—create sound effects or provide structure in a poem.

Rhyme scheme is the arrangement of rhyming words in a stanza or poem. Usually the rhyming words are at the end of a line, but it is possible for internal rhymes to be part of the scheme. A frequently used rhyme scheme is present in quatrains, in which the first and third lines rhyme and the second and fourth lines rhyme, creating an *abab* pattern. The repeating pattern of sound creates a sense of balance and musicality; it produces an aesthetic effect that allows the reader to predict the upcoming sounds, thereby freeing him or her to focus on the ideas themselves.

Technically, **slant rhyme** is not true rhyme. In slant rhyme, the poet substitutes assonance or consonance (defined below) for real rhyme.

Internal rhyme is rhyming two or more words in the same line of poetry.

Rhythm is the drumbeat or heartbeat of a poem; it is the pattern of accentuated sounds, which creates or heightens the emotional effect of the language. **Meter** is an established rhythm within a poem, in which accentuated syllables are repetitive and predictable. Each unit of the meter, called a foot, has stressed and unstressed syllables. A familiar poetic foot is an **iamb**, which occurs when an unaccented syllable is followed by an accented one, as in the word *contain* (con-TAIN).

The meter of a poem is often named by the type and number of feet in one line of the poem. For example, a line that contains five iambs (ten syllables, beginning with an unstressed syllable and alternating for the rest of the line) is written in iambic pentameter. For the most part, Shakespeare's verse is written in this meter. An example from Romeo and Juliet is, "But, soft! what light through yonder window breaks?" or "But, SOFT! what LIGHT through YONder WINdow BREAKS?"

Blank verse is poetry that is written in iambic pentameter and is unrhymed. Many English dramas, including Shakespeare's plays and Milton's *Paradise Lost* are written in blank verse.

Free verse is poetry without patterns of rhyme or regular meter. Free verse poets write poems that have unpredictable rhythms.

Poets also use **repetition** to emphasize important ideas and heighten the emotional effect of their language. Sometimes, the repetition is of words themselves; a particularly important or charged word might be repeated to draw the reader's attention to it. Other times, repetition can be found only in sounds, as when poets employ assonance or consonance.

Assonance is the inclusion of words with the same vowel sounds within one or two lines of poetry. An example is the line "The only other sound's the sweep/ Of easy wind and downy flake" from Robert Frost's poem "Stopping by Woods on a Snowy Evening." Assonance lends a musicality to the language in a poem.

Consonance is repetition of the same consonant sounds at the end of a stressed syllable, but following different vowel sounds, in words that are fairly close together. Robert Frost also employs consonance in his poem "Stopping by Woods on a Snowy Evening": "Whose woods these are I think I know." Poets use consonance to highlight particular words, and like the other sound devices, it creates a pleasing lyrical effect.

In his poem "A Noiseless Patient Spider," Walt Whitman's speaker reveals the yearning of his soul using a combination of diction, repetition, and consonance.

The repetition of the word "filament" emphasizes the amount of thread that is coming from the spider's body. The use of the words "tirelessly" and "ceaselessly" highlight the similarity between the spider's ongoing efforts to spin her web and the speaker's ongoing effort to connect with the external world. The six present progressive verbs—the repetition of the *-ing* sound—enhance the reader's sense of the relentless efforts on the parts of the spider and the speaker to improve their situations.

A Noiseless Patient Spider

A noiseless patient spider,

I mark'd where on a little promontory it stood isolated,

Mark'd how to explore the vacant vast surrounding,

It launch'd forth filament, filament, filament, out of itself,

Ever unreeling them, ever tirelessly speeding them.

And you O my soul where you stand,

Surrounded, detached, in measureless oceans of space,

Ceaselessly musing, venturing, throwing, seeking the spheres to connect them,

Till the bridge you will need be form'd, till the ductile anchor hold,

Till the gossamer thread you fling catch somewhere, O my soul.

While some poets rely on established formats for their work, others prefer to create their own rules. **Closed form** poetry is poetry that follows a given form or shape. Closed form poems usually have a specified number of lines and a designated number of feet in each line; they also follow a consistent rhyme and meter. Examples of closed forms include blank verse, couplets, the villanelle, the quatrain, the sonnet, and the ballad.

Open form poetry does not have restrictions. The poets of open form poetry create unique arrangements of words and lines that flow naturally or communicate a particular feeling. Often, they use the lengths of the lines to emphasize ideas.

Poets design their poems according to the ideas they are communicating and the mood they hope to convey. Today, poets can choose any form, open or closed, they wish. Some past and present poets chose to reinforce their ideas using pattern poems. For example, in the seventeenth century, George Herbert wrote "Easter Wings." The first stanza follows:

Easter Wings

Lord, who createdst man in wealth and store,

  Though foolishly he lost the same,

    Decaying more and more,

> Till he became
>
> Most poore:
>
> With thee
>
> O let me rise
>
> As larks, harmoniously,
>
> And sing this day thy victories:
>
> Then shall the fall further the flight in me.

Poets employ, in addition to these poetic devices, many other kinds of figurative language that are common in literature including metaphors, similes, symbols, and analogies.

SAMPLE QUESTIONS

20) **What is the difference between closed form and open form poetry?**

   A.   A closed form poem comes to a natural ending, but an open form poem is just a random description.

   B.   An open form poem has lines in couplets, but closed form poems must have more than two lines in a stanza.

   C.   An open form poem uses distinct arrangements of words, while closed form poems must repeat at least two words or sounds in each line.

   D.   A closed form poem has a required number of lines, while an open form poem can have any number of lines.

   Answers

   A.   Incorrect. The words of a poem are meaningful, not random.

   B.   Incorrect. Both open and closed forms can include couplets.

   C.   Incorrect. An open form poem does use distinct arrangements of words, and a closed form poem does not have to repeat at least two words or sounds in each line.

   D.   **Correct.** With closed form poems, the number of lines is determined, but open form poems can have any number of lines.

21) **What creates the musical qualities of poetry?**

   A.   the rhythm and use of figurative language

   B.   the rhythm and use of sound devices

   C.   the stanzas and meter

   D.   the symbols and the sound devices

→ Go on

Answers

A. Incorrect. Rhythm is a characteristic of music. Figurative language creates meaning; it is unrelated to sound.

B. Correct. The repetition of sound and rhythm of accented sounds in regular intervals is musical.

C. Incorrect. The stanzas of poems are related to their forms and patterns, not their sounds.

D. Incorrect. Symbols are related to ideas and have little effect on musicality.

The following questions refer to this stanza from the poem "Fairest of the Rural Maids" by William Cullen Bryant.

The twilight of the trees and rocks
Is in the light shade of thy locks;
Thy step is as the wind, that weaves
Its playful way among the leaves.

22) **What sound device is used in the lines "The twilight of the trees and rocks/ Is in the light shade of thy locks"?**

A. internal rhyme

B. consonance

C. slant rhyme

D. simile

Answers

A. Incorrect. There is no internal rhyme. The words "rocks" and "locks" are at the end of the lines.

B. Correct. Consonance is repetition of the same consonant sounds at the end of a stressed syllable. "Twilight" ends with the same sound as "light."

C. Incorrect. Slant rhyme is not true rhyme. With slant rhyme the poet uses assonance or consonance instead of real rhyme. This poem uses actual rhyme: "rocks" with "locks" and "weaves" with "leaves."

D. Incorrect. A simile is a poetic device, not a sound device.

23) **What does the poet use to create a musical effect in the lines "The twilight of the trees and rocks/Is in the light shade of thy locks"?**

A. a metaphor

B. a stanza

C. assonance

D. a symbol

Answers

A.   Incorrect. A metaphor is not a sound device.

B.   Incorrect. The poem is written in stanzas, but stanzas are not sound devices.

C.   Correct. Assonance is the inclusion of words with the same vowel sounds within one or two lines of poetry. In this case the long /i/ sound is repeated in "twilight," "light" and "thy."

D.   Incorrect. A symbol in a poem may be repeated, but it is not a sound device.

READING STRATEGIES

Effective teachers provide ongoing, systematic instruction in a variety of reading strategies in order to equip their students to become active readers. **Active readers** get involved with a text by making connections between what they know and what they are learning or experiencing; they seek meaning in what they read in order to solve a problem, to gain new knowledge, or to answer a compelling question about something that matters to them. Teachers can instill active reading skills in their students throughout the reading process—before, during, and after reading.

Pre-reading strategies, such as previewing and setting a purpose, should be modelled and practiced throughout the school year, prior to beginning each new class text. **Previewing** a text involves taking time to identify the author, the genre, and the general subject matter of the work. It also includes reading headings and chapter titles, examining related graphics, researching the author and the context of the work, and anticipating the author's purpose. Previewing general information about a text allows an active reader to **set a purpose** for his or her reading. To instill this practice in students, an effective teacher might introduce each new text with a guiding question (*What does it mean to be evil?*) or hypothetical situation that pushes students to examine their own value systems (*Imagine you are a business owner. Should you be required to hire a certain number of individuals with disabilities?*). After facilitating a discussion about the question or scenario, the teacher would direct students to a particular text or section of text to examine how the author or characters would respond. By setting a purpose for the class's reading, the teacher is guiding students toward the thematic elements of the text and pushing them to draw connections between the author's choices and his or her overall message.

Prior to reading a new text, and throughout the reading process, students should also spend time **making predictions** about what they are reading. A prediction is a particular kind of inference that is specifically concerned with what is going to happen next in a given text. Making predictions is a valuable active reading skill because it requires readers to be constantly aware of what is going on in the story and what the author is foreshadowing through his or her specific choices.

In addition to making predictions as they read, students should be using what is referred to as the monitor and clarify strategy, also known as **metacognition**.

In metacognition, readers think about what they are thinking as they read so that they can recognize immediately any confusion or uncertainty. If they come to an unfamiliar word, for example, they use the context to decide what the word means or look it up and select a synonym that makes sense in the context. If they are unsure about what a particular pronoun is referring to, they reread until the pronoun reference is clear. Likewise, if readers realize they have stopped paying attention or sentences are not making sense, they backtrack to ensure they don't miss any significant details. Metacognitive readers are also aware of their purpose for reading; they may be reading to find information, to consider the arguments on all sides of an issue, or to enjoy a creative, imaginative experience.

Annotating is another important strategy that takes place during reading. To provide effective instruction in annotation and ensure that students are mastering the skill, teachers should set clear guidelines and expectations for annotation practice. For example, an effective teacher may require students to make VISA annotations, making note of interesting or novel **vocabulary**, important **inferences**, helpful **summaries**, and brief **analyses**.

Summarization is a reading strategy that requires readers to determine what is important in the text. Using their own words, readers reduce a text or section of text to its main points or central ideas. To accomplish this, they exclude insignificant details and redundancies; they look for general ideas as opposed to specific facts and examples. Student-produced summaries often provide valuable insight into comprehension levels; students who actively comprehend what they read will produce accurate summaries, while students who struggle with comprehension may leave out important ideas or leave in unnecessary information. Thus, summaries should be used throughout the study of a text and in the post-reading process in order to gauge how well students understood the basic ideas of the work.

In addition to having students summarize a text upon completion of reading, effective teachers might also have students engage with the text in other ways. They may ask students to **reflect** on their experience of the text and compose formal or informal responses. They may also ask students to return to the guiding question, **synthesizing** their understanding of the text and its thematic and cultural relevance. They might also ask students to **make connections** between the text, themselves (text-to-self), the world (text-to-world), and other literature (text-to-text). In all cases, students should be encouraged to use **text evidence** in their post-reading exercises, even in their personal responses, in order to ensure that their conclusions and understandings are fully informed and truly based in the text itself. In fact, as readers consider textual evidence, they may modify or extend their original interpretations. Thus, examination of textual evidence is an essential part of the process of constructing meaning.

SAMPLE QUESTIONS

The questions below refer to the following excerpt from Self-Reliance *by Ralph Waldo Emerson.*

There is a time in every man's education when he arrives at the conviction that envy is ignorance; that imitation is suicide; that he must take himself for better, for worse, as his portion; that though the wide universe is full of good, no kernel of nourishing corn can come to him but through his toil bestowed on that plot of ground which is given to him to till. The power which resides in him is new in nature, and none but he knows what that is which he can do, nor does he know until he has tried.

24) **How can teachers help students connect to Emerson's idea of self-reliance?**

   A.   Teachers can have their students summarize Emerson's text.

   B.   Students can take opportunities to read some of Emerson's poetry.

   C.   Students can research Emerson's life and learn about his accomplishments.

   D.   Teachers can ask their students to respond to Emerson's ideas by discussing ways these ideas can be applied to their everyday lives.

Answers

   A.   Incorrect. A summary is a restatement of the text and doesn't involve making connections.

   B.   Incorrect. Reading more of Emerson's texts may provide a better understanding of Emerson's poetry overall, but it may not necessarily give students any more insight into the topic of self-reliance in particular.

   C.   Incorrect. Knowing about Emerson's life will increase students' knowledge about Emerson but not about the topic of self-reliance.

   D.   Correct. Students will be making text-to-self connections as they consider how to apply Emerson's ideas to their own lives.

24) **Which of the statements below is a personal response to Emerson's assertions?**

   A.   Emerson uses persuasive writing techniques to convince readers that they can be self-reliant.

   B.   In my opinion, Emerson is stating that each individual has a unique power.

   C.   Emerson's metaphor of a person being a plot of ground is his way of telling readers to cultivate their talents.

   D.   I feel a burden to discover my talents and to accept myself.

Answers

A.   Incorrect. This statement is a comment about Emerson's purpose.

B.   Incorrect. This statement is not an opinion; it expresses a main point of the text. Restating an idea from the text is not the same thing as expressing an opinion. An opinion is a statement of agreement, disagreement, or qualification of the author's idea. To actually be an opinion, this statement would have to include some reaction to Emerson's assertion that each individual has a unique power.

C.   Incorrect. This statement is an analysis of a literary device that Emerson used to convince readers to be self-reliant.

D.   **Correct.** This is a personal response to Emerson; it expresses the reader's personal understanding and reaction to what he or she read.

Research-Based Strategies

Recent research in cognition and studies of the practices of effective teachers have established the efficacy of teaching strategies that enhance traditional lessons with targeted reviews, rigorous and regular questioning, guided and independent practice, and differentiated supports. In today's English classroom, the goal of instruction is to link new learning to existing knowledge and to build networks of connected points of information.

Importantly, contemporary research into reading instruction has shown that knowledge and skills are most effectively taught in the context of the class's reading. Therefore, lessons should, in general, be structured around a particular text, with examples and exercises being taken directly from the text itself or from a related text. Daily lesson objectives should be focused, active, clear, and achievable; the most effective lessons cover only one new skill or topic and allow for plentiful student practice using texts that are relevant to the broader unit of study.

The strategy of beginning lessons with a **targeted review of previous learning** is imperative. When a teacher regularly revisits or reviews a concept, which is highly recommended for the most essential skills, he or she is **spiraling** that concept throughout his or her instruction. Prior to beginning a new lesson, an effective teacher might remind students of relevant definitions, revisit previous examples, or have students activate their prior knowledge on the subject through brief writing or discussion activities. Before introducing a poem with an extended metaphor, for example, the teacher might review the definition of a metaphor and have students cite examples from earlier lessons before predicting what an extended metaphor might look like. By reviewing significant concepts prior to a new lesson, the teacher prevents confusion and saves valuable instructional time. Once relevant concepts have been reviewed, the teacher must sharpen the focus of the new lesson by stating the objective explicitly and by establishing the value of the new learning.

In teaching the new material, the instructor might incorporate a think-aloud into his or her lesson, **modelling** the thought process for students using a related example; in this process, the teacher breaks down the new skill into key steps, which he or she then demonstrates for the class. Throughout the lesson, the teacher might also employ **questioning strategies** that allow him or her to check the students' understanding of the new material so that future lessons can be adjusted in order to meet the instructional needs of the class. When the teacher is sure that most students have a basic grasp of the new material, he or she should provide opportunities for group, partner, and independent practice so that students have plenty of chances to apply their new knowledge or rehearse their new skill.

In some cases, teachers will need to provide differentiated supports as a means of helping all their students succeed. Some evidence-based strategies for differentiation include providing graphic organizers, listing steps in a process, offering sentence frames for responses, and allowing students to have additional time or to correct their errors on an assignment.

SAMPLE QUESTION

25) **What is an example of a metacognitive practice?**

    A.   a reader asking himself questions while reading

    B.   a reader taking notes during a lecture about the historical background of the text she will soon read

    C.   a teacher providing pop quizzes to determine who has read a text

    D.   a teacher explaining the characteristics of a given genre before students are asked to comprehend the genre

Answers

    A.   **Correct.** When readers ask themselves questions as they read, they are monitoring their own understanding.

    B.   Incorrect. Students should take notes; however, taking notes is passively receiving information as opposed to actively regulating their own thinking and learning.

    C.   Incorrect. Pop quizzes allow the teacher to evaluate student understanding, while metacognitive practices involve the student being aware of and evaluating his or her own understanding.

    D.   Incorrect. This is a good practice, but it is not metacognitive. The reader is not observing his or her own understanding.

LITERARY THEORY

The ability to recognize and empathize with multiple perspectives is an imperative of living in a diverse world; it is also a powerful way to deepen one's understanding of works of art and literature. **Literary theory** is using a set of principles or a system of ideas to interpret literature from a unique angle. By viewing a single text through a variety of different lenses, readers gain a depth of understanding that far exceeds that which can be developed based on straightforward analysis. By teaching literary theory, instructors can highlight for students how the assumptions that people make can color their interpretation of literary works and of the world as a whole.

Before thinking about a literary text from different theoretical perspectives, students must first have a general understanding of the text. In other words, before introducing a particular theoretical framework, teachers should engage students in the processes of literary criticism. Specifically, he or she may have students engage in activities or discussions that prime their thinking to prepare them for the theory that they will be applying. For example, an effective teacher might prepare students to analyze *The Great Gatsby* via a Marxist approach to criticism by asking them to consider the relationship between financial wealth and social status.

Reader-response theory is centered on the idea that as readers read, they experience a transaction with the text. The feelings and associations readers experience and make as they read influence their interpretation of what they are reading: in the process of constructing meaning, the reader's responses blend with the author's intended meanings so that the reader ends up participating in the creative process. Thus, there is no single correct interpretation of a text; any individual's understanding will be unique to him or her. Still, all interpretations must be grounded in text evidence.

Feminist literary theory involves asking questions about the degree to which a literary text perpetuates the ideas that women are inferior to and dependent on men or that the perspective of a woman is not as interesting or significant as that of a man. One goal of feminist theory is to challenge the view that being female is the opposite of being male, that having characteristics of sensitivity or a desire to nurture others makes an individual "feminine" and weak. A related intention is to free both males and females from the rigid thinking that traditional concepts of gender identity perpetuate. Feminists maintain that as students are confronted by feminist criticism, they will begin to recognize biases in their own thinking and in popular culture, making them more equipped to evaluate and challenge traditional gender roles.

Closely related to feminist theory is **queer theory**, which investigates texts by asking questions about both gender and sexuality. This lens of analysis involves recognizing and challenging all cultural assumptions related to sex and gender, especially those related to identity. One pillar of queer theory is that a person is not defined by one's sexuality and cannot be categorized in such terms because one's sexual identity is in a constant state of change. A queer analysis of a literary text challenges assumptions about the rigidity of sexuality and identifies alternative ways of thinking about the characters or their situations. For example, most commentary on Walt

DID YOU KNOW?

Note that literary criticism is distinguished from literary theory in that literary criticism is the process of analysis, while literary theory is the study of various analytical perspectives.

Whitman's poem "Song of Myself" points to Whitman's homosexual imagery; a queer analysis might come to the conclusion that Whitman finds all experiences to be erotic, even the undulating waves of the ocean, and that homosexuality constitutes only one small part of his sexual identity.

Deconstructionist literary criticism focuses on dissecting and uncovering the writer's assumptions about what is true and false, good and bad. Deconstructionists begin by examining language, which they consider a distortion of reality. They explain that meaning in language comes from differences: people understand *good* as the absence of *bad*; that is, one thing is understood as the absence of its opposite. By traditional thinking, reason or logic is the absence of emotion. By extension, if it is good to be rational, then it is not good to be emotional. The goal of deconstructionism is to identify these binaries in language and thinking in order to inspire investigation into possible other alternatives. As deconstructionist critics read a literary text, they examine linguistic contradictions and ambiguities in order to uncover incongruities in the underlying reasoning. Deconstructionists argue that, because of these inconsistencies, no text can be reduced to one correct meaning or interpretation.

Semiotic analysis is the study of signs, signals, visual messages, and gestures. In semiotics, a sign system is a set of behaviors or things which are analyzed as if they are symbols that represent ideas. In Ernest Hemingway's novel *The Old Man and the Sea*, the sign system of the man's struggle with the fish and his determination to show the boy what a man can do signifies many ideas about human potential. To interpret a message using semiotic analysis, consider the following:

▶ Who created the message?

▶ For whom was it created?

▶ What was the context?

Marxist theory focuses on the economic systems that structure society and the ways human behavior is motivated by a desire for economic power. According to this theory, life cannot be understood through abstract principles or ideals but can instead be understood only in terms of the concrete, actual conditions that people experience. Marxists literary theorists examine how the experiences of and relationships between characters are influenced by socioeconomic class.

Formalism or **New Criticism** emphasizes closely reading the text and analyzing how literary elements create meaning in it; it is unconcerned with the text's effect on the reader.

SAMPLE QUESTIONS

The following questions refer to this excerpt from the poem "In an Artist's Studio" by Christina Rossetti.

One face looks out from all his canvasses,
One selfsame figure sits or walks or leans;

We found her hidden just behind those screens,

That mirror gave back all her loveliness.

A queen in opal or in ruby dress,

A nameless girl in freshest summer greens,

A saint, an angel;–every canvass means

The same one meaning, neither more nor less.

26) **A critic comments that, in the poem, the famous artist's paintings of the woman suggest that he views her as an object to be admired and not as a real person. This critic asserts that the poem reveals a dangerous and biased assumption—that by portraying women in artistic ways, men are honoring women. The critic argues that, on the contrary, to make a woman the center of a piece of art is to objectify her.**

What literary theory does this critic represent?

A.   Marxist

B.   feminist

C.   deconstructionist

D.   reader-response

Answers

A.   Incorrect. A Marxist critic would write about issues related to social class, not issues related to gender.

B.   Correct. This argument reflects feminist theory because it discusses popular perceptions of women and evaluates how those perceptions might be detrimental to the fight for gender equality.

C.   Incorrect. A deconstructionist would be interested in the words and language structures of the poem and would focus on the terms like "saint" and "angel."

D.   Incorrect. A reader-response analysis would focus on how the reader feels about and interprets the images described in the poem.

27) **To analyze the poet's specific choices about the clothing the woman wears in the different paintings is to do a _____ analysis of the poem.**

A   semiotic

B.   queer

C.   deconstructive

D.   critical

Answers

A.   Correct. A semiotic analysis would pay attention to the clothing described in the poem in terms of the ideas that are communicated by the poet's specific choices.

B.   Incorrect. Queer theory focuses on social ideas of what is normal and abnormal sexual behavior; these lines do not relate to that focus.

C.   Incorrect. The deconstructionist looks for ambiguities, contradictions, and unexpected connections between different elements of a text, not so much symbolic representations.

D.   Incorrect. Although a critical analysis does examine the specific elements of a text, including symbols, it does not focus so much on the isolated ideas that the symbols signify as much as on how the symbolism relates to the author's purpose or overall meaning.

INFORMATIONAL TEXTS AND RHETORIC

In today's information-rich world, students benefit from having a solid understanding of the aims and structures of informational texts. It fact, it is just as important for students to know the format of a current event article, an editorial, or a speech as it is for them to know the structure of a sonnet or a short story. To interpret informational texts, students benefit from making connections between texts; thus, an effective teacher might assign multiple articles on the same subject and ask students to make comparisons.

In general, informational texts are written for one of three purposes: to inform, to argue, or to persuade.

Writing to **inform** is as straightforward a purpose as the term suggests: the author sets out simply to communicate information to his or her audience. Purely informative writing can be found in many textbooks and news articles.

Other writers of informational texts write to **argue** a particular point. Argumentation is the act of giving readers specific reasons and supporting evidence as to why they should act or think a certain way. It relies heavily on logical reasoning and involves disproving or countering opposing arguments.

Writers who write to **persuade** also attempt to convince the reader to act or think a certain way. However, unlike argumentative writing, persuasive writing does not necessarily rely as heavily on logical reasoning and evidentiary support; instead, it relies on rhetoric, language chosen specifically for its effect, to influence the minds of readers.

TEXTUAL EVIDENCE

The goal in courtrooms, science labs, and classrooms is not just to arrive at conclusions, but to come to *evidence-based* conclusions. Within the constructivist framework, students are urged to formulate responses to and interpretations of the texts they read; then, they must cite specific evidence to support their conclusions. In the early grades, students begin by referring to the text when looking for answers to teacher-provided questions. When they get older, they move to asking their own questions and quoting text to articulate their answers. By middle school, they should be able to cite details in the text in order to explain and justify their thinking.

In addition to using evidence themselves, students must also be able to identify and interpret an author's use of evidence in the context of an informational text. They must learn how to evaluate arguments based on the evidence and claims made in support of those arguments. One of the most efficient ways of having students evaluate the reliability of an article is to have them explore how well the writer supported his or her ideas. An effective teacher might have students first identify the claims of an article, then look for the evidence the writer includes to substantiate the claim. Evidence can then be evaluated based on its source.

Students should be aware that, even in informational texts, they will have to draw their own **inferences** to fully make sense of what they are reading. Readers draw inferences when they use their own knowledge in combination with details from the text to understand the meaning of a sentence, paragraph, or passage.

SAMPLE QUESTIONS

The questions below refer to the following excerpt from the speech "Advice to Youth" by Mark Twain.

> Being told I would be expected to talk here, I inquired what sort of talk I ought to make. They said it should be something suitable to youth—something didactic, instructive, or something in the nature of good advice. Very well. I have a few things in my mind which I have often longed to say for the instruction of the young; for it is in one's tender early years that such things will best take root and be most enduring and most valuable. First, then. I will say to you my young friends—and I say it beseechingly, urgently—Always obey your parents, when they are present. This is the best policy in the long run, because if you don't, they will make you. Most parents think they know better than you do, and you can generally make more by humoring that superstition than you can by acting on your own better judgment.

28) **In the previous text, what does Twain suggest is a child's perspective on obedience?**

   A. It's better to do as one wants because parents do not understand what daily life is like for youths.

   B. In the long run, one's parents don't find out everything one does, so it's not worth worrying about.

   C. One's parents really don't know what's best.

   D. Obedience to one's parents is a value that one must accept and live with, knowing that parents will become more permissive with time.

Answers

A.   Incorrect. Readers can infer that children think their parents do not understand their experiences, but there is no indication that children think disobedience is the better thing.

B.   Incorrect. This cannot be inferred because the passage specifies that when parents are present, they know what their children are doing.

C.   Correct. Children will obey when they must, but not because they think their parents are right about things or know what's better for them.

D.   Incorrect. Twain indicates obedience to parents is an expectation that will endure.

29) **What is the literal meaning of the passage?**

A.   It is essential for children to be reminded to obey their parents.

B.   If children are not taught to obey their parents when they are young, they will make bad decisions.

C.   Children should obey their parents because they will ultimately benefit from being obedient.

D.   Although people who do not have children give speeches about how children must be taught to obey, these people have no idea how difficult it is to control children.

Answers

A.   Incorrect. Mark Twain was asked to give good advice to children, but Twain chose the topic to discuss.

B.   Incorrect. Twain did say that his remarks were urgent, but his tone is not serious.

C.   Correct. Twain indicates that children benefit from obedience when he says, "you can generally make more by humoring [the] superstition" that "they know better than you do."

D.   Incorrect. There is no indication in the text that Twain's remarks have anything to do with his own experiences raising children (or lack thereof).

ORGANIZATIONAL AND TEXT STRUCTURES

Students should be taught to consider the patterns and structures of informational texts, as these details can provide valuable insight into the author's purpose and the overall meaning of a text. Teaching students the common structures that are used in informative texts helps them to quickly make sense of new texts by looking at the organization of their arguments.

Patterns are recurring elements in a text that form a design. One kind of pattern is text organization, which refers to how the details of a text are arranged.

Text organization may be chronological, problem-solution, cause-effect, general-specific, or compare-contrast. Authors choose the organizational structure of their text according to their purpose; for example, an author who hopes to convince people to begin recycling might begin by talking about the problems that are caused by excessive waste and end by offering recycling as a reasonable solution. **Problem-solution** is an organizational structure that begins with examining the details of something and concludes by offering a possible solution to the issue. **Cause-effect** is a text structure that shows a causal chain of events or ideas. One action causes another, which brings about a third action and so on, with each event connected to or leading to another. **Sequential order** is an arrangement of events in the order in which they occur, either in consecutive or logical order. Often one thing has to happen in order for the next to occur, like the steps of a procedure. **Chronological order** is applied when events are presented in the order in which they occurred in time.

Visual aids are pictures and graphics that are used to enhance a text. They attract, focus, and hold the attention of the reader and can help the reader develop a clearer understanding of the author's message. As concrete representations, visual aids also support memory. Thus, students should be asked to interpret and evaluate visual aids, just as they would the text itself.

SAMPLE QUESTIONS

The questions below refer to the following excerpt, from Chapter IV of the essay Nature *by Ralph Waldo Emerson.*

> Words are signs of natural facts. The use of natural history is to give us aid in supernatural history: the use of the outer creation, to give us language for the beings and changes of the inward creation. Every word which is used to express a moral or intellectual fact, if traced to its root, is found to be borrowed from some material appearance. *Right* means *straight*; *wrong* means *twisted*. *Spirit* primarily means *wind*; *transgression*, the crossing of a *line*; *supercilious*, the *raising of the eyebrow*. We say the *heart* to express emotion, the *head* to denote thought; and *thought* and *emotion* are words borrowed from sensible things, and now appropriated to spiritual nature. Most of the process by which this transformation is made, is hidden from us in the remote time when language was framed; but the same tendency may be daily observed in children. Children and savages use only nouns or names of things, which they convert into verbs, and apply to analogous mental acts.

30) **How does Emerson create coherence in his text?**

  A.   Emerson develops his point that words express facts in nature.

  B.   The sentences are linked by repeated words, parallelism, and the logical connection of general to specific.

  C.   Emerson gives specific examples of his points.

  D.   The sentences are logical and include descriptions that elaborate on the ideas communicated.

Answers

A.   Incorrect. This is a statement of the central idea, but it doesn't explain how Emerson develops the idea coherently.

B.   Correct. Emerson repeats words to link one sentence to another. One sentence ends with "observed in children." The next sentence begins with the word *children*. In another sentence, the phrases "*heart* to express emotion" and "the *head* to denote thought" are parallel. A specific example follows a general point.

C.   Incorrect. He does provide examples, but it's the connection between the specific example and the general idea that creates coherence.

D.   Incorrect. This is true, but it doesn't explain how the transitions are created.

31)   **How does Emerson structure the information in this section of text?**

A.   from general to specific

B.   sequentially

C.   chronologically

D.   using spatial details

Answers

A.   Correct. Emerson begins by making a general assertion about language and then goes on to provide specific examples of words that support his assertion.

B.   Incorrect. Emerson does not explain the sequence of steps or actions that led to the "the process by which this transformation is made," only that it "is hidden from us."

C.   Incorrect. Emerson does not explain how language was formed over time, only that connections between words and natural facts happened in the remote past.

D.   Incorrect. Emerson does not rely on any spatial details in his discussion of language.

ARGUMENTATION

Debating or distinguishing between opposing viewpoints may be the central challenge of the pluralistic world of the twenty-first century. Multiple belief systems exist for almost every scenario, so people are faced with the task of understanding the various arguments, deciding how they will act, and articulating, perhaps even defending, their own positions.

A written argument begins with a proposition, thesis, or assertion that will be defended throughout the work. A set of assumptions may then be established. Next, research and evidence are presented in an organized way. Opposing arguments are often mentioned and countered.

In learning to evaluate arguments, students should receive plentiful instruction and practice in critical thinking. **Critical thinking** involves asking questions about the quality of reasoning or the validity of a belief or an assumption. Rather than accepting information as necessarily true, students should be taught to ask questions and to formulate responses to arguments presented in any text. Effective teachers provide questions to guide critical thinking:

- What are the conclusions the author is making and what evidence is being provided?
- What assumptions are being made in order for this reasoning to work?
- Is there any fallacious reasoning, deceptive, ambiguous, or omitted information?
- Is the evidence accurate and reliable?
- What other causes or conclusions are possible?

Students must be able to evaluate evidence, identify errors in reasoning, and recognize the rhetorical strategies that are being used in a given piece of informative writing.

In evaluating evidence, students should ask questions about its relevancy and its reliability. **Evidence relevancy** depends on how closely the evidence is related to the argument and how recently the information was established. Evidence must be representative, meaning that it speaks directly to the situation or claim being discussed; thus, evidence that is irrelevant or too dated should be viewed with a skeptical eye. Additionally, evidence must come from a reliable source, the definition of which will vary depending on the topic and the kind of evidence that is being gathered.

CONSIDER THIS

Aristotle stated, "It is the mark of an educated mind to be able to entertain a thought without accepting it." Consider how Aristotle's statement relates to critical thinking and rhetoric.

A **logical fallacy** is an error or breakdown in logical reasoning. With deductive reasoning, the argument begins with a general statement or premise that is proven. Then, by applying the premise to a set of circumstances, specific conclusions can be drawn. If the initial premise is not valid, the reasoning is not sound or logical. With inductive reasoning, facts are gathered and conclusions are drawn from these facts. If there are enough facts to prove a conclusion, the conclusion is supported. Reasoning breaks down when there is contradictory or incomplete evidence.

Students should learn to recognize logical fallacies in order to evaluate the effectiveness of evidence in informative texts. Many types of errors in reasoning exist (and are discussed in depth later in this book):

- the **slippery slope**, in which the main argument is based on the assumption that if one particular thing happens, a series of other specific things will follow

- ▶ the **hasty generalization**, in which an individual comes to a conclusion without enough evidence, based on prior experiences or assumptions
- ▶ **the circular argument**, in which the argument is simply restated repeatedly with no inclusion of new evidence
- ▶ the **red herring**, in which distracting information is introduced, moving the focus away from the most important points of the argument

Dichotomous thinking begins with thinking in dichotomies or pairs of opposing terms, like good/evil, true/false. Dichotomous thinking allows people to only see the extremes of a situation rather than its complexities and subtleties. In argumentation, dichotomous thinking is considered fallacious because it simplifies a complex problem to the degree that only two options are possible. Readers are led to believe that there are no other options.

SAMPLE QUESTIONS

The questions below refer to the following excerpt from the speech "What to the Negro Is the Fourth of July?" by Frederick Douglass, July 5, 1852

Mr. President, Friends and Fellow Citizens:

The papers and placards say, that I am to deliver a Fourth of July oration. This certainly, sounds large, and out of the common way, for me... The fact is, ladies and gentlemen, the distance between this platform and the slave plantation, from which I escaped, is considerable—and the difficulties to be overcome in getting from the latter to the former, are by no means slight. That I am here to-day is, to me, a matter of astonishment as well as of gratitude...

This, for the purpose of this celebration, is the Fourth of July. It is the birthday of your National Independence, and of your political freedom. This, to you, is what the Passover was to the emancipated people of God. It carries your minds back to the day, and to the act of your great deliverance; and to the signs, and to the wonders, associated with that act, and that day. This celebration also marks the beginning of another year of your national life; and reminds you that the Republic of America is now seventy-six years old...

Fellow-citizens; above your national, tumultuous joy, I hear the mournful wail of millions! whose chains, heavy and grievous yesterday, are, to-day, rendered more intolerable by the jubilee shouts that reach them. If I do forget, if I do not faithfully remember those bleeding children of sorrow this day, "may my right hand forget her cunning, and may my tongue cleave to the roof of my mouth!" To forget them, to pass lightly over their wrongs, and to chime in with the popular theme, would be treason most scandalous and shocking, and would make me a reproach before God and the world. My subject, then, fellow-citizens, is AMERICAN SLAVERY. I shall see, this day, and its popular characteristics, from the slave's point of view. Standing, there, identified with the American bondman, making his wrongs mine, I do not hesitate to declare, with all my soul, that the character and conduct of this nation never looked blacker to me than on this Fourth of July! Whether we turn to the declarations of the past, or to the professions of the present, the conduct of the nation seems equally hideous and revolting. America is false to the past, false to the present, and solemnly binds herself to be false to the future. Standing with God and the crushed and bleeding slave on this occasion, I will, in the name of humanity which is outraged, in the name of liberty which is fettered, in the name of the Constitution and the Bible, which are disregarded and trampled upon, dare to call in question and to denounce, with all the emphasis I can command, everything that serves to perpetuate slavery—the great sin and shame of America! "I will not equivocate; I will not excuse;" I will use the severest language I can command; and yet not one word shall escape me that any man, whose judgment is not blinded by prejudice, or who is not at heart a slaveholder, shall not confess to be right and just...

32) **What is Frederick Douglass' purpose?**

    A.   to express his gratitude for being free

    B.   to celebrate Independence Day with his audience

    C.   to express admiration for America's belief in freedom and justice

    D.   to persuade his audience that slavery is against American principles

Answers

    A.   Incorrect. Initially, he mentions gratitude but goes on to express his real purpose in the second and third paragraphs.

    B.   Incorrect. Douglass speaks of Independence Day in order to draw his audience's attention to the various perspectives on the meaning of the day.

    C.   Incorrect. He does admire American ideals, but he does not admire the fact that many people in America are being denied freedom.

    D.   Correct. He says, "I will, … dare to call in question and to denounce, with all the emphasis I can command, everything that serves to perpetuate slavery—the great sin and shame of America!"

33) **Douglass' mention of the American Revolution illustrates _____.**

    A.   dichotomous thinking.

    B.   evidentiary relevancy.

    C.   fallacious reasoning.

    D.   critical thinking.

Answers

    A.   Incorrect. Douglass is not simplifying a complex problem; he is arguing against a practice.

B. **Correct.** Mention of the American Revolution is relevant and is being used as evidence to prove that Americans fought against tyranny and therefore must know it is wrong.

C. Incorrect. In this introductory section of his speech, Douglass has already offered well-supported and relevant evidence of the American belief in freedom.

D. Incorrect. Douglass is not evaluating slavery or arguments about it; he is arguing for an end to slavery.

RHETORICAL STRATEGIES

In addition to giving careful thought to the words chosen, writers consider how to position words in a sentence in order to make the biggest impact. For example, to emphasize a word, a writer might place it at the end of a sentence and may repeat the word. He or she may use parallel sentence construction to accentuate the key facets of an issue. Figures of speech may be used to engage the reader's attention and connect new ideas to what is familiar. A series of vivid images may be included to describe events in more detail. A writer might also include personal anecdotes to illustrate his or her points. In rhetoric, a deliberate effort is made to show the connection between points, to relate each point to the central idea, and to use words that will elicit a response from an audience.

After the assassination of Martin Luther King, in a speech to Americans, Robert Kennedy said, "We can move in that direction as a country, in greater polarization—black people amongst blacks, and white amongst whites, filled with hatred toward one another. Or we can make an effort, as Martin Luther King did, to understand, and to comprehend, and replace that violence, that stain of bloodshed that has spread across our land, with an effort to understand, compassion, and love." Kennedy uses several rhetorical strategies to convince his audience to change their approach to the issue of race. He contrasts words hate and hatred with the words love and compassion; uses a vivid image to describe the "stain of bloodshed" to describe the approach of the past; he defines the concept of polarization, repeats the word *understand*, and creates a parallel between the verbs understand, comprehend, and replace in order to emphasize his goals for race relations in the United States.

> **QUICK REVIEW**
>
> Note that rhetoric is the powerful use of language, the purposeful expression of ideas, which are meant to command the reader's attention.

To provide **rhetorical support** is to support generalizations, claims, and arguments with examples, details, and other evidence. In rhetoric, arguments are supported using **logos** (logical appeals), **pathos** (emotional appeals), and **ethos** (ethical appeals). Because these rhetorical appeals are present in nearly all kinds of informative texts, students should receive significant instruction in and practice at identifying various appeals and their purpose in context. In Kennedy's speech mentioned above, the young politician relies heavily on pathos, emotional appeal, to remind his audience that violence is unnecessary and that compassion and love can overcome it.

As consumers of popular media, students need to understand that they do not have to be convinced by rhetoric, that they can withhold their judgments, and that they are free to disagree with some or all of what they read or hear. In fact, an audience can appreciate the craft, artistry, or power of a rhetorical text and still choose not to be persuaded. The goal in rhetorical instruction is to equip students with the skills to recognize, interpret, and evaluate rhetoric so that they can make informed decisions that are not clouded by the subtle influence of others.

SAMPLE QUESTIONS

These questions refer to the following excerpt from the speech "The Oldest Inhabitant-The Weather of New England" by Mark Twain.

Mind, in this speech I have been trying merely to do honor to the New England weather—no language could do it justice. But, after all, there is at least one or two things about that weather (or, if you please, effects produced by it) which we residents would not like to part with. If we hadn't our bewitching autumn foliage, we should still have to credit the weather with one feature which compensates for all its bullying vagaries—the ice-storm: when a leafless tree is clothed with ice from the bottom to the top—ice that is as bright and clear as crystal; when every bough and twig is strung with ice-beads, frozen dew-drops, and the whole tree sparkles cold and white, like the Shah of Persia's diamond plume. Then the wind waves the branches and the sun comes out and turns all those myriads of beads and drops to prisms that glow and burn and flash with all manner of colored fires, which change and change again with inconceivable rapidity from blue to red, from red to green, and green to gold—the tree becomes a spraying fountain, a very explosion of dazzling jewels; and it stands there the acme, the climax, the supremest possibility in art or nature, of bewildering, intoxicating, intolerable magnificence. One cannot make the words too strong.

34) What are **TWO** rhetorical strategies that Mark Twain uses in his speech?

    A.   logical and ethical appeals

    B.   irony and understatement

    C.   symbolism and irony

    D.   hyperbole and metaphor

Answers

    A.   Incorrect. Logical and ethical appeals are rhetorical supports, not strategies.

    B.   Incorrect. Twain is being straightforward when he says there are one or two positive effects of New England weather.

C. Incorrect. There is no indication that Twain is using the ice storms to represent any idea, and there is no apparent contradiction between what he says and what he means.

D. Correct. The hyperbole is "it stands there the acme, the climax, the supremest possibility in art or nature, of bewildering, intoxicating, intolerable magnificence. One cannot make the words too strong." The metaphor is "when every bough and twig is strung with ice-beads, frozen dew-drops…"

35) **Twain supports his view that "there is at least one or two things about that weather (or, if you please, effects produced by it) which we residents would not like to part with" by**

A. including a response to opposing arguments.

B. incorporating logical appeals.

C. providing details.

D. incorporating ethical appeals.

Answers

A. Incorrect. There is no indication that Twain is countering an opposing argument.

B. Incorrect. Twain's rhetoric is meant to impress and entertain, not to persuade.

C. Correct. Twain provides a detailed description of an ice storm.

D. Incorrect. Twain is not dealing with moral issues, nor does he need to establish credibility for the purpose of this work.

Audience Appeal

The principles that guide rhetorical practice rely heavily on a writer's understanding of his or her audience. A **perspective** is a person's point of view, frame of reference, position, or attitude towards an idea or occurrence. To most effectively appeal to a particular audience, a writer must understand the audience's perspective and be able to appeal to them in ways that will be most appropriate for their unique circumstances. For example, a congressman addressing a group of his or her campaign supporters will appeal very differently to them than he or she would in attempting to persuade a congressional committee.

Facts are based in truth and can usually be proven. They are pieces of information that have been confirmed or validated. An **opinion** is a judgment, belief, or viewpoint that is not based on evidence. Opinions are often stated in descriptive, subjective language that is difficult to define or prove. While opinions can be included in informative texts, they are often of little impact unless they are supported by some kind of evidence. Students should learn to differentiate between facts and opinions in order to more effectively analyze an author's argument.

A **testimonial** is a statement about the quality or value of a person, idea, or thing. When someone with a good reputation recommends a method for doing something or a belief, it strengthens an argument or claim. Students should learn to identify testimonials and the reasons writers might employ testimonials in trying to convince an audience of a particular idea.

Technical language is language related to a specific field of study, from computer technology to mechanics to engineering. **Non-technical language** is language that does not require specialized knowledge. Students should learn to identify technical and non-technical language in an informative text, as these can provide insight into the author's intended purpose and audience. In writing for a group of his or her peers, for example, a scientist might rely heavily on technical language, as doing so will enhance his or her credibility as a professional in the field; on the other hand, if he or she is writing to a popular audience, technical language might be a hindrance to the reader's understanding and will, thus, be left out.

In all cases, students should be aware that writers of informative texts have a heightened awareness of their audience, as this awareness allows them to shape their writing to be most effective for their intended purposes. By considering an author's specific choices, students can likely identify the author's audience and, subsequently, his or her purpose in writing.

SAMPLE QUESTIONS

These questions refer to the following excerpt from the speech "House Divided" by Abraham Lincoln.

Mr. President and Gentlemen of the Convention:

If we could first know *where* we are, and *whither* we are tending, we could then better judge *what* to do, and *how* to do it.

We are now far into the *fifth* year, since a policy was initiated, with the *avowed* object, and *confident* promise, of putting an end to slavery agitation.

Under the operation of that policy, that agitation has not only, *not ceased*, but has *constantly augmented*.

In *my* opinion, it *will* not cease, until a *crisis* shall have been reached, and passed.

"A house divided against itself cannot stand."

I believe this government cannot endure, permanently half *slave* and half *free*.

I do not expect the Union to be *dissolved*—I do not expect the house to *fall*—but I *do* expect it will cease to be divided.

It will become *all* one thing or *all* the other.

Either the *opponents* of slavery, will arrest the further spread of it, and place it where the public mind shall rest in the belief that it is in the course of ultimate extinction; or its *advocates* will push it forward, till it shall become alike lawful in *all* the States, *old* as well as *new*—*North* as well as *South.*

Have we no *tendency* to the latter condition?

Let anyone who doubts, carefully contemplate that now almost complete legal combination—piece of *machinery* so to speak—compounded of the Nebraska doctrine, and the Dred Scott decision. Let him consider not only *what* work the machinery is adapted to do, and *how well* adapted; but also, let him study the *history* of its construction, and trace, if he can, or rather *fail*, if he can, to trace the evidence of design and concert of action, among its chief architects, from the beginning.

36) **What is Lincoln doing in this section of his speech?**

    A.   giving a testimonial

    B.   sharing his opinion

    C.   using technical language

    D.   applying inductive reasoning

Answers

    A.   Incorrect. A testimonial is a personal statement in support of an idea. Lincoln does not use a personal statement to support the idea that there could be some free states and some slave states.

    B.   **Correct.** He says, "I believe this government cannot endure, permanently half slave and half free."

    C.   Incorrect. The language in this text is straightforward and does not include any specialized terminology.

    D.   Incorrect. Lincoln is not drawing a conclusion from evidence gathered; rather, he is using deductive reasoning, starting with the premise that a house divided cannot stand and applying that premise to the idea of slave and free states.

37) **What evidence does Lincoln have to support his claim that America will not stay divided?**

    A.   the extinction of slavery

    B.   the history of the Constitution

    C.   the work of abolitionists

    D.   the dissolution of the Union

Answers

    A.   Incorrect. He does not say slavery is extinct; he only mentions the possibility that slavery could become extinct.

    B.   **Correct.** Lincoln says, "[L]et him study the history of its construction, and trace, if he can, or rather fail, if he can, to trace the evidences of design, and concert of action, among its chief bosses, from the beginning."

C.   Incorrect. Lincoln did not say these groups would prevent America from being divided. He only mentioned that these groups were working against slavery.

D.   Incorrect. Lincoln said, "I do not expect the Union to be dissolved—I do not expect the house to fall."

WORD CHOICE

Authors consider a number of factors when selecting words. First, they consider both the denotation and the connotation of a word. The **denotation** of a word is its meaning, the meaning that can be found in the dictionary. The **connotation** of a word, on the other hand, is its suggested or implied meaning. Connotation can be positive or negative, based on the emotional associations of the word.

QUICK REVIEW

Consider Emily Dickinson's thoughts on word choice as expressed in her poem:

A word is dead when it is said

Some say—

I say it just begins to live

That day.

Mark Twain once said, "The difference between the *almost*-right word and the *right* word is really a large matter—it's the difference between the lightning bug and the lightning." Writers choose words based on how effectively they convey the feelings, ideas, and associations they want to express; when it comes to word choice, precision is of the utmost importance. For example, Dr. Martin Luther King Jr. said, "I have a dream"; he didn't say "I have a plan." The word *plan* suggests something practical and quotidian, while the word *dream* communicates a much larger desire, a more abstract idea, and a greater vision.

An author might also consider whether to write explicitly or implicitly about the subject based on the degree to which he or she wants the reader to think independently about the subject. **Explicit** language is clear, detailed, and exact; explicit wording is designed to prevent confusion and ambiguity. Alternatively, with **implicit** language, meanings are implied, so the reader is left more to his or her own conclusions. If a writer intends only to inform the reader, he or she may choose explicit language so that the reader can clearly understand the information being presented. On the other hand, if the writer hopes to change the reader's behavior, he or she might use implicit language with the hope of leading readers to their own conclusions of how they should change.

SAMPLE QUESTIONS

The following questions refer to the excerpt from the poem "Ode to the West Wind," by Percy Bysshe Shelley.

O wild West Wind, thou breath of Autumn's being,
Thou, from whose unseen presence the leaves dead
Are driven, like ghosts from an enchanter fleeing,

Yellow, and black, and pale, and hectic red,
Pestilence-stricken multitudes:
O thou, Who chariotest to their dark wintry bed

The wingèd seeds, where they lie cold and low,
Each like a corpse within its grave, until
Thine azure sister of the Spring shall blow

Her clarion o'er the dreaming earth, and fill
(Driving sweet buds like flocks to feed in air)
With living hues and odours plain and hill:

Wild Spirit, which art moving everywhere;
Destroyer and Preserver; hear, O hear!

38) **What is the connotation of the words "Pestilence-stricken" in the lines, "Thou, from whose unseen presence the leaves dead/Are driven, like ghosts from an enchanter fleeing,/…Pestilence-stricken multitudes:"?**

   A. carrying a contagious disease

   B. having received a death blow

   C. pathetic and sorrowful

   D. ghastly, to be feared

   Answers

   A. Incorrect. This is the literal meaning of "Pestilence-stricken." *Connotations* are suggested meanings.

   B. Incorrect. This is an explanation of the literal meaning of "Pestilence-stricken."

   C. Incorrect. Although anything struck with pestilence could be considered hopeless, in this context the multitudes that are "Pestilence-stricken" are something to be feared because they are contagious, something to flee from.

   D. Correct. The dead leaves are moving like they are escaping something horrific. "Pestilence-stricken" must connote something the reader would flee.

39) **What is the implication of the lines, "The wingèd seeds, where they lie cold and low,/… until Thine azure sister of the Spring shall blow/Her clarion o'er the dreaming earth, and fill/ (Driving sweet buds like flocks to feed in air)…"?**

    A.   The seeds are being blown in the air.

    B.   The seeds will come to life in the spring.

    C.   The spring is lovely.

    D.   The spring is the time for following dreams.

Answers

    A.   Incorrect. This might be true, but that's not all: the lines imply that eventually, the seeds begin to grow.

    B.   **Correct.** Spring awakens the earth; the seeds come to life and begin to grow. The plants form buds that seem to be feeding on air.

    C.   Incorrect. This answer is too general a description of the lines' meaning.

    D.   Incorrect. The text does not support this statement because the subject of the lines is the seeds in the ground. The earth was asleep and "dreaming" until it was awakened by spring.

ROLE OF MEDIA

In the twenty-first century, ideas are communicated through both texts and media, which includes visual images, music, film, video, television, radio, and the Internet. **Media influence** refers to the impact the media has on an audience's thinking and behavior; today, culture is shaped significantly by the media, and the Internet is a key source of knowledge.

Media sources—like newspaper and magazine articles, television or radio broadcasts, interviews, and photographs—can be considered primary source documents; they record events and people's reactions to those events as they occur. Students should be made aware that media sources use the same rhetorical strategies that writers use, but the media can enhance the verbal message with graphics, images, and music, making their ideas even more compelling.

QUICK REVIEW

Given the influence of the media in the twenty-first century, consider evidence that supports Mark Twain's assertion that "There are only two forces that can carry light to all corners of the globe, the sun in the heavens and the Associated Press down here."

Visual persuasion is the use of visual images to influence the thinking and choices of viewers. On the Internet and social media, information is communicated constantly and quickly; many words can be replaced by a single picture. Thus, along with teaching students to understand text, teachers must help students to understand and interpret media and visuals. For instance, the concepts of frame, color contrast, focus, depth-of-field, and point of view can all be used to analyze and interpret an image or graphic and to provide the audience further insight into the author's purpose.

Finally, especially in the study of informational texts, teachers should incorporate media as a way of helping their students further understand and relate to what they are reading. One exciting way to introduce a new text, for example, is with a Gallery Walk. Teachers place images, video clips, or quotations related to the text in stations around the room; students then walk around, studying the items and recording their impressions. Finally, students share what about the images stood out to them and what they think about them.

SAMPLE QUESTIONS

The following questions refer to the cartoon "Emerson as a Transparent Eyeball" by Christopher Cranch and an excerpt from Nature *by Ralph Waldo Emerson.*

Standing on the bare ground, my head bathed by the blithe air, and uplifted into infinite space, all mean egotism vanishes. I become a transparent eyeball-I am nothing; I see all; the currents of the Universal Being circulate through me-I am part or particle of God. The name of the nearest friend sounds then foreign and accidental: to be brothers, to be acquaintances-master or servant, is then a trifle, and a disturbance. I am a lover of uncontained and immortal beauty. In the wilderness, I have something more connate and dear than in the streets or villages. In the tranquil landscape, and especially in the distant line of the horizon, man beholds somewhat as beautiful as his own nature.

40) **How does the cartoon of Emerson reinforce the transcendental ideas that are expressed in his essay *Nature*?**

  A.   Emerson has no arms; as a Transcendentalist, he can do nothing practical.

  B.   The cartoon shows Emerson to be an eyeball.

  C.   The cartoon shows Emerson alone, lost in space.

  D.   Emerson is shown to be larger than his surroundings, indicating that he is God.

Answers

  A.   Incorrect. This statement expresses a humorous critique of Emerson and his Transcendentalist ideas, but it does not reinforce or align with the ideas expressed in the passage from the essay.

  B.   **Correct.** In the passage from *Nature*, Emerson claimed to have become an eyeball that is "nothing" in itself but can "see all."

  C.   Incorrect. This statement does not reflect the ideas expressed in the passage from *Nature*.

  D.   Incorrect. Emerson did not claim to be God, only to be at one with and connected to God while transcending.

41) **In reference to the text below the cartoon, what TWO persuasive techniques is Emerson using to convince readers to spend time in nature?**

  A.   an emotional appeal and figurative language

  B.   a logical appeal and humor

  C.   an ethical appeal and a rhetorical question

  D.   a logical appeal and imagery

Answers

  A.   **Correct.** Emerson uses the metaphor of becoming a transparent eyeball to appeal to readers' desire to feel uplifted and connected to God.

  B.   Incorrect. Emerson's ideas are purposely not based on rational arguments; as a Romantic, Emerson opposed the use of reason to understand truth. Although the cartoon is humorous, Emerson was completely serious about his ideas.

  C.   Incorrect. It is possible for readers to associate time spent seeking spiritual experience as "right," but ethics has more to do with morality than spirituality. There is no rhetorical question in this excerpt.

D.   Incorrect. The word picture of Emerson standing alone in nature is imagery, but Emerson's ideas are not based on logic.

2

Language Use and Vocabulary

Much is encompassed in the study of a language, especially a language as complex and varied as English. Indeed, when communicating verbally, students of English must simultaneously consider everything from word choice to sentence construction to cultural context. In modern life, the importance of verbal communication skills can hardly be overstated: email communication, professional reports, court documents, business memos, and all other forms of written correspondence require a certain level of expertise in the use of language in order to be most effective. Though the many rules and guidelines of English language usage can pose a challenge to writers, the study of these structures can lead to increased confidence in verbal communication, a benefit that will extend to nearly all areas of life.

GRAMMAR

Grammar refers to the structures and systems that make up a language. In English, two schools of thought emerge when linguists discuss proper grammar: descriptivism and prescriptivism. Grammarians who promote prescriptivism encourage language usage that observes grammatical correctness and adheres strictly to time-honored rules. Grammarians who promote descriptivism, on the other hand, argue that language should be taught in a way that mirrors how it is used in a day-to-day social context—how people speak and write to be understood by others in their culture. Despite the differences in these two schools of thought, they are not necessarily in competition with one another. In fact, to communicate to a broad audience, descriptive and prescriptive grammar usage in tandem will communicate both professionalism and sensitivity to the intended audiences.

PARTS OF SPEECH

The **parts of speech** are the building blocks of sentences, paragraphs, and entire texts. Grammarians have typically defined eight parts of speech—nouns, pronouns, verbs, adverbs, adjectives, conjunctions, prepositions, and interjections—all of which play unique roles in the context of a sentence. Thus, a fundamental understanding of the parts of speech is necessary in order to form an understanding of basic sentence construction.

Though some words fall easily into one category or another, many words can function as different parts of speech based on their usage within a sentence.

Nouns are the words we use to give names to people, places, things, and ideas. Most often, nouns fill the position of subject or object within a sentence. The category of nouns has several subcategories: common nouns (*chair, car, house*), proper nouns (*Julie, David*), abstract nouns (*love, intelligence, sadness*), concrete nouns (*paper clip, bread, person*), compound nouns (*brother-in-law, rollercoaster*), non-countable nouns (*money, water*), countable nouns (*dollars, cubes*), and verbal nouns (*writing, diving*). There is much crossover between these subcategories (for example, *chair* is common, concrete, and countable), and other subcategories do exist.

> **QUICK REVIEW**
>
> Sometimes, a word that is typically used as a noun will be used to modify another noun. The word then would be labelled as an adjective because of its usage within the sentence. Here is an example using the word *cabin*: *The family visited the cabin (noun) by the lake. Our cabin (adjective) stove overheated during vacation.*

Pronouns replace nouns in a sentence or paragraph, allowing a writer to achieve a smooth flow throughout a text by avoiding unnecessary repetition. The unique aspect of the pronoun as a part of speech is that the list of pronouns is finite: while there are innumerable nouns in the English language, the list of pronouns is rather limited in contrast.

Pronoun categories are the following: personal, possessive, reflexive/intensive, relative, interrogative, demonstrative, and indefinite.

Personal pronouns act as subjects or objects in a sentence. (*She received a letter; I gave the letter to her.*)

Possessive pronouns indicate possession. (*My coat is red; our car is blue.*)

Reflexive or **intensive pronouns** intensify a noun or reflect back upon a noun. (*I myself made the dessert. I made the dessert myself.*)

Table 2.1. Personal, Possessive, and Reflexive/Intensive Pronouns

Case	First Person		Second Person		Third Person	
	singular	*plural*	*singular*	*plural*	*singular*	*plural*
subject	I	we	you	you (all)	he, she, it	they
object	me	us	you	you (all)	him, her, it	them
possessive	my	our	your	your	his, her, its	their
reflexive/ intensive	myself	ourselves	yourself	yourselves	himself, herself, itself	them-selves

Relative pronouns begin dependent clauses. Like other pronouns, they may appear in subject or object case, depending on the clause.

Take, for example, the sentence *Charlie, <u>who made the clocks</u>, works in the basement.* Here, the relative pronoun *who* is substituting for Charlie; that word indicates that Charlie makes the clocks, and so *who* is in the subject case because it is performing the action (*makes the clocks*).

In cases where a person is the object of a relative clause, the writer would use the relative pronoun *whom*. For example, read the sentence *My father, <u>whom</u> I care for, is sick.* Even though *my father* is the subject of the sentence, in the relative clause the relative pronoun *whom* is the object of the preposition *for*. Therefore that pronoun appears in the object case.

When a relative clause refers to a non-human, *that* or *which* is used. (*I live in Texas, <u>which</u> is a large state.*) The relative pronoun *whose* indicates possession. (*I don't know <u>whose</u> car that is.*)

Table 2.2. Relative Pronouns

Pronoun Type	Subject	Object
person	who	whom
thing	which, that	which, that
possessive	whose	whose

Interrogative pronouns begin questions. (*<u>Who</u> worked last evening?*) They request information about people, places, things, ideas, location, time, means, and purposes.

Table 2.3. Interrogative Pronouns

Interrogative Pronoun	Example
who	<u>Who</u> lives there?
whom	To <u>whom</u> shall I send the letter?
what	<u>What</u> is your favorite color?
where	<u>Where</u> do you go to school?
when	<u>When</u> will we meet for dinner?
which	<u>Which</u> movie would you like to see?
why	<u>Why</u> are you going to be late?
how	<u>How</u> did the ancient Egyptians build the pyramids?

Demonstrative pronouns point out or draw attention to something or someone. They can also indicate proximity or distance.

Table 2.4. Demonstrative Pronouns

Number	Subject/ Proximity	Example	Object/ Distance	Example
singular	this (subject)	<u>This</u> is my apartment—please come in!	that (object)	I gave <u>that</u> to him yesterday.
	this (proximity)	<u>This</u> is the computer you will use right here, not the one in the other office.	that (distance)	<u>That</u> is the Statue of Liberty across the harbor.
plural	these (subject)	<u>These</u> are flawless diamonds.	those (object)	Give <u>those</u> to me later.
	these (proximity)	<u>These</u> right here are the books we want, not the ones over there.	those (distance)	<u>Those</u> mountains across the plains are called the Rockies.

Indefinite pronouns simply replace nouns to avoid unnecessary repetition. (*Several* came to the party to see *both*.)

Table 2.5. Common Indefinite Pronouns

Singular		Plural	Singular or Plural
each	everybody		some
either	nobody		any
neither	somebody	both	none
one	anybody	few	all
everyone	everything	several	most
no one	nothing	many	more
someone	something		*These pronouns take their singularity or plurality from the object of the prepositions that follow: Some of the pies were eaten.*
anyone	anything		
	another		

Remember that a pronoun takes the place of the noun. For example, instead of writing *Mary, Sue, Ralph, Peter, Michael, and Stephen visited the museum*, within the context of the story, the author could write the following: <u>*All*</u> *visited the museum.* An indefinite pronoun works well to replace a list of names or objects.

QUICK REVIEW

In the following sentence, *that* is a relative pronoun, not a demonstrative pronoun, because it is beginning a relative clause. *All of the wagons* <u>*that*</u> *survived the fire made the trip to Colorado Springs.*

Verbs express action (*run, jump, play*) or state of being (*is, seems*).

Verbs also convey mood.

▶ Indicative verbs state facts: *My brother plays tennis.*

▶ Subjunctive verbs make a statement of speculation or wish. The subjunctive mood is formed with other words like *that*. However, the verb itself does not usually change. Example:

The doctor recommends that you take the medication twice a day.

I wish that I had a dog.

▶ Conditional sentences, which use the auxiliaries *would, could*, and *should*, use the subjunctive. Example:

If I took a road trip, I could visit the Grand Canyon.

▶ Imperative verbs state a command: *Play tennis!*

Finally, verbs are conjugated in active or passive voice.

▶ Active voice expresses a dynamic action: *They played tennis.*

▶ Passive voice is used to indicate that the subject is acted upon: *Tennis was played at the club.* It is rarely used and is most frequently seen (when used properly) in math and science where the subject has limited agency in the matter at hand. (*The math problem is easily solved.*) However, overuse of the passive voice is common.

Verbs are conjugated to indicate *person* (first, second, and third person) and *number* (whether they are singular or plural).

Table 2.6. Verb Conjugation (Present Tense)

Person	Singular	Plural
first person	I give	we give
second person	you give	you (all) give
third person	he/she/it/ gives	they give

Verb tense indicates the time of the action.

Table 2.7. Verb Tenses

Tense	Past	Present	Future
simple	I <u>gave</u> her a gift yesterday.	I <u>give</u> her a gift every day.	I <u>will give</u> her a gift on her birthday.
continuous	I <u>was giving</u> her a gift when you got here.	I <u>am giving</u> her a gift; come in!	I <u>will be giving</u> her a gift at dinner.
perfect	I <u>had given</u> her a gift before you got there.	I <u>have given</u> her a gift already.	I <u>will have given</u> her a gift by midnight.
perfect continuous	Her friends <u>had been giving</u> her gifts all night when I arrived.	I <u>have been giving</u> her gifts every year for nine years.	I <u>will have been giving</u> her gifts on holidays for ten years next year.

Linking verbs join the subject to the subject complement: for example, *The dog is cute.* The following chart helps to distinguish among linking, helping, and action verbs.

Table 2.8. Linking, Helping, and Action Verbs

Linking or Helping	Action or Helping	Helping	Linking or Action
am, is, are, was, were, be, being, been	have, has, had, do, does, did	shall, will, should, would, may, might, must, can, could	taste, feel, smell, sound, look, appear, become, seem, grow, remain, stay

Transitive verbs take an object; intransitive verbs do not. Such troublesome verbs include combinations such as *lie* or *lay*, *rise* or *raise*, and *sit* or *set*. The following chart may help to clarify the differences in some pairs of troublesome verbs.

Table 2.9. Intransitive and Transitive Verbs

Intransitive Verbs	Transitive Verbs
lie – to recline	lay – to put lay <u>something</u>
rise – to go or get up	raise – to lift raise <u>something</u>
sit – to be seated	set – to put set <u>something</u>
Hint: These intransitive verbs have *i* as the second letter. *Intransitive* begins with *I*.	Hint: The word *transitive* begins with a *T*, and it *TAKES* an object.

Verbs may be regular, following the conventions of regular verbs and their four parts (simple present, present participle, simple past, and past participle) and endings (*walk*, *walked*, *walking*, *have walked*). Some examples follow.

Table 2.10. Regular Verbs and Their Endings

Simple Present	Present Participle	Simple Past	Past Participle
sit	sitting	sat	(have) sat
set	setting	set	(have) set
lie	lying	lay	(have) lain
lay	laying	laid	(have) laid
rise	rising	rose	(have) risen
raise	raising	raised	(have) raised

Also, verbs may be irregular, not following the convention of the four parts and endings (*swim*, *swam*, *swimming*, *have swum*).

SAMPLE QUESTIONS

Choose the correct verb.

1) Yesterday, I (laid/lay) on the couch for hours.

2) (Lying/Laying) the picture down, he smiled with admiration.

3) The city workers had (laid/lain) the plans for the civic center.

4) (Lying/laying) in the basket, the flowers dried beautifully.

5) For five years she (lay/laid) in a coma.

6) We (sat/set) the ladder upright.

7) Where was the pitcher (setting/sitting)?

8) The bottle had (set/sat) there under the shelf undiscovered.

9) (Setting/Sitting) the chairs in a row took precision.

10) The boy (sat/set) his puppy beside him.

11) The egg was (rising/raising) in the water as it boiled.

12) Will all the people on the committee (raise/rise) a hand?

13) Will the bread (rise/raise)?

14) (Rise/Raise) early at dawn to see the pigs.

15) We (rise/raise) the flag high into the sky on our farm.

Answers:

1) The correct response is **lay**, the intransitive (here, in the past tense), which does not take an object.

2) The correct response is **laying**, the transitive, which takes an object (*the picture*).

3) The correct response is **laid**, the transitive, which takes an object (*the plans*).

4) The correct response is **lying**, the intransitive, which does not take an object.

5) The correct response is **lay**, the intransitive, which does not take an object.

6) The correct response is **set**, the transitive, which takes an object (*the ladder*).

7) The correct response is **sitting**, the intransitive, which does not take an object.

8) The correct response is **sat**, the intransitive, which does not take an object.

9)   The correct response is **setting**, the transitive, which takes an object (*the chairs*).

10)   The correct response is **set**, in the transitive form, which takes an object (*puppy*).

11)   The correct response is **rising**, the intransitive, which does not take an object.

12)   The correct response is **raise**, the transitive, which takes an object (*a hand*).

13)   The correct response is **rise**, the intransitive, which does not take an object.

14)   The correct response is **rise**, the intransitive, which does not take an object.

15)   The correct response is **raise**, the transitive, which takes an object (*the flag*).

Adverbs take on a modifying or describing role. These parts of speech describe the verb (*He quickly ran to the house next door.*), adjectives (*Her very effective speech earned her a new job.*), other adverbs (*Several puppies arrived rather happily after they had eaten dog treats.*), and entire sentences. (*Instead, the owner kept his shop.*)

Adverbs typically answer the questions *Where? When? Why? How? How often? To what extent? Under what conditions?*

Like adverbs, **adjectives** modify or describe, but they add to the meaning of nouns (*Five thoughtful students came to work at the farm.*) and pronouns only. (*The idea from the committee proved a smart one.*) One very important note regarding the adjective is that any word used to describe a noun or pronoun will be classified as an adjective. *Her* could be used as a pronoun or an adjective depending on usage. (*Her [used as an adjective] dog barks until midnight. We gave several books to her [used as a pronoun and object of the preposition to].*) Also, *a, and,* and *the* are always limiting adjectives.

Adjectives typically answer the questions *What kind? Which one? How many? How much? Whose?*

Conjunctions join words into phrases, clauses, and sentences by use of three mechanisms: coordinating conjunctions (*and, but, or, for, nor, yet, so*), correlative conjunctions (*whether/or, either/or, neither/nor, both/and, not only/but also*), and subordinating conjunctions, which join dependent clauses (typically adverbial clauses) to the independent clauses to which they are related. (*Because we love pizza, we treat ourselves during football season to several orders.*)

The following is a list of common subordinating conjunctions:

⟶

Go on

Table 2.11. Subordinating Conjunctions

Time	after, as, as long as, as soon as, before, since, until, when, whenever, while
Manner	as, as if, as though
Cause	because
Condition	although, as long as, even if, even though, if, provided that, though, unless, while
Purpose	in order that, so that, that
Comparison	as, than

When using correlative conjunctions, be sure that the structure of the word, phrase, or clause that follows the first part of the conjunction mirrors the structure of the word, phrase, or clause that follows the second part. Here is a **correct** example: *I will neither <u>mow the grass</u> nor <u>pull the weeds</u> today.* Here is an **incorrect** example: *I will neither <u>mow the grass</u> nor <u>undertake the pulling of the weeds</u> today.*

Prepositions set up relationships in time (*<u>after</u> the party*) or space (*<u>under</u> the cushions*) within a sentence. A preposition will always function as part of a prepositional phrase—the preposition along with the object of the preposition. If a word that usually acts as a preposition is standing alone in a sentence, the word is likely functioning as an adverb. (*She hid <u>underneath</u>.*)

The following is a list of common prepositions:

about	beyond	of	to
among	by	off	toward
around	despite	on	under
at	down	onto	underneath
before	during	out	until
behind	except	outside	up
below	for	over	upon
beneath	from	past	with
beside	in	since	within
besides	into	through	without
between	near	till	

The following is a list of common compound prepositions:

according to	because of	in place of	on account of
as of	by means of	in respect to	out of
as well as	in addition to	in spite of	prior to
aside from	in front of	instead of	with regard to

A preposition acts as an adverb when it provides more information about a verb: *Several days ago, we took the turkey bones <u>outside</u> because of the smelly garbage.* Here, the preposition explains where the bones were taken.

Interjections have no grammatical attachment to the sentence itself other than to add expressions of emotion. These parts of speech may be punctuated with commas or exclamation points and may fall anywhere within the sentence itself. Here are a few examples of the usage of the interjection: *Ouch! He stepped on my toe. She shopped at the stores after Christmas and, hooray, found many items on sale. I have seen his love for his father in many expressions of concern—Wow!*

> **HELPFUL HINT**
>
> Interjections should generally be avoided in academic writing. However, they are great for adding emotion and excitement to creative writing, journals, and diaries.

SAMPLE QUESTIONS

16) **List all of the adjectives used in the following sentence:**

Her camera fell into the turbulent water, so her frantic friend quickly grabbed the damp item.

- A.　turbulent, frantic, damp
- B.　turbulent, frantic, quickly, damp
- C.　her, turbulent, her, frantic, damp
- D.　her, the, turbulent, her, frantic, the, damp

Answers:

- A.　Incorrect. This list is incomplete.
- B.　Incorrect. This list is incomplete and inaccurate; *quickly* is an adverb.
- C.　Incorrect. This list is incomplete.
- **D.**　**Correct.** *Turbulent, frantic,* and *damp* are adjectives; *her* is modifying first *camera* and then *friend*; and *the* is always a limiting adjective—the definite article.

17) **List all of the pronouns used in the following sentence:**

Several of the administrators who had spoken clearly on the budget increase gave both of the opposing committee members a list of their ideas.

- A.　several, of, their
- B.　several, who, both
- C.　several, who, both, their
- D.　several, both

Go on ⟶

Answers:

A.   Incorrect. The word *of* is a preposition; the word *their* is being used as a possessive adjective.

B.   Correct. *Several* is an indefinite plural pronoun; *who* is a relative pronoun introducing the adjectival clause *who had spoken clearly on the budget increase*; *both* is an indefinite plural pronoun.

C.   Incorrect. The word *their* is being used as a possessive adjective.

D.   Incorrect. The list is missing the word *who* which is a relative pronoun introducing the adjectival clause *who had spoken clearly on the budget increase*.

18)   **List all of the conjunctions in the following sentence, and indicate after each conjunction whether the conjunctions are coordinating, correlative, or subordinating:**

   The political parties do not know if the most popular candidates will survive until the election, but neither the voters nor the candidates will give up their push for popularity.

A.   if (subordinating), until (subordinating), but (coordinating), neither/nor (correlative), for (coordinating)

B.   if (subordinating), but (coordinating), neither/nor (correlative), for (coordinating)

C.   if (subordinating), but (coordinating), neither/nor (correlative)

D.   if (subordinating), until (subordinating), but (coordinating), neither/nor (correlative), up (subordinating), for (coordinating)

Answers:

A.   Incorrect. *Until* and *for* in this sentence are acting as prepositions.

B.   Incorrect. *For* is acting as a preposition.

C.   Correct. *If* is acting as a subordinating conjunction; *but* is acting as a coordinating conjunction; and *neither/nor* is a correlative conjunction pair.

D.   Incorrect. *Up* is acting as an adverb.

19) **List all of the parts of speech following each word for all of the words in the following sentence:**

Since we like cheesecake, we will not have regular cake at our reception.

    A.   since (subordinating conjunction), we (pronoun), like (verb), cheesecake (noun), we (pronoun), will (verb), not (adverb), have (verb), regular (adjective), cake (noun), at (preposition), our (adjective), reception (noun)

    B.   since (subordinating conjunction), we (pronoun), like (verb), cheesecake (noun), we (pronoun), will (verb), not (adverb), have (verb), regular (adjective), cake (noun), at (preposition), our (pronoun), reception (noun)

    C.   since (subordinating conjunction), we (pronoun), like (verb), cheesecake (noun), we (pronoun), will (verb), not (verb), have (verb), regular (adjective), cake (noun), at (preposition), our (adjective), reception (noun)

    D.   since (preposition), we (pronoun), like (verb), cheesecake (noun), we (pronoun), will (verb), not (adverb), have (verb), regular (adjective), cake (noun), at (preposition), our (adjective), reception (noun)

Answers:

    A.   **Correct.** The sentence is deconstructed and the parts of speech are correctly labeled.

    B.   Incorrect. *Our* is not a pronoun; *our* is acting as a possessive adjective.

    C.   Incorrect. *Not* is not a verb; *not* negates the verb, acting as an adverb.

    D.   Incorrect. *Since* is not a preposition as it precedes a subject and verb; *since* is acting as a subordinating conjunction, introducing the adverbial clause.

SYNTAX

Syntax is the study of how words are combined to create sentences. In English, words are used to build phrases and clauses, which, in turn, are combined to create sentences. By varying the order and length of phrases and clauses, writers can create sentences that are diverse and interesting.

PHRASES

A **phrase** is a group of words that communicates a partial idea and lacks either a subject or a predicate.

- ▶ Noun phrase: *the large bridge*
- ▶ Infinitive phrase: *to eat the fish*
- ▶ Prepositional phrase: *on the wharf*

Several phrases may be strung together, one after another, to add detail and interest to a sentence: *The animals crossed the large bridge to eat the fish on the wharf.*

Phrases have general groupings usually depending on the word that begins the phrase itself.

1. **Prepositional phrases**: A prepositional phrase begins with a preposition and ends with an object of the preposition. These phrases set out relationships in time and space: when and where. Examples: *at noon time*; *under the porch*; *before breakfast*; *over the mountain*

2. **Verb phrases**: A verb phrase is composed of the main verb along with its helping verbs. Example: *The chef would have created another soufflé, but the staff protested.*

3. **Noun phrases**: A noun phrase consists of a noun and its modifiers. Example: *The big, red barn rests beside the vacant chicken house.*

4. **Appositive phrases**: Appositive phrases rename the word or group of words that precedes them. Example: *My dad, a clock maker, loves antiques.*

5. **Gerund phrases**: The gerund phrase is one type of **verbal phrase**, a phrase that begins with a word that would normally act as a verb but is instead filling another role within the sentence. Gerund phrases begin with gerunds (verbs ending in *–ing* and acting as nouns). Examples:

    Writing numerous Christmas cards occupies her aunt's time each year. (Here, the gerund phrase is acting as the subject of the verb *occupies*.)

    She remembers enjoying the sounds of the loons on the Maine lake. (Here, the gerund phrase is acting as the direct object of the verb *remembers*.)

    She was worried about becoming like her mother. (Here, the gerund phrase is acting as the object of the preposition *about*.)

> **HELPFUL HINT**
>
> The word *gerund* has an *n* in it, a helpful reminder that the gerund acts as a noun. Therefore, the gerund phrase might act as the subject, the direct object, or the object of the preposition just as another noun would.

6. **Participial phrases**: The participial phrase is a type of verbal phrase that acts as an adjective. Present participles end in *–ing* while past participles end in *–ed*, *–d*, *–en*, *–t*, or other endings. These phrases can be extracted from the sentence, and the sentence will still make sense because the participial phrase is playing only a modifying role. Example:

    Enjoying the stars that filled the sky, Dave lingered outside for quite a while.

    Jon, known for his golf expertise, played in a Vero Beach tournament last month.

7. **Infinitive phrases**: The infinitive phrase is a verbal phrase that may act as a noun, an adjective, or an adverb. Infinitive phrases begin with the

word *to*, followed by a simple form of a verb (*to eat, to jump, to skip, to laugh, to sing*). Examples:

I wanted <u>to see the Christmas lights on each home.</u> (Here, the infinitive phrase is acting as a noun and the direct object of *wanted*.)

<u>To enjoy the multi-berry pie in the evening,</u> she refused dessert at noon. (Here, the infinitive phrase is acting as an adverb, modifying *refused*.)

The student packed the special albums <u>to sort later on.</u> (Here, the infinitive phrase is acting as an adjective, modifying *albums*.)

8. **Absolute phrases**: The absolute phrase usually follows a very simple pattern—noun plus participle—in which a participle follows the noun that it modifies. The entire phrase modifies the entire clause to which it is attached, so the phrase acts as an adverb, usually answering the question *under what conditions?* Examples:

    <u>Her eyes closing,</u> Sandra laid her head down on the pillow, ready for a good night's sleep.

    We sprinted enthusiastically through the finish line, <u>our goal accomplished</u>.

> **HELPFUL HINT**
>
> Verbal phrases often take on complements and modifiers of their own. For example, the direct object of the gerund in the sentence *Making wreaths requires a lot of hard work* is *wreaths*, because those objects are being acted upon (they are being created).

CLAUSES

Clauses come in the form of dependent clauses and independent clauses. All clauses contain both a subject and a verb, even if the subject is implied. However, dependent or subordinate clauses cannot and should not stand alone. Dependent clauses can be grouped by type: adverb, noun, and adjective.

Adverb clauses are introduced by subordinating conjunctions; they modify the independent clauses to which they are attached by answering adverb questions.

- ▶ *<u>Because she loves pizza,</u> we took her to the Pizza Palace.*
- ▶ *She moved to the city <u>after her car broke down completely.</u>*

The following is a list of words that commonly begin adverb clauses:

after	if	than	where
although	in order that	that	whereas
as	once	though	wherever
because	provided that	unless	whether
before	since	until	while
even if	so	when	
even though	so that	whenever	

Noun clauses are introduced by relative pronouns and relative adverbs. They play a vital role in the sentence by filling the position of subject, object of a preposition, or direct object. Because they are acting as nouns, they do not modify.

▶ *When she will move has not been determined.* (Here, the noun clause is acting as the subject of the verb *has*.)

▶ *She gave the prize to whomever he chose.* (Here, the noun clause is acting as the object of the preposition *to*.)

▶ *The judge ruled that she should go to jail.* (Here, the noun clause is acting as the direct object of the verb *ruled*.)

The following commonly begin noun clauses:

▶ Relative Pronouns: *who, whoever, whom, whomever, whose, which, that*

▶ Relative Adverbs: *when, where, why, how*

Adjective clauses are introduced by relative pronouns and relative adverbs. They play a describing or modifying role by following—and providing more information about—a noun or pronoun in the sentence.

▶ *My dad, who built clocks, came from Sweden.* (Modifies *dad*)

▶ *The restaurant where we ate serves salmon.* (Modifies *restaurant*)

  Note: In this sentence above, the temptation is to label the clause adverbial. But that label would be incorrect. The relative adverb—*where*—introduces the adjective clause answering the question which restaurant?

The following commonly begin adjective clauses:

▶ Relative Pronouns: *who, whoever, whom, whomever, whose, which, that*

▶ Relative Adverbs: *when, where, why, how*

SENTENCE STRUCTURE

Writers can diversify their use of phrases and clauses in order to introduce variety into their writing. Variety in **sentence structure** not only makes writing more interesting but also allows writers to emphasize that which deserves emphasis. In a paragraph of complex sentences, a short, simple sentence can be a powerful way to draw attention to a major point.

The following table will help you remember the four sentence structures and the differences among them. Note the patterns in each column.

Table 2.12. Sentence Structure and Clauses

Sentence Structure	Independent Clauses	Dependent Clauses
simple	1	0
compound	2+	0
complex	1	1+
compound-complex	2+	1+

The **simple sentence** will have only one independent clause and no dependent clauses. The sentence may contain phrases, complements, and modifiers, but it will comprise only one independent clause, one complete idea. Example:

The <u>cat</u> (under the back porch) <u>jumped</u> (against the glass) (yesterday).

The **compound sentence** will have two or more independent clauses and no dependent clauses.

Example: *The <u>cat</u> (under the back porch) <u>jumped</u> (against the glass) (yesterday), and <u>he</u> <u>scared</u> my Grandma; <u>he</u> even <u>scared</u> my Grandpa.*

The **complex sentence** will have only one independent clause and one or more dependent clauses.

Example: *Cole, the <u>cat</u> (under the porch), [<u>who loves</u> tuna], <u>jumped</u> (against the glass) (yesterday).*

The **compound-complex sentence** will have two or more independent clauses and one or more dependent.

Example: *<u>Cole,</u> the cat (under the back porch), [<u>who loves</u> tuna], <u>jumped</u> (against the glass) yesterday; <u>he</u> <u>left</u> a mark (on the window) (with his dirty nose).*

SAMPLE QUESTIONS

20) Identify the underlined phrases in the following sentence:

   <u>Wrapping packages for the soldiers,</u> the kind woman tightly rolled the tee-shirts <u>to see how much space</u> remained <u>for the homemade cookies</u>.

   A. participial, infinitive, prepositional
   B. gerund, infinitive, prepositional
   C. gerund, prepositional, prepositional
   D. participial, prepositional, adverbial

→

Go on

Answers:

A. **Correct.** The underlined phrases are participial, infinitive, and prepositional, respectively.

B. Incorrect. *Wrapping packages for the soldiers* is modifying the subject *woman*.

C. Incorrect. *Wrapping packages for the soldiers* is modifying the subject *woman; to see* is the verbal beginning the infinitive phrase.

D. Incorrect. *...for the homemade cookies* is indeed acting adverbially, but the phrase is technically a prepositional phrase, beginning with a preposition and ending with an object.

21) **Which sentence is correct in its sentence structure label?**

A. The grandchildren and their cousins enjoyed their day at the beach. Compound

B. Most of the grass has lost its deep color despite the fall lasting into December. Complex

C. The members who had served selflessly were cheering as the sequestration ended. Simple

D. Do as you please. Complex

Answers:

A. Incorrect. This sentence is simple with only one independent clause.

B. Incorrect. This sentence is simple with only one independent clause but several phrases.

C. Incorrect. This sentence is complex, having only one independent clause and two dependent clauses.

D. **Correct.** This sentence is complex because it has one independent clause (*Do*) and one dependent (*as you please*).

Mechanics and Usage

Mechanics and usage conventions are important in written communication. **Mechanics** are those rules that govern that minutia of written English: punctuation, capitalization, and spelling. **Usage conventions** guide writers and speakers more broadly in the area of word choice to ensure accuracy and agreement within a sentence.

Punctuation

Many of the mechanical choices writers must make relate to **punctuation**. While creative writers have liberty to play with punctuation to achieve their desired ends, academic and technical writers must adhere to stricter conventions.

The **period** is the most common **terminal punctuation** mark, used to end declarative (statement) and imperative (command) sentences. Examples:

- ▶ *Sarah and I are attending a concert.*
- ▶ *Meet me outside the concert hall one hour before the show.*

The **question mark**, another common terminal punctuation mark, is used to end interrogative sentences (questions). Example: *How many people are attending the concert?*

While the difference between the period and the question mark is usually obvious, confusion sometimes occurs when questions are stated indirectly. In that case, the period is usually preferable. Example: *I wonder how many people are attending the concert.*

Exclamation points end exclamatory sentences, in which the writer or speaker is exhibiting intense emotion or energy; thus, writers should carefully consider their use of exclamations. In fact, the exclamation point should be used reservedly or not at all in academic writing unless the exclamation point is within a quotation that a writer incorporates into the text. The emphatic usage of *what* or *how* without asking a question, however, demands the usage of the exclamation point. Example: *What a great show that was!*

> **HELPFUL HINT**
>
> The exclamation point has impact only in contrast to its frequency of usage. That is, if the exclamation point is used frequently, each exclamation will be less impactful. On the other hand, if the exclamation point is used sparingly, its use will draw the reader's attention and emphasize the information contained in the sentence.

The **colon** and the **semi-colon**, though often confused, each have a unique set of rules surrounding their use. While both punctuation marks are used to join clauses, the construction of the clauses and the relationship between them varies.

The **semi-colon** is used to show a general relationship between two independent clauses (IC; IC). Example: *The disgruntled customer tapped angrily on the counter; she had to wait nearly ten minutes to speak to the manager.*

When using the semi-colon with a conjunctive adverb to join two independent clauses, the pattern is as follows: independent clause, semi-colon, conjunctive adverb, comma, independent clause. Example: *She may not have to take the course this <u>year; however,</u> she eventually will have to sign up for that specific course.*

The **colon**, somewhat less limited than the semi-colon in its usage, is used to show a relationship between two clauses and, moreover, to highlight the information contained in the second clause—usually a list, definition, or clarification. While the clause preceding the colon must be an independent clause, the clause that follows doesn't have to be. Examples:

▶ Incorrect. *The buffet offers three choices that include: ham, turkey, or roast beef.*

▶ Correct. *The buffet offers three choices: ham, turkey, or roast beef.*

▶ Correct. *The buffet offers three choices that include the following: ham, turkey, or roast beef.*

A writer should also use the colon to separate a title from a subtitle (Title: Subtitle), to separate the hour and the minutes (9:30 a.m.), to follow certain parts of a letter or memo (To:, From:, Date:, RE:), and to follow a formal salutation (To whom it may concern:).

Neither the semi-colon nor the colon should be used to set off an introductory phrase from the rest of the sentence.

▶ Incorrect. *After the trip to the raceway; we realized that we should have brought ear plugs.*

▶ Incorrect. *After the trip to the raceway: we realized that we should have brought ear plugs.*

▶ Correct. *After the trip to the raceway, we realized that we should have brought ear plugs.*

HELPFUL HINT

Let's eat Grandma, OR *Let's eat, Grandma.* While this well-known example is humorous, it also demonstrates the drastic need for comma accuracy.

Many people are taught that, when reading, a comma represents a pause for breath. While this trick may be useful as a way of helping young readers build fluency, it is not a helpful guide for comma usage when writing. Rather, proper comma usage is guided by a set of specific rules.

The following list summarizes the most important comma rules for accurate comma placement.

1. Commas should be used to separate two independent clauses along with a coordinating conjunction.

   George ordered the steak, but Bruce preferred the ham.

2. Commas should be used to separate coordinate adjectives.

   The shiny, regal horse ran majestically through the wide, open field.

3. Commas should be used to separate items in a series.

   The list of groceries included cream, coffee, donuts, and tea.

4. Commas should be used to negate a statement.

   A hockey game has periods, not quarters.

5. Commas should be used to separate introductory words from the rest of the sentence.

   Slowly, Nathan became aware of his surroundings after the concussion.

6. Commas should be used to separate introductory phrases from the rest of the sentence.

   Within an hour, the authorities will descend on the home.

7. Commas should be used to separate introductory clauses from the rest of the sentence.

   After Alice swam the channel, nothing intimidated her.

8. Commas should be used to separate introductory, participial phrases for the rest of the sentence.

   Smiling from ear to ear, the teen showed his new driver's license to his mother.

9. Commas should be used to separate transitional statements from the rest of the sentence.

   For example, we have thirty students who demand a change.

10. Commas should be used to set off non-essential information (non-restrictive information).

    Estelle, our newly elected chairperson, will be in attendance.

11. Commas should be used to set off appositives.

    Ida, my neighbor, watched the children for me last week.

12. Commas should be used to set off parenthetical elements including words and phrases.

    The movie was, nonetheless, an improvement over the book.

13. Commas should be used to set off nouns of direct address (vocatives).

    Attention, ladies and gentlemen, as we explain the directions.

14. Commas should be used to set off introductory words from quoted words if the introductory words are not an independent clause.

    Elizabeth said sadly, "I want to go home right now for spring break."

15. Commas should be used to set off titles of famous individuals.

    Charles, Prince of Wales, visited Canada several times in the last ten years.

16. Commas should be used to set off the day and month of a date within a text.

    My birthday makes me feel quite old because I was born on February 16, 1958, in Minnesota.

17. Commas should be used to set off the items in an address within a text.

    The package should be delivered to the Department of English, University of Chicago, 1000 Main Street, Chicago, IL 55555.

18. Commas should be used to set up numbers in a text of more than four digits.

    We expect 25,000 visitors to the new museum.

Quotation marks are used for many purposes, the most common of which are related to academic writing and citation. First, quotation marks enclose titles of short, or relatively short, literary works such as short stories, chapters, and poems. (The titles of longer works, like novels and anthologies, are italicized.) Additionally, quotation marks are used to enclose direct quotations within the text of a document where the quotation is integrated into the text. If a quotation is within another quotation, then the inner quotation uses single quotation marks.

Writers also use quotation marks to set off dialogue. Occasionally, quotation marks are used to enclose words used in special sense or for a non-literary purpose. (*The shady dealings of his Ponzi scheme earned him his ironic name "Honest Abe."*)

When considering quotation marks versus italics in notating a title, the question of short versus long is a useful guide. A chapter title is written in quotation marks, while the book title itself is italicized. Short poetry titles are written in quotation marks; long epic poem titles are italicized. An article title is written in quotation marks, while the name of the newspaper is italicized.

Apostrophes, sometimes referred to as single quotation marks, show possession; replace missing letters, numerals, and signs; and form plurals of letters, numerals, and signs in certain instances.

1. To signify possession by a singular noun not ending in s, add 's. (boy = boy's)

2. To signify possession by a singular noun ending in s, add 's. (class = class's)

3. To signify possessions by an indefinite pronoun not ending in s, add 's. (someone = someone's)

4. To signify possession by a plural noun not ending in s, add 's. (children = children's)

5. To signify possession by a plural nouns ending in s, add only the apostrophe. (boys = boys')

6. To signify possession by singular, compound words and phrases, add 's to the last word in the phrase. (everybody else = everybody else's)

7. To signify joint possession, add 's only to the last noun. (John and Mary's house)

8. To signify individual possession, add 's to each noun. (John's and Mary's houses)

9. To signify missing letters in a contraction, place the apostrophe where the letters are missing. (do not = don't)

10. To signify missing numerals, place the apostrophe where the numerals are missing. (1989 = '89)

11. There are differing schools of thought regarding the pluralization of numerals and dates, but be consistent within the document with whichever method you choose. (1990's/1990s) (A's/As)

Other marks of punctuation include the **en dash** (to indicate a range of dates, for example), the **em dash** (to indicate an abrupt break in a sentence and emphasize the words within the em dashes), the **parentheses** (to enclose insignificant information), the **brackets** (to enclose added words to a quotation and to add insignificant information within parentheses), the **slash** (to separate lines of poetry within a text or to indicate interchangeable terminology), and the **ellipses** (to indicate information removed from a quotation, to indicate a missing line of poetry, or to create a reflective pause).

SAMPLE QUESTIONS

22) **Identify the marks of punctuation needed in the following sentence:**

Freds brother wanted the following items for Christmas a red car a condo and a puppy.

   A.   Fred's / Christmas; / car, /condo,

   B.   Fred's / Christmas: / car, / condo,

   C.   Fred's / Christmas: / car,

   D.   Fred's / items' / Christmas: / car, / condo,

Answers:

   A.   Incorrect. *Christmas* must have a colon after it and not a semi-colon. A semi-colon must have an independent clause that precedes and follows.

   B.   Correct. To be possessive, *Fred's* requires an apostrophe before the s. *Christmas* needs a colon to indicate the upcoming list, and *car and condo* should be followed by commas since they are items in a series.

   C.   Incorrect. The correct comma placement for items in a series is a, b, and c.

   D.   Incorrect. The word *items* is simply plural without showing possession.

23) **Identify the marks of punctuation needed in the following sentence:**

No one in the class could believe that the professor who was a well-known scholar did not know that Mark Twains short story The Celebrated Jumping Frog of Calaveras County was recently noted in the article Famous Stories of Local Color.

   A.   professor, / scholar, / "Famous Stories' of Local Color"

   B.   professor, / scholar, / Twain's / "The Celebrated Jumping Frog of Calaveras County" "Famous Stories' of Local Color"

   C.   professor, / scholar, / "Famous Stories of Local Color."

   D.   professor, / scholar, / Twain's / "The Celebrated Jumping Frog of Calaveras County" / "Famous Stories of Local Color."

→

Go on

Answers:

A. Incorrect. *Twain's* is possessive; the name of the short story would be in quotation marks; and the word *Stories* is a simple plural without showing possession.

B. Incorrect. The word *Stories* is a simple plural without showing possession.

C. Incorrect. *Twain's* is possessive; the name of the short story would be in quotation marks.

D. Correct.

Usage Conventions

In addition to learning mechanics, students and teachers of English must seek to gain mastery over **usage conventions**, which govern word choice and order. In particular, these guidelines are intended to create coherence and agreement across sentences and paragraphs.

First, verbs must agree in number with their subjects. (In some other languages, such a Spanish, verbs must also agree with their subjects in gender.) **Subject/verb agreement** rules can be found below:

1. Single subjects agree with single verbs; plural subjects agree with plural verbs.

   The *girl walks* her dog.

   The *girls walk* their dogs.

2. Ignore words between the subject and the verb: agreement must exist between the subject and verb.

   The new *library* ~~with its many books and rooms~~ *fills* a long-felt need.

3. Compound subjects joined by *and* typically take a plural verb unless considered one item.

   Correctness and precision are required for all good writing.

   Macaroni and cheese makes a great snack for children.

4. Compound subjects joined by *or* or *nor* agree with the nearer or nearest subject.

   Neither *I nor my friends are* looking forward to our final exams.

   Neither *my friends nor I am* looking forward to our final exams.

5. For sentences with inverted word order, the verb will agree with the subject that follows it.

   Where *are Bob and his friends going?* Where *is Bob going?*

6. In expletive construction (which is not preferable in most cases), the subject is delayed.

There are several students who are sleeping in class.

There is one student who is sleeping in class.

7. All single, indefinite pronouns agree with single verbs.

   Neither of the students is happy about the play.

   Each of the many cars is on the grass.

   Every one of the administrators speaks highly of Trevor.

8. All plural, indefinite pronouns agree with plural verbs.

   Several of the students are happy about the play.

   Both of the cars are on the grass.

   Many of the administrators speak highly of Trevor.

9. Some of the singular, indefinite pronouns (*all, most, some, more, any*) change agreement depending on the object of the preposition.

   All of the pie is gone.

   All of the pies are gone.

   Some of the bucket is dirty.

   Some of the buckets are dirty.

10. Collective nouns agree with singular verbs when the collective acts as one unit. Collective nouns agree with plural verbs when the collective acts as individuals within the group.

    The band plans a party after the final football game.

    The band play their instruments even if it rains.

    The jury announces its decision after sequestration.

    The jury make phone calls during their break time.

11. The linking verbs agree with the subject and not the subject complement (predicate nominative).

    My favorite is strawberries and apples.

    My favorites are strawberries and apples.

12. Nouns that are plural in form but singular in meaning will agree with singular verbs.

    Measles is a painful disease.

    Sixty dollars is too much to pay for that book.

13. Singular verbs come after titles, business corporations, and words used as terms.

    "Three Little Kittens" is a favorite nursery rhyme for many children.

    General Motors is a major employer for the city.

14. When a relative pronoun (*who, whom, which, that*) is used as the subject of the clause, the verb will agree with the antecedent of the relative pronoun.

    This is the <u>student who is receiving</u> an award.

    These are the <u>students who are receiving</u> awards.

Similarly, pronouns must agree with their antecedents (the words they replaced) in number; however, some pronouns also require gender agreement (*him, her*). **Pronoun/antecedent agreement** rules can be found below:

1. Antecedents joined by *and* typically require a plural pronoun.

   The <u>children and their dogs</u> enjoyed <u>their</u> day at the beach.

   If the two nouns refer to the same person, a singular pronoun is preferable.

   My <u>best friend and confidant</u> still lives in <u>her</u> log cabin.

2. For compound antecedents joined by *or*, the pronoun agrees with the nearer or nearest antecedent.

   Either the resident mice <u>or the manager's cat</u> gets <u>itself</u> a meal of good leftovers.

3. When indefinite pronouns function in a sentence, the pronoun must agree with the number of the pronoun.

   <u>Neither</u> student finished <u>his or her</u> assignment.

   <u>Both</u> of the students finished <u>their</u> assignments.

4. When collective nouns function as antecedents, the pronoun choice will be singular or plural depending on the function of the collective.

   The <u>audience</u> was cheering as <u>it</u> rose to <u>its</u> feet in unison.

   Our <u>family</u> are spending <u>their</u> vacations in Maine, Hawaii, and Rome.

5. When *each* and *every* precede the antecedent, the pronoun agreement will be singular.

   <u>Each and every man, woman, and child</u> brings unique qualities to <u>his or her</u> family.

   <u>Every creative writer, technical writer, and research writer</u> is attending <u>his or her</u> assigned lecture.

HELPFUL HINT

For native English speakers, some or all of these rules may feel like second-nature. For ELLs, however, memorization and extended practice may be required to master subject-verb and pronoun-antecedent agreement.

One common debate between descriptive and prescriptive approaches to grammar involves something called the generic singular. As an example, "Every boy and girl should check _____ homework before turning it in." In technically correct terms, the pronoun that goes in the blank should mirror the gender uncertainty that exists in the phrase "every boy and girl"; the phrase does not refer to an individual of one gender or the other, so the pronoun in the blank should be, properly, "his or her." Thus, the sentence should read: "Every boy and girl should check his or her homework before turning it in." However, the generic singular (their) eliminates what some would call unnecessary wordiness, while avoiding the sexually-insensitive option of defaulting to the male pronoun. Thus, the sentence might also correctly read: "Every boy and girl should check their homework before turning it in."

SAMPLE QUESTIONS

24) **Which sentence in the following list is correct in its subject and verb agreement?**

   A.   My sister and my best friend lives in Chicago.

   B.   My parents or my brother is going to pick me up from the airport.

   C.   Neither of the students refuse to take the exam.

   D.   The team were playing a great game until the rain started.

Answers:

   A.   Incorrect. Because the sentence reads *My sister and my best friend*, the subject is plural and needs a plural verb (*live*).

   B.   Correct. The verb agrees with the closest subject—in this case, the singular *brother*.

   C.   Incorrect. *Neither* is a singular, indefinite pronoun, so the agreement is singular. *Neither refuses...*

   D.   Incorrect. In the context of a game, the team is functioning as a singular, so it should take a singular verb. *The team was...*

25) **Which sentence in the following list is correct in its pronoun and antecedent agreement?**

   A.   The grandchildren and their cousins enjoyed their day at the beach.

   B.   Most of the grass has lost their deep color.

   C.   The jury was cheering as their commitment came to a close.

   D.   Every boy and girl must learn to behave themselves in school.

Answers:

   A.   Correct. *Grandchildren and cousins/their*

   B.   Incorrect. *Most of the grass has lost its deep color.*

   C.   Incorrect. *The jury was cheering as its commitment came to a close.*

   D.   Incorrect. *Every boy and girl must learn to behave himself or herself in school.*

Writers must also consider **verb tense** when choosing their words. In a broad sense, verb tense tells the reader when the action occurred: in the **past**, in the **present**, or in the **future** (*I smiled*; *I smile*; *I will smile*).

The **progressive tense** tells the reader if the action is, was, or will be progressing (*She is smiling*; *she was smiling*; *she will be smiling*). The **perfect tense** tells the reader if the action has been or will be completed (*He had eaten his food*; *he has eaten his food*; *he will have eaten his food*). A progressive aspect can also be added to the perfect tenses to create the perfect progressive tense (*They had been eating their food*; *they have been eating their food*; *they will have been eating their food*).

HELPFUL HINT

Remember that many times because of tense construction, verbs will come in phrase form. For example, in the sentence that follows the verb phrase is multiple words: *She should have been walking the dog more regularly.*

SAMPLE QUESTIONS

Use the regular verb to study, *and insert the correct tenses accordingly.*

26) Present Progressive Tense First Person Singular

27) Future Tense Second Person

28) Present Perfect Tense Third Person Plural

29) Present Tense Second Person

30) Future Perfect Tense Third Person Singular

31) Past Perfect Progressive Tense First Person Singular

32) Past Tense Second Person

33) Future Progressive Tense Second Person

34) Past Progressive Tense First Person Singular

35) Future Perfect Progressive Tense First Person Plural

Answers:

26) I am studying.

27) You will study.

28) They have studied.

29) You study.

30) She will have studied.

31) I had been studying.

32) You studied.

33) You will be studying.

34) I was studying.

35) We will have been studying.

The choice of whether to use active or passive voice is an important consideration a writer must make. Active voice, in which the subject is doing the action, is preferable most of the time over passive voice, in which the subject is being acted upon. In general, passive voice is useful for imposing a tone of objectivity and emotional distance; thus it is used most often in scientific writing and in professional and legal settings. Active voice, on the other hand, creates a sense of action and engagement. Active voice is a subject-action verb-direct object sentence pattern; passive voice is a subject-be verb-past participle pattern. Here is a simple illustration:

Active voice: *The janitor mopped the floor.*

Passive Voice: *The floor was mopped.* OR *The floor was mopped by the janitor.*

COMMON ERRORS

The ability to guide students by providing feedback is essential to a teacher's success. Thus, recognizing the most common grammar errors is a valuable skill for educators.

Errors in diction and usage are common, especially in classrooms with high numbers of ELLs. A list of commonly confused and misused words is below:

- ▶ *a, an*: *a* is used before words beginning with consonants or consonant sounds; *an* is used before words beginning with vowels or vowel sounds.

- ▶ *affect, effect*: *affect* is most often a verb; *effect* is usually a noun. (*The experience affected me significantly* OR *The experience had a significant effect on me.*)

- ▶ *among, amongst, between*: *among* is used for a group of more than two people; *amongst* is archaic and not commonly used in modern writing; *between* is reserved to distinguish two people or groups.

- ▶ *amount, number*: *amount* is used for non-countable sums; *number* is used with countable nouns.

- ▶ *cite, site*: *cite* is a verb used in documentation to credit an author of a quotation, paraphrase, or summary; *site* is a location.

- ▶ *elicit, illicit*: *elicit* means to draw out a response from an audience or a listener; *illicit* refers to illegal activity.

- ▶ *every day, everyday*: *every day* is an indefinite adjective modifying a noun—*each day* could be used interchangeably with *every day*; *everyday* is a one-word adjective to imply frequent occurrence. (*Our visit to the Minnesota State Fair is an everyday activity during August.*)

- ▶ *fewer, less*: *fewer* is used with a countable noun; *less* is used with a non-countable noun. (*Fewer parents are experiencing stress since the new teacher was hired; parents are experiencing less stress since the new teacher was hired.*)

- ▶ *firstly, secondly*: These words are archaic; today, *first* and *second* are more commonly used.

- **good, well**: *good* is always the adjective; *well* is always the adverb except in cases of health. (*She felt well after the surgery.*)

- **implied, inferred**: *implied* is something a speaker does; *inferred* is something the listener does after assessing the speaker's message. (*The speaker implied something mysterious, but I inferred the wrong thing.*)

- **irregardless, regardless**: *irregardless* is non-standard usage and should be avoided; *regardless* is the proper usage of the transitional statement.

- **its, it's**: *its* is a possessive case pronoun; *it's* is a contraction for *it is*.

- **moral, morale**: *moral* is a summative lesson from a story or life event; *morale* is the emotional attitude of a person or group of people.

- **principal, principle**: *principal* is the leader of a school in the noun usage; *principal* means *main* in the adjectival usage; *principle* is a noun meaning idea or tenet. (*The principal of the school spoke on the principal meaning of the main principles of the school.*)

- **quote, quotation**: *quote* is a verb and should be used as a verb; *quotation* is the noun and should be used as a noun.

- **reason why**: *reason why* is a redundant expression—use one or the other. (*The reason we left is a secret. Why we left is a secret.*)

- **should of, should have**: *should of* is improper usage, likely resulting from misunderstood speech—*of* is not a helping verb and therefore cannot complete the verb phrase; *should have* is the proper usage. (*He should have driven.*)

- **than, then**: *than* sets up a comparison of some kind; *then* indicates a reference to a point in time. (*When I said that I liked the hat better than the gloves, my sister laughed; then she bought both for me.*)

- **their, there, they're**: *their* is the possessive case of the pronoun *they*. *There* is the demonstrative pronoun indicating location or place. *They're* is a contraction of the words *they are*, the third-person plural subject pronoun and third-person plural, present-tense conjugation of the verb *to be*. These words are very commonly confused in written English.

- **to lie (to recline), to lay (to place)**: *to lie* is the intransitive verb meaning *to recline*, so an object is not taken by the verb; *to lay* is the transitive verb meaning *to place something*. (*I lie out in the sun; I lay my towel on the beach.*)

- **to try and**: *to try and* is sometimes used erroneously in place of *to try to*. (*She should try to succeed daily.*)

- **unique**: *unique* is an ultimate superlative. The word *unique* should not be modified technically. (*The experience was very unique.*)

- **who, whom**: *who* is the subject relative pronoun. (*My son, who is a good student, studies hard.*) Here, the son is carrying out the action of studying, so the pronoun is a subject pronoun (*who*). *Whom* is the object relative pronoun. (*My son, whom the other students admire, studies hard.*) Here, *son* is the object of the other students' admiration, so the pronoun standing in for him, *whom*, is an object pronoun.

▶ *your, you're*: *your* is the possessive case of the pronoun *you*. *You're* is a contraction of the words *you are*, the second-person subject pronoun and the second-person singular, present-tense conjugation of the verb *to be*. These words are commonly confused in written English.

Agreement errors are those errors that involve faulty subject/verb or pronoun/antecedent agreement.

Incorrect: *The stove and the pan on top of it was scorching hot.*

Correct: *The stove and the pan on top of it were scorching hot.*

Incorrect: *Everyone in the class turned out their pockets as the teacher searched for the missing stapler.*

Correct: *Everyone in the class turned out his or her pockets as the teacher searched for the missing stapler.*

Errors in parallelism prevent a writer from creating a smooth flow, or coherence, from word to word and sentence to sentence. Thus, writers must seek to create parallel structure in their words (*The walls were painted green and gold.*), phrases (*Her home is up the hill and beyond the trees.*), and clauses (*If we shop on Friday and if we have enough time, we will then visit the aquarium.*)—wherever two or more similar and equally important ideas exist next to each other in a sentence.

Sentence errors fall into three categories: fragments, comma splices (comma fault), and fused sentences (run-on). A **fragment** occurs when a group of words does not have both a subject and verb as needed to construct a complete sentence or thought. Many times a writer will mirror conversation and write down only a dependent clause, for example, which will have a subject and verb but will not have a complete thought grammatically. That dependent clause is technically a fragment: *Why are you not going to the mall? Because I do not like shopping.* The second group of words has both a subject and verb but does not have a complete thought. The word *because* creates a dependent, adverbial clause, needing an independent clause to compete the thought technically. A corrected version of the fragment might read, *Because I do not like shopping, I will not plan to go to the mall.*

A **comma splice** (comma fault) occurs when two independent clauses are joined together in a paragraph with only a comma to "splice" them together. Here is an example of a comma splice: *My family eats turkey at Thanksgiving, we eat ham at Christmas.* To avoid the comma splice, this writer has three choices: to join the clauses using a comma plus a coordinating conjunction (*My family eats turkey at Thanksgiving, and we eat ham at Christmas.*); to separate the clauses into two sentences by employing a period and capital letter to begin the next clause (*My family eats turkey at Thanksgiving. We eat ham at Christmas.*); or to join the two clauses using a colon or semi-colon. (*My family eats turkey at Thanksgiving; we eat ham at Christmas.*)

Fused (run-on) sentences occur when two independent clauses are joined with no punctuation whatsoever. *Run jump!* is an example of a fused sentence: two imperative sentences are joined without the proper punctuation. *Run; jump!* is the corrected sentence.

SAMPLE QUESTIONS

36) **What is the verb tense expressed in the following sentence?**

    They <u>will have swum</u> fifty laps during the practice session.

    A.   future tense

    B.   future progressive tense

    C.   future perfect tense

    D.   future perfect progressive tense

    Answers:

    A.   Incorrect. Future tense would be *will swim*.

    B.   Incorrect. Future progressive tense would be *will be swimming*.

    C.   Correct. This is the future perfect tense.

    D.   Incorrect. Future perfect progressive tense would be *will have been swimming*.

37) **Which of the following sentence errors is labelled correctly?**

    A.   Since she went to the store. (fused)

    B.   The football game ended in a tie, the underdog caught up in the fourth quarter. (fragment)

    C.   The football game ended in a tie the underdog caught up in the fourth quarter. (fused)

    D.   When the players dropped their gloves, a fight broke out on the ice hockey rink floor. (comma splice)

    Answers:

    A.   Incorrect. The group of words in A is not a complete thought and would, therefore, be classified as a fragment.

    B.   Incorrect. The sentence in B joins two complete thoughts with only a comma and would, therefore, be classified as a comma splice.

    C.   Correct. These two independent clauses in C are fused because there is no punctuation where the two clauses meet.

    D.   Incorrect. The sentence in D is punctuated properly and constructed correctly. The introductory, adverbial clause is punctuated with a comma; then an independent clause follows.

VOCABULARY

In addition to grammar, vocabulary plays an important role in language development. Students, both native English speakers and ELLs, benefit from continuous word acquisition, especially when they are seeing, learning, and studying new words in context. Thus, teachers must be able to provide support to students by instructing them in the use of word clues and reference materials to acquire new vocabulary.

AFFIXES, CONTEXT, AND SYNTAX

Learning to recognize and define words by observing their form, context, and function is an important goal for students of English; it is a skill that allows the reader to grow his or her vocabulary more efficiently and, in many cases, more effectively than the process of studying words' definitions out of context.

To determine a word's meaning, a reader can use one, or a combination, of tactics. First, he or she might attempt to determine the word's **root** and **affixes** (prefixes and suffixes) to gain a general, though not necessarily exact, understanding of the word's meaning.

Philanthropist = *phil* (meaning love) + *anthropo* (meaning man or humanity) + *ist* (meaning one who)

Philanthropist = lover of humanity

The following chart of prefixes and suffixes summarizes the typical affixes that a reader might encounter.

Table 2.13. Common Prefixes and Suffixes

Prefix	Meaning	Example	Suffix	Meaning	Example
a-, anti-	not, against	atypical, antihero	-able, -ible	able to be done	presentable, visible
bi-	two, twice	bisect, biannual, bicycle	-al, -ial	similar to, exhibiting characteristics of	biblical, potential
circa, circum-	around	circumspect	-ed	verbal (past tense)	danced
de-	reverse, opposite	deconstruct	-er	adjectival (comparative)	faster
dia-	across	diameter	-er	noun (person)	dancer, worker
dis-	not	discover (uncover, reveal)	-est	adjectival (superlative)	fastest, biggest

Prefix	Meaning	Example	Suffix	Meaning	Example
en-, em-	make happen, cause to	encompass, empower	-ful	with attributes of ('full of")	fanciful, watchful
in-, im-, ir-	not	inappropriate, imperfect, irrelevant	-ic	similar to, exhibiting characteristics of	lunatic, enthusiastic
inter-	between	interstate, interrupt	-ing	verbal (present participle/gerund)	dancing
mid-	middle	midterm	-ion, -tion, -ation, -ition	the act or process of an action	liberation, validation
mis-	in error	misappropriate, mistake	-ity, -ty	a state of existence or being	equality, liberty
non-	wrong, not	nonentity	-less	lacking, without	regardless, limitless
pre-	before	precede	-ly	indicative of, characteristic of	slowly, painfully
re-	again, doing over	repeat, review	-ment	the act or process of an action	supplement, augment
semi-	half	semicolon	-ness	state of being, condition	weakness, wellness
sub-	under	subsume, submerge	-ous, -eous, -ious	characteristic of	nauseous, disastrous, various
super-	above	supersede	-s, -es	plural	trees, foxes
trans-	across	transit, translate, transportation			
un-	reverse, opposite, not	unwell, unneeded, unwilling			
under-	limited, underneath	underused			

In addition to looking at the parts of the word, the reader might observe the word's **context** in an attempt to determine the meaning of an unfamiliar word.

> *The philanthropist <u>donated a large sum of money</u> in the hope <u>of improving the lives of those living in poverty</u>.*

The reader may also use syntactical clues to gain a better understanding of a new word.

> *Philanthropists (<u>noun</u>) from all over the world gathered at the fundraiser for cancer research.*

Importantly, learning words in context allows students to learn not only the **denotations** (literal definitions) but also the **connotations** (implied meanings) of the words. This additional knowledge expands the students' understanding of the nuances of word meaning and choice.

Figures of speech are expressions that communicate meaning in a way that is indirect or imaginative rather than literal. When used effectively, figures of speech can be valuable tools in communicating feeling beyond meaning. Some common types of figurative language are defined below:

- ▶ **Alliteration:** repetition of the same sound, usually the initial letter
- ▶ **Antithesis:** contrast in parallel phrases or clauses
- ▶ **Assonance:** repetition of vowels or vowel sounds
- ▶ **Euphemism:** a pleasant-sounding expression for words that might be unpleasant in meaning
- ▶ **Euphony:** words sound pleasant because of their letter sounds
- ▶ **Metaphor:** a comparison not using *like* or *as*
- ▶ **Oxymoron:** juxtaposition of seemingly contradictory words
- ▶ **Paradox:** a seemingly contradictory statement
- ▶ **Simile:** a comparison using *like* or *as*
- ▶ **Verbal Irony:** the use of words that have an entirely different meaning from their literal interpretation

SAMPLE QUESTION

38) **In which answer choice is the figure of speech correctly identified?**
   - A. The stars were like diamonds on black velvet. (metaphor)
   - B. Donald denied doing the dastardly deed. (alliteration)
   - C. The stars were diamonds on black velvet. (simile)
   - D. The raging brook lay at our feet. (euphony)

Answers:
   - A. Incorrect. Similes, not metaphors, use *like*.
   - B. **Correct.** The repetition of the *D* sound indicates alliteration here.

C.   Incorrect. Similes use *like*.

   D.   Incorrect. This is an oxymoron (*raging brook*—a brook does not rage), not euphony.

RESOURCES

Despite their best efforts, students will inevitably encounter a word that they cannot decipher based on usage alone. Thus, in order to assist students in the acquisition of new words, a teacher must also be knowledgeable about the tools and resources that are at his or her students' disposal in the modern age. He or she must understand the purpose and usage of each kind of resource, the limits of the various tools, and the advantages and disadvantages of dependence on reference materials.

Spell checkers come as a default on many word processing systems and can be helpful as a first line of defense against spelling (and even grammar) errors. However, spell checkers should not be used in isolation, as they are limited in their ability to catch certain kinds of errors. For example, a spell checker might recognize *therre* as an incorrect spelling of *there*, but it would not recognize *their* as incorrect. Though improvements are always being made to automatic spelling and grammar checking technology, students would be prudent to continue doing their own editing as well.

Style manuals are guidebooks for general language usage and documentation of sources within a written document, anthology, or field of study. While some style manuals exist to serve a general readership, like *The Chicago Manual of Style*, many serve specific audiences or professional groups, like the *Publication Manual of the American Psychological Association*, which is used in most social science publications. Students should be familiarized with some of the more common style manuals and be able to apply them to their own work.

Dictionaries provide the definitions of words along with a few other important details like part of speech and other forms of the word. Thus, dictionaries are especially useful tools for ELLs. With a good dictionary students can do the following:

- ▶ look up the meaning of a word
- ▶ check the spelling of a word
- ▶ check the plural of a noun or past tense of a verb
- ▶ find out other grammatical information about a word
- ▶ find the synonym or antonym of a word
- ▶ check the part of speech of a word
- ▶ find out how to say a word
- ▶ find out about the register of a word (e.g., formal or informal)
- ▶ find examples of a word's usage

Bilingual dictionaries can be used to translate words and phrases between two languages. While some bilingual dictionaries allow the user to translate only from the one language to the other, many actually allow the reader to translate both directions, to and from the secondary language.

Thesauri (singular: **thesaurus**) are useful when considering alternate word choices. They provide synonyms and antonyms and are useful when a writer needs to vary his or her language or when he or she is looking for just the right word to communicate a particular idea. Students should be taught, however, that thesauri should be used cautiously: sometimes, replacing words for the sake of choosing more interesting or advanced words can complicate the true meaning of the text.

Ineffective: *The man walked toward his house in the wind and snow.*

Ineffective: *The fellow ambulated in the orientation of his household, against the strident gale and frigid precipitation.*

Most effective: *The man trudged toward his distant house, against the harsh wind and unrelenting snow.*

Enhancing word choice without overwriting is challenging but generally makes for the most effective writing. Indeed, as long as the voice of the writer is maintained, the thesaurus can become a tool to add creativity to the text.

Glossaries are useful for researching terms in a specific book or field of study.

Emphasize that these resources are tools for students, not substitutes for their own knowledge. For instance, after looking up a new word in the dictionary, students should make an effort to learn the word. Students may refer to these resources throughout their academic careers, but do their best to enhance their own knowledge.

SAMPLE QUESTION

39) A student in Mr. Moreno's class is writing an essay and needs to find a suitable replacement for the word justify. Where should the student look first?

   A. the dictionary
   B. a glossary
   C. a bilingual dictionary
   D. a thesaurus

Answers:

   A. Incorrect. A dictionary provides definitions and a limited number of synonyms, but it is not the most appropriate place to look.
   B. Incorrect. Glossaries provide definitions for specialized terms.
   C. Incorrect. Bilingual dictionaries provide translations across languages but do not provide synonyms.
   D. Correct. Thesauri provide a list of synonyms and antonyms for each word.

Diversity

In today's language classrooms, diversity extends both to language itself and to the learning process as a whole. Teachers must understand variations in language usage across time and place and must be able to instruct students not only to use language in the context of their own culture and community but also to understand and adapt to the unique characteristics of language usage in other places and times as well. All the while, teachers must also be conscious of how language and culture are impacting their own classrooms and must be able to employ diversified, research-based instructional techniques to meet the diverse needs of their students.

Sociolinguistics

In the United States alone, **language diversification** has led to interesting variances in usage across dialects, accents, regionalisms, and cultures. One area of the country may use the word *soda* while another area of the country may use the word *pop* or *coke*; one area may use the word *sneaker* while another area may say *tennis shoe*; another area of the country may say *grinder* to refer to a long sandwich while another may use the word *hero* or *sub*. A writer should consider both **purpose** and **audience** in deciding whether to employ colloquialisms or to adhere to prescriptive conventions: proper prescriptive usage may be beneficial during a presentation to a potential investor, for example, but a campaign speech in a local town might be heightened by the use of regionalisms.

Sociolinguistics is the study of language and its relation to society and culture. One reason sociolinguistics is important is because sociocultural factors determine language policy. **Language policy** is what a government does to regulate what language(s) is/are spoken and where and when in a country. In a country with a multilingual population, the exclusion of or attempt to exclude languages can cause social and political conflict. Indeed, language has played a crucial part in the separatist movements of regions in many countries, namely Quebec in Canada and the Basque in Spain.

Another important point of study in sociolinguistics is that of regional and social dialects. **Regional and social dialects** are varieties of a language that people in a certain region or social group speak. Dialects are real sociolinguistic phenomena studied and written about and easily heard by laypeople, but they also carry the weight of sociocultural stereotypes and prejudice. For example, in the United States, the "Southern drawl" is well-liked but often associated with ignorance and backwardness in news, television, film, and literature.

When people of two or more language groups need to communicate, they often develop a **pidgin** language, a grammatically simplified mode of communicating that may use elements of both languages. A pidgin is not a person's native language; it is a language of necessity which allows speakers of different languages to communicate. The most common situation that would call for a pidgin would be trade, such as occurred with the development of Chinese Pidgin English when the British began to trade heavily in China in the eighteenth century.

Another area in which dialect plays a part is the idea of **World Englishes**; there are many varieties of English spoken in the world as first and other languages. It may surprise many to know that after the United States, India has the world's highest number of English speakers. Because of colonialization by England and the United States, many countries in the world speak English as a first or second language. Moreover, because of the prevalence of English as a *lingua franca* in business, entertainment, commerce, and academia throughout the world, many more people also learn to speak English as a second language. As the world becomes more globally connected, both native English speakers and those speaking English as a second language must become accustomed to understanding these varying dialects of English.

> **HELPFUL HINT**
>
> If a pidgin language becomes nativized and people begin speaking it as a first language, it is then known as a **creole**. For example, the Gullah language spoken on the South Carolina coast is a creole.

COMMUNICATIVE COMPETENCE

Communicative competence means being able to speak a language both appropriately in a social context as well as correctly in terms of rules and structure. Linguists break down communicative competence into four distinct areas. **Linguistic competence** refers to knowledge of the linguistic components of a language such as syntax, semantics, and so on. **Sociolinguistic competence** means using the language in a socially appropriate way and includes understanding **register:** degrees of formality, differences in setting, appropriate context and so on. **Discourse competence** deals with the knowledge of how to construct smaller units of language like phrases and sentences into cohesive works like letters, speeches, conversations, and articles. **Strategic competence** is the ability to recognize and repair instances of "communication breakdown" by strategic planning and/or redirecting.

SAMPLE QUESTION

40) Which of the four components of communicative competence would address the appropriate way for a student to speak to the principal while visiting a class at school?

　　A.　linguistic competence

　　B.　sociolinguistic competence

　　C.　discourse competence

　　D.　strategic competence

→ Go on

Answers:

A.   Incorrect. Linguistic competence deals with syntax, semantics, and so on.

B.   **Correct.** Sociolinguistic competence deals with using language in a socially appropriate way.

C.   Incorrect. Discourse competence deals with using language in longer forms such as letters and speeches.

D.   Incorrect. Strategic competence deals with recognizing and repairing communication breakdowns.

RESEARCH–BASED ACQUISITION

Differentiated instruction can transform the language acquisition process from one that is rigid and unchanging to one that responds to individual student needs so that everyone can thrive. Indeed, the authenticity of the teacher and the capacity of that teacher to provide differentiated instruction may vastly change the learning outcome and the student performance.

Some differentiated instructional techniques are listed: charting or graphing, comparing, contrasting, debating, demonstrating, discussing, dramatizing, drilling, experimenting, analyzing a film, playing learning games, collaborative group work, illustrating, lecturing, interactive lecturing, listening to music, studying art, having panel discussions, questioning, quizzing, reviewing, role playing, planning a skit, providing study guides, team teaching, testing, assessing with other means than paper tests, video recording, and completing worksheets.

ORGANIZING AND COLLABORATING

Organizing instruction around content and objectives is one way that teachers can ensure that their students are getting the most language and content instruction. In order to do this successfully, teachers must have clearly defined content and language objectives that fall under the umbrella of the academic standards.

Content area standards identify what students are supposed to learn throughout a given time period in a specific subject area. Each content area has its own set of standards. They can be yearly standards, such as the Common Core State Standards, which identify goals and expectations for students' annual learning. Or, they can be unit standards created by the teacher that clearly lay out expectations for students' achievement in a single unit. Either way, they are intended to guide instruction and clearly define goals for students' learning. Content area learning is intended to be aligned to these standards to ensure that all students are learning the same material.

Content objectives identify what students should be able to do at the end of a content area lesson. These objectives are usually the same for all students in the classroom and are related to the key concepts being taught. These objectives should also be clearly stated so that students can understand them without explanation, and they should have measurable goals that are achievable in the given time for the lesson. One example of a well-written content objective is, "Students will explain three contributions made by George Washington that improved the lives of people living in the United States." This objective clearly states what students should be able to do at the end of the lesson and can be measured in a number of ways.

Language objectives tell how students will learn and/or demonstrate their mastery of materials by reading, writing, speaking, or listening. Effective language objectives meet several criteria:

1. They are formed using the tasks of the content area lesson.
2. They emphasize the communicative skills of speaking and writing without neglecting the importance of listening and reading.
3. The use active verbs to name targeted functions.
4. They specify the target language that students will need to complete the task.
5. They focus on language that is suitable for students' use in other contexts.

A strongly written language objective provides a precise look at the expectations for students' learning. For example, the objective "Students will make predictions about the events in the short story using future tense and conditional verbs," states what students will be expected to do, what materials they will use, and what kind of language they will be expected to use. Each element of the objective is clear and measureable.

SAMPLE QUESTION

41) **Which of the following statements is a clearly written language objective?**

   A. Students will learn about the Battle of Antietam.
   B. Students will write a summary of their science lab.
   C. Students will identify and define the adjectives used in character description.
   D. Students will listen to two pianists' interpretations of Beethoven's Fifth Symphony.

Answers:

   A. Incorrect. This objective is not measureable.
   B. Incorrect. This objective does not indicate target language.
   C. Correct. This objective is clear, measurable, transferable to other contexts, and indicates the target language for students' use.
   D. Incorrect. This objective is not focused on communicative linguistic skills.

PROMOTING MENTAL DEVELOPMENT OF STUDENTS

While students can develop many mental skills on their own, teachers can always promote this development through lessons and activities that are aimed toward increasing understanding and awareness of cognitive and metacognitive strategies. Strategies differ from the skills students use inherently as they require some thought to determine what strategy will be used.

Cognitive strategies help students remember and organize both content and language learning information. Deliberate instruction in cognitive strategies can help all students become more successful in their learning. For example, it is common to skim the title, headings, and pictures for information when reading. This strategy is taught to children as they are learning to read and often becomes habitual with good readers. It develops into a skill. Skimming assists students in anticipating what they are about to read and aids them in making predictions. Another common practice is grouping information. When presented with large amounts of material, it is helpful to separate the information into chunks that relate to one another. Some teachers show students how to do this with graphic organizers, diagrams, or outlines. Regardless of the strategy, direct instruction in cognitive practices aids students in understanding the content and linguistics they are learning. There are five types of strategies to aid students in their learning.

1. **Comprehension strategies** help students understand and remember content. These strategies are usually broken into the subcategories of monitoring, using text structure, summarizing, elaborating, and explaining. When explicitly taught to use these strategies, students can retain and comprehend information more easily.

2. **Writing strategies** help students complete unstructured tasks. These teach students the importance of planning in order to conceive and organize ideas. After they plan their work, students begin generating a piece. After the initial draft, revisions and edits are made before presenting the final product. Students who complete all of the steps in writing strategies are more likely to create comprehensive, well-composed pieces.

3. **Problem-solving strategies** help students to see ways in which they can achieve a specific goal. Students are presented with a problem and must identify steps to solve it. There are several effective problem-solving strategies, but the most popular steps involve teaching students to understand the problem, then to develop a plan for solving it. Students then carry out the plan and look back to see what can be learned from their process and their solution.

4. **Reasoning strategies** help students determine what they believe to be true or false, correct or incorrect. Successful reasoning involves the creation of arguments and counterarguments, fair evaluation of evidence, and consideration of sources.

5. **Self-regulation strategies** help students monitor their behaviors. Students who master self-regulation are capable of successful self-monitoring and evaluations, time management, and goal setting. These skills aid them in their learning endeavors by contributing to their metacognitive processes and focus.

Metacognitive strategies are those that focus on thinking about thinking. They involve one's knowledge of one's own thinking processes, one's own knowledge itself, and the limitations of that knowledge. Metacognition is not an inherent process; students must be taught how to analyze their knowledge in order to successfully plan, monitor, evaluate, and revise their thinking to meet various learning environments and subjects. Metacognitive strategies teach students how to identify their prior knowledge of a topic, recognize what they don't know about something, and what it is that they still need to learn. They help students to plan their learning, self-regulate, and choose appropriate cognitive strategies to aid them as they study new material.

Direct instruction in metacognitive strategies can lead to increases in students' learning. Teaching students several strategies can lead them to both success and self-sufficiency in implementing these approaches.

1. **Identify what is known and what is not.** Students need to recognize their prior learning and then move forward in determining what they don't know, what they need clarification on, and what knowledge has stuck with them.

2. **Plan.** Estimating the time a task will take, organizing materials, scheduling group or individual work time, and determining procedures for completing a task all require planning. Students should assume responsibility for these components of planning in order to become self-directed. Criteria for evaluating their planning process should be established and taught as students proceed through an activity.

3. **Keep a thought journal.** Logging their own thoughts and ideas can help students reflect upon their thinking and understanding of a topic. It can also help them to understand any difficulties they are struggling with as they work through a problem or process.

4. **Talk about thinking.** This process must be modeled for students. Teachers should think aloud during problem-solving and planning activities to show students what this process looks like. This will enable them to understand what it means to talk about their thinking and demonstrate the benefits of doing it.

5. **Self-evaluate.** Show students what it means to self-evaluate by modelling the process. Providing them with checklists or one-on-one conferences can help them to develop the skills necessary for determining their own understanding as well. And as students come to recognize how to implement strategies and where they are most useful,

they will develop the ability to evaluate their use of strategies for success as well as their understanding.

6. **Debrief.** Activities that focus on closure help students to develop awareness of the strategies they implemented, as well as where their successes and areas of improvement are. It also helps them to recognize the cross-curricular uses of many of the strategies they employ.

Activating students' prior knowledge can help them make connections between what they already know and what they are going to learn. In order to activate students' prior knowledge, there are several strategies that teachers can use to encourage students to think about what they already know.

1. **Introduce vocabulary before content.** Presenting students with words and learning about them prior to being expected to apply them allow students to gain comfort and familiarity with new words and to demonstrate their understanding and practice words they already knew. It can help them to recall familiar topics within given content.

2. **Use graphic organizers, outlines, and diagrams.** Helping students to visualize content can aid them in recall. By creating a visual aid to organize information, students are able to see the material in the topic and potentially recall prior learning.

3. **Brainstorm ideas about the topic or content.** Students are able to toss out ideas that they have and make connections with what they already know when completing brainstorming activities. It may help them to generate connections that they did not know existed.

4. **Ask questions about the content or topic and things related to it.** This kind of exercise can help students to use vocabulary that they already know and prepare them to use what they are going to learn in communicative ways.

SAMPLE QUESTIONS

42) Mr. Carson wants to conduct a classroom experiment to see how many students are able to get an inflated balloon from one side of the room to the other without using their arms, legs, or mouths. He has set some obstacles in the room for students to get around, including a large blue tarp on the floor that he has named "the quicksand." Any student who touches the quicksand is automatically out.

What kind of cognitive strategy should Mr. Carson model for students before allowing them to attempt the activity?

A. comprehension strategy

B. problem-solving strategy

C. reasoning strategy

D. writing strategy

Answers:

A) Incorrect. Students conducting this experiment do not need to recall content information.

B) Correct. Students conducting this experiment need to work out how to solve the problem presented using a series of logical steps.

C) Incorrect. Students conducting this experiment do not need to conclude what they think is true or false.

D) Incorrect. Students conducting this experiment are not working on an unstructured or written task.

43) **Which of the following strategies is NOT intended to aid students in activating prior knowledge?**

A) asking questions about the content

B) introducing vocabulary before content

C) using graphic organizers, diagrams, and outlines

D) listening to an expert speaker discuss the content

Answers:

A) Incorrect. Asking questions allows students to recall and process through discussion information that they already learned.

B) Incorrect. Previewing vocabulary allows students to gain familiarity with new materials and may allow them to make connections between what they are going to learn and what they have previously learned.

C) Incorrect. The use of graphic organizers allows students to create visual representations of what they have learned and allows them to add to their prior knowledge in an organized way.

D) Correct. Listening to an expert speaker discuss a topic may be beneficial to students' understanding of the material, but it will not activate their prior knowledge.

Writing, Speaking, and Listening

Effective language use at the most basic level—the sentence—is essential to effective communication. However, beyond these basics, students must spend a significant amount of time—both inside and outside of school—developing the writing, speaking, and listening skills that will allow them to succeed in the adult world.

WRITING

An ELA classroom emphasizes building students' written communication skills. These skills extend far beyond the basics of grammar and vocabulary: indeed, producing meaningful writing is a task that requires extensive planning and revising.

PURPOSE, AUDIENCE, AND TASK

In order to produce meaningful work, a writer must first have a clear understanding of its **purpose**. Purpose usually falls into one of three modes: narrative, informative, or argumentative.

Narrative writing tells a story; it includes a plot and characters, and its purpose may be to entertain the reader. In **informative** writing, the writer provides the reader with information on a given topic. **Argumentative** writing is intended to convince the reader to agree with a certain perspective or opinion.

All three modes of writing described above share a common trait: they are intended for an audience. Second only to purpose, **audience** is the most important factor a writer must consider when embarking on a new project. He or she must study and know the intended audience well: the writer's perception of his or her reader will guide elements of the writing, from topic to syntax to diction. The **tone** of a history professor's account of the Boston Tea Party, for example, will vary widely based on whether it is written for graduate students or kindergartners; a scientific article intended for a popular audience will be far less complex than one intended for an audience of professionals. Sometimes, there are even special limits or requirements based on audience. For example, a teacher might decide that an essay assignment is limited to ten pages and must adhere to MLA guidelines.

Together with the writer's personal preferences, the combination of purpose and audience might lend itself to a particular writing **task**, the specific form that the project will take.

If the writer hopes to express his or her creativity, he or she might produce a narrative in the form of a **short story** or **novel**.

Journals take different forms depending on their audience. A personal journal is an outlet for a writer to record his or her experiences and thoughts; this type of journal is usually intended only for the writer, not any outside readers. **Professional journals** are comprised of articles on a given subject, in which professionals provide colleagues with research-based conclusions about their fields of study.

An **essay** is a short piece of writing that, like a professional journal, addresses a scholarly audience. In an essay, a writer explores a single topic in order to inform or persuade the reader.

Writers may also construct a piece of short writing that is intended to be delivered orally: a **speech**. The production of a speech differs from other writing tasks in that the speech writer must consider nuances of tone, facial expression, pacing, and audience reaction when designing and delivering the speech. See below for more information on oral delivery of speeches.

QUICK REVIEW

Consider the most appropriate type of writing task for students assigned to *describe* a political party. Consider the appropriate mode of writing for students assigned to *convince* the reader of the best candidate to vote for in an upcoming election.

A **blog** provides an online outlet for the expression of personal ideas, experiences, and opinions. Writers often design their blogs to focus on a particular theme or audience. Unlike other forms of writing, blogs allow dialogue and discourse between the writer and reader (and even among readers themselves). Often blog writers read and respond to feedback from readers, who post their own ideas as comments. Blog writers may even imbed hyperlinks through their writing in order to draw attention to their blog, to a business, or to a cause. See below for more information on using blogs.

SAMPLE QUESTION

1) **Which of the following is the most common purpose for a writing task?**

A.   to inform

B.   to persuade

C.   to argue a point

D.   to narrate a story

Answers

A.   **Correct.** The most common purpose for writing tasks is informative, the dissemination of information for the general public in magazines, newspapers, and journal articles.

B.   Incorrect. While persuasion is common in advertising and politics, it is not as common as informative writing.

C.   Incorrect. Like persuasive writing, argumentative writing has a very specific purpose but is not as common as informative writing.

D.   Incorrect. While creative writers focus on scripts, novels, short stories, and poems, informative writing is more common.

UNITY, COHERENCE, AND DEVELOPMENT

To accurately and effectively convey information and meaning, a writer must carefully develop sentences, paragraphs, and whole texts.

The **writing process** typically involves the following steps: **planning** (mapping or brainstorming), **drafting** (writing and constructing), **revising** (moving, cutting, replacing, and adding), **editing** (checking grammar and punctuation), and **proofreading** (checking the final draft for typos).

Throughout the writing process, it is essential that a writer ensure unity in a text. **Unity** demands that the details included in a sentence, paragraph, or text share a main idea: all ideas within a paragraph, for example, must support the main idea that is expressed in the paragraph's topic sentence (often the first sentence of the paragraph). Similarly, the thesis statement for a larger work will unify ideas across paragraphs and across the full text.

There are many kinds of details that a writer can use to support his or her main idea. Many writers refer to the acronym **RENNS** to recall these various types: *Reasons, Examples, Names, Numbers,* and *Senses.* By varying the types of details they use, writers can make their writing more interesting and convincing.

Coherence refers to the logical progression of words, sentences, and paragraphs. It is important to write as clearly as possible to allow the reader to follow the logic and progress of the text. To assist with coherence, writers employ transitional expressions, some of which are listed below.

Table 3.1. Transitional Expressions

Meaning	Expressions
addition	and, furthermore, moreover, too, also, in addition, next, besides, first, second
contrast	although, in contrast, but, conversely, nevertheless, however, on the contrary, on the other hand
time	later, earlier, when, while, soon, thereafter, meanwhile, whenever, during, now, until now, subsequently
location	nearby, adjacent to, beyond, above, below
comparison	similarly, in the same manner, in like manner, likewise
cause	because, since, on account of, for that reason
illustration	specifically, for instance, for example
effect	therefore, consequently, accordingly, as a result
summation	in summary, in brief, to sum up
conclusion	in conclusion, finally
referring back to an object or idea	this, that, these, those (The pronoun reference must be near the antecedent and clear to avoid a pronoun reference error.)
to replace a noun	Use personal pronouns for coherence to avoid unnecessary redundancies.

One of the biggest detriments to coherence is **overwriting**. Overwriting occurs when a writer tries to imbue his or her work with inappropriately and awkwardly ornate language or complex, technical terms. Not only might this kind of writing seem disingenuous to the audience, but it will also likely become difficult to follow.

Writing for the general audience means that the author's honest voice neither belittles nor overwhelms. A creative writer addresses a topic honestly and simply: *The sunshine revealed dew drops clinging to each spider web.* Avoid overwriting: *The glorious rays from the happy, beaming face of the morning light radiated joy as the water blobs rested on the stringy spider webs.*

ORGANIZING WRITING

Aside from unity and coherence, writers have other considerations when developing a piece of writing, especially in terms of the overall organization of ideas and paragraphs in the text.

Almost all writing begins with an **introduction**, which sets the tone, topic, direction, style, and mood for the writing that is to follow. Most importantly, the introduction provides the first impression of the writer to the reader. Thus, writers must create introductions that are engaging and appropriate for their particular audience.

A **conclusion** leaves the reader with a sense of closure by reiterating the author's thesis and sometimes even providing a summary of his or her main points.

Between the introduction and the conclusion, a writer may develop a text using a number of different organizational patterns, some of which are described below:

- **Chronological order** is employed when a writer organizes events in a text in the order in which they occurred.
- **Spatial sequence** is employed when a writer organizes information according to its position in space.
- **Compare and contrast** organization starts by highlighting the similarities between two things and then addresses their differences.
- **Cause and effect** organization begins by discussing the causes or reasons for a given phenomenon and ends with the revelation of the effect.
- **Problem and solution** organization starts by introducing a problem and concludes by exploring solutions to that problem.

A particularly useful tool for organizing ideas is the outline. An **outline** is an overall map of the content of a text; it may be informal or formal, phrasal or clausal. A formal outline for a written essay should include the following elements: an introduction, a thesis statement, main points in grammatically similar structure, sub-points in grammatically similar structure, active voice, action verbs, a restatement of the thesis, and a conclusion. Below is an example of a formal outline for an argumentative writing task:

I. The first paragraph introduces the reader to the topic (here, *Cats make better pets than dogs*).
   A. An anecdote may get a reader's attention; here, the writer could relate a personal story about an experience with a dog or cat.
   B. Thesis statement: While dogs are loyal and protective, cats are smarter, more affordable, independent, and cuter, so they make better pets.

II. Cats are smarter than dogs.
   A. Dogs often get sick from eating foreign objects, incurring costly vet bills; cats rarely eat such items.
   B. If dogs are left outside alone, they may get lost and are at risk of injury or death due to traffic; cats are able to protect themselves better and almost always find their way home.

III. Cats are easier to care for than dogs.

    A.   Cats are smaller and lazier; they do not require walks.

    B.   Cats can be left alone for several days with ample food, water, and litter; dogs require daily attention and thus a dog sitter.

IV. Cats are more pleasant to live with than dogs.

    A.   Cats have softer fur and are therefore cuddlier.

    B.   Cats are quieter than dogs; they meow, while dogs bark.

V. The final paragraph concludes the essay and discusses the broad implications of the issue.

    A.   <u>Restatement of Thesis</u>: Even though dog ownership has many benefits, the convenience, affordability, and enjoyment cats offer makes them the superior pet.

    B.   With so much to offer, cats will surely become even more popular than they are today.

Figure 3.1. Sample Outline

If students struggle with the outline format, **graphic organizers** are useful tools for helping students understand text organization visually.

SAMPLE QUESTION

2) **Which of the following is NOT true about the use of transitional expressions?**

    A.   Writers should use them to transition from paragraph to paragraph.

    B.   Writers should use them to transition from sentence to sentence.

    C.   Writers should use them to create the proper direction of thought.

    D.   Writers should use them only at the end of each paragraph.

Answers

    A.   Incorrect. Transitional expressions make for smooth reading from paragraph to paragraph.

    B.   Incorrect. Transitional expressions make for smooth reading from sentence to sentence.

    C.   Incorrect. Transitional expressions create direction of thought such as contrast or addition.

    D.   **Correct.** Using transitions at the ends of paragraphs is generally not a good idea. Using them to open paragraphs develops coherence more effectively.

EFFECTIVE RESEARCH

It is crucial for a research writer to form a specific and answerable **research question** as part of the planning process. This question will focus the author's research. For example, the topic *education* is too **broad** to result in meaningful research findings. Thus, the writer must **narrow** his or her topic to *higher education* or, even further, to *higher education in the twenty-first century*. Then, the writer must further hone his or her focus by formulating a specific question to explore: *What are some of the changes that institutions of higher education must address to stay relevant in the twenty-first century?*

After formulating a research question, a research writer must embark on the task of searching for relevant, impactful information from credible sources.

With today's student relying heavily on the Internet for information, teachers have the responsibility not only to guide students in the appropriate use of digital resources but also to ensure students understand the importance of print resources and how to utilize them. Most importantly in research writing, teachers must equip students to evaluate the credibility of a text based on its source, contemporaneity, and purpose. In general, **print resources** may be more credible because they go through numerous reviews before arriving in the hands of the researcher. Print resources include books, magazines, newspapers, and journals. **Digital and online resources**, on the other hand, can pose a bigger challenge for young researchers, as the Internet provides little-to-no oversight regarding who can post information online or its reliability. Thus, students must remain especially aware of inaccuracies and bias when using the Internet for research; teachers must direct them to credible sources. Such sources may include peer-reviewed journals or reputable news outlets and blogs.

Ethical research practices exist to ensure that fairness and truth are employed in the pursuit of knowledge. Some research practices that might be considered **unethical** are the following: buying and selling research papers for purposes other than the dissemination of knowledge; knowingly using and disseminating biased material that falsely spreads shallow, unsubstantiated claims as academically-researched empirical evidence; using resources that stem from a company's desire to sell something or to promote a private agenda; removing a fact or piece of writing from its context in order to manipulate an audience's interpretation of it; and passing off the work of another as one's own or failing to properly credit another whose work is being referenced (plagiarism).

A significant amount of time in research-based writing is devoted to ensuring that resources and reference materials are properly cited. Proper **citations** have two parts: first, the original source must be credited within the document itself (**in-text citation**); then, the source must be credited at the end of the document using a reference page, a bibliography page, or a works cited page. Many word processing programs have tools and references to assist writers in adhering to various writing styles and their citation formats. Various websites and applications are also available to assist in the easy formation of accurate citations.

Style manuals function as guidebooks for the documentation of sources within a written document. The most common style guides are the following: APA (*Publication Manual of the American Psychological Association*), which writers use for the fields of education, psychology, and other social sciences; MLA (*Modern Language Association Style Manual and Guide to Scholarly Publishing*), which writers use for arts, humanities, and literature; Chicago (*The Chicago Manual of Style*), which writers use for the sciences, history, literature, and art; and Turabian (*A Manual for Writers of Research Papers, Theses, and Dissertations* by Kate Turabian), which writers use for history and theological studies. Other style manuals apply more narrowly to anthropology and specific fields of scientific study.

STYLES OF IN-TEXT CITATIONS
Example 1: Literary or Linguistic Studies (MLA)

When using MLA style for documentation and research, the author of the writing task must attribute summaries, paraphrases, and quotations to the original author or group. In-text citations following the summary, paraphrase, or quotation identify the origin of the material. An in-text citation in MLA format looks like the following:

> The popularity of fantasy opened up "other worlds" to readers: "He was a faun. And when he saw Lucy he gave such a start of surprise that he dropped all of his parcels" (Lewis 114).

The parenthetical citation after the quotation refers to the author (C.S. Lewis) and a page number for this particular printing of the text (114). If the writer uses the name of the author to introduce the quotation, the parenthetical reference contains only a page number for a print source.

The second part of proper citation in MLA format requires that the author of the writing task include the publication information of his or her source in a *Works Cited* page, alphabetized according to the source author's last name (or the first significant word in a title if there is no author). The entry on the *Works Cited* page would look like the following for the in-text citation above:

> Lewis, C.S. *The Chronicles of Narnia*. New York: Harper Collins, 1994. Print.

Example 2: Psychology and Social Sciences (APA)

As with MLA, a writer using APA who quotes, paraphrases, or summarizes the work of another must cite that source. However, APA in-text citation varies in format from that of MLA. In-text citation in APA format looks like the following:

> The general trend in the early 1900s was to consult the student, an action that had, up to that time, been looked upon as "soft pedagogy" (Tolman, 1902, p. 159).

The same writer might, alternatively, include some citation information in the text itself.

> The general trend in the early 1900s was to consult the student,
> an action that had, up to that time, been looked upon as what
> Tolman (1902) called "soft pedagogy" (p. 159).

The parenthetical citation refers to the author (Tolman), the year of publication (1902), and the page number from the referenced text (p. 159).

In APA, as in MLA, documentation occurs not only with an in-text citation, but also after the document as part of the *References* page. The author of the writing task must include the proper publication information of all references, alphabetized according to the author's or first author's last name (if more than one author) or the first significant word in a title if there is no author. The entry on the *References* page would look like the following for the in-text citation above:

> Tolman, A. (1902). The revival of English grammar. *The School
> Review, 10*(2), 157-165.

Example 3: History (Chicago)

When using Chicago style for documentation and research, the author of the writing task must attribute summaries, paraphrases, and quotations to the original author or group. By way of footnotes indicated by superscript following the summary, paraphrase, or quotation, the author of the writing task identifies the origin of the material. In-text citation in Chicago style looks like the following:

> The power of the naval forces could not be underestimated. "So
> great was the force of the big naval guns that surgeons swore
> they had seen men killed by the wind of a passing shot."[1]

The superscript ([1]) would then correspond to a footnote at the bottom of the corresponding page to the quoted material. At the bottom of the page, an entry would appear with the publication information immediately at hand for the reader's convenience.

> [1]Toll, Ian W. *Six Frigates: The Epic History of the Founding of the U.S.
> Navy*. New York: W. W. Norton & Company, 2006.

Example 4: History and Theology (Turabian)

Kate Turabian's style manual is very similar to Chicago style. The difference between the Chicago and Turabian styles is the largely stand-alone nature of Turabian. The reader of an article written in Chicago style may have to reference other materials to fully understand what he or she is reading. The reader of an article written in Turabian style will find stand-alone information within the text itself. Overall, the Turabian-style article is more comprehensive.

A theological work in Turabian style presents citations in footnotes. If the author and publication information have been referenced previously in the text, the footnote may contain more information regarding the citation:

> It is difficult to understand Hoekema's "new-self." For example, Hoekema acknowledges the difficulty of differentiating between the objective and subjective parts of sanctification.[25]

Further information would be provided in the footnote as in the following:

> [25]The objective or definitive part of sanctification is that which is finished at salvation. Hoekema explains this in the Reformed view in pages 73 – 74 of the *Five Views on Sanctification*. He terms progressive sanctification as "subjective."

Then the Hoekema reference would be listed under the bibliographical entries as the following:

> Hoekema, Anthony A. "Reformed Perspective." In *Five Views on Sanctification*, ed. Stanley N. Gundry, 59 – 90. Grand Rapids: Zondervan, 1987.

ELECTRONIC SOURCES: GENERAL GUIDELINES

Sources that are primarily accessed online are **electronic sources**. With the rapid development of internet communication and publishing in recent years, style manuals have had to evolve quickly to accommodate new reference formats: websites, online books, journal articles, DVDs, online magazines, online newspapers, interviews, and more. While many style guides have turned away from requiring URLs and other complicated details, some citations still require a DOI (Digital Object Identifier). Thus, writers must consult specific manuals for specific instructions and details.

Generally, when citing electronic sources, writers should take note of the following elements:

- ▶ the author(s), compiler(s), or editor(s) of a text, keeping in mind that the authors may be a corporation or group
- ▶ the title of the book, article, website posting, or blog title, especially if it differs from the name of the website or the website sponsor
- ▶ the name of the website, often revealed in the URL (www.apa.studies)
- ▶ the sponsor of the website or an associated organization, institution, or company
- ▶ the date that the electronic source was posted (as in website articles) or published (as in articles from online periodicals)

▶ the date that the researcher accessed the source

▶ the format of the source (Note: if a resource is a PDF, it may be because this source is actually a print source. Otherwise, online reference materials fall under the web format.)

The following is an example of citing an electronic source with a DOI (Digital Object Identifier):

> Kuh, G. (1999). How are we doing? Tracking the quality of the undergraduate experience, 1960s to the present. *The Review of Higher Education, 22*(2), 99-120. doi: 10.1353/rhe.1999.0003

ETHICAL USE OF SOURCES

When a research writer summarizes, paraphrases, or quotes the ideas or conclusions of another but neglects to credit the original source, that writer is committing **plagiarism**. Whether the result of malice or ignorance, plagiarism is a serious offense with serious consequences. Academic, professional, and even legal consequences can arise from the improper and unethical use of another person's work.

One type of information that does not need to be cited, however, is **common knowledge.** *Common knowledge* refers to the set of facts and information that is reiterated frequently and is assumed to be true among a group or within a culture. In the general public, common knowledge is broad: it is information that the typical person can be expected to know. Within a group of medical professionals, on the other hand, common knowledge takes on a different meaning—one in which a basic understanding of medical terminology is assumed. When in doubt, it is always safer to credit a relevant source or consult with a style manual.

In discussing the use of reference materials, teachers must also understand and address the topic of **source integration**, that is, how a resource is used effectively without overwhelming the writer's own voice and ideas. In simple, but vague, terms, resources should not be overused or underused: they should support the writer's ideas appropriately without overshadowing them or replacing them altogether. Whenever possible, writers should avoid beginning and/or ending paragraphs with cited material. This practice ensures that the resources are truly integrated and that the ideas that are shaping the paragraphs via the topic sentences are the writer's own.

Sources can be integrated into a research paper in three different ways: by quoting, paraphrasing, or summarizing. A quotation is an exact (or near exact) transfer of content and punctuation from a resource into a research paper. Quotations should be less than four lines long and are denoted directly in the text using quotation marks and a parenthetical citation. Sometimes, longer quotes are included if they are especially impactful; they should be offset to signify a significant break from the writer's own words. Quotes are most effective when integrated completely into sentences and paragraphs of a research text. Thus, bracket and ellipses rules exist to clarify any sections of a quotation that the writer might have altered in order to lend coherence to the sentence or paragraph.

A **paraphrase** is not simply a synchronistic syllable replacement of words. Rather, paraphrasing involves changing both the wording and the syntax used to express an idea: a writer restates a specific piece of information from a source in his or her unique voice.

Summaries are similar to paraphrases in that they require the author to use his or her own voice; however, summaries usually cover much more material. While a writer may paraphrase a particular point or idea from an article, for example, he or she may summarize the article as a whole.

All three types of source integration—**quotations**, **paraphrases**, and **summaries**—require citation according to the appropriate style guide.

The basic order of events in research writing should follow a particular progression, especially for the beginner research writer, to aid in the prevention of plagiarism and the smooth integration of source materials. Students should do the following:

1. Narrow down a topic and formulate a research question that will drive all of the research.

2. Gather credible source material—compiling significant ideas in the form of summaries, paraphrases, and quotes.

3. Write source citation entries according to the appropriate writing style for a reference page, bibliography page, or works cited, and store them alphabetically. This step saves time when it comes time to finalize a document.

4. Formulate an outline with a thesis and main points.

5. Draft the project from the outline alone, NOT using any outside sources. This will ensure that the ideas in the essay will have as their foundation the author's own thoughts and conclusions.

6. Add transitional expressions within paragraphs and between paragraphs for coherence.

7. Integrate summaries, paraphrases, and quotations from the research that support and enhance the points that the author is trying to make.

8. Revise the essay for clarity, coherence, and organization.

9. Edit the paper using an extensive editing checklist.

10. Proofread the final product for typographical errors.

SAMPLE QUESTIONS

3)   Which of the following sources would NOT be a good choice for an authoritative digital source in a research project?

A.   a peer-reviewed journal article retrieved from JSTOR that has multiple reputable sources listed in the reference page for the article

B.   an article retrieved through a general Google search that quotes from *Wikipedia*

C.   an article posted by the U.S. Department of Education with the statistics that include the number of high school dropouts from across the country

D.   an extensive study posted by a car company that includes dates, statistics, and a lengthy reference page

Answers

A.   Incorrect. A peer reviewed journal article from JSTOR, a journal bank, is a reputable source.

B.   Correct. A general Google search does not necessarily provide any reliable sources; furthermore, *Wikipedia* is not a reliable source. Google Scholar may have some usable articles.

C.   Incorrect. The Department of Education is usually considered a reputable source; websites ending with *.gov* are U.S. government websites.

D.   Incorrect. The data from this source is probably usable; however, the researcher should be cautious about using any interpretation of the statistics, given that the company may be biased.

4)   Which of the following sources would NOT be a good choice for an authoritative print source in a research project?

A.   a book published by the NRA that cites examples and statistics from Canada to support a pro-gun agenda

B.   a recent magazine article from *Psychology Today* that includes the latest mental health assessment tools

C.   a dissertation regarding the use of sentence diagramming with adult learners that includes the research conducted during a true experiment

D.   a sacred text that illustrates the basic tenets of the religion of the region

Answers

A.   Correct. A book written by a special interest group may be biased.

B.   Incorrect. A peer-reviewed article is a reliable informative source.

C.   Incorrect. A true experiment controls for external threats to validity, so the research could be very reliable as a source.

D.   Incorrect. A sacred text is a primary source, and therefore would be an excellent choice.

5)   **Which of the following would be an effective way to introduce and integrate a source into a research paper?**

A.   Some people think "…

B.   This quotation says it well: "…

C.   I don't know how to say this, but this author says it best: "…

D.   Dr. Philip Stern, author of twenty books on the subject of sleep deprivation and graduate of Famous State University, concluded after his experiment that "…

Answer

A.   Incorrect. "Some people think" is a weak introduction because it makes a generalization and lacks a specific reference.

B.   Incorrect. "This quotation says it well" is a weak introduction, lacking a reference to a specific author or authoritative source.

C.   Incorrect. "I don't know how to say this, but this author says it best" is weak because it weakens the author's authority and challenges his or her competence completely.

D.   Correct. This example includes a specific authoritative source, an active verb, and integrates the quotation into the text.

6)   **Which of the following answer choices accurately paraphrases the following quotation?**

"Eighty-eight percent of the adult learners in the control group scored below the adult learners in the experiment group."

A.   Lots of folks did well in the experiment group.

B.   Eighty-eight percent of the adults in the control group did better than the adults in the experiment group.

C.   Hurray for the experiment group; they did super fantastic!

D.   After the researcher had administered the final test, the control group scored eighty-eight percent worse than the group that received the intervention.

Answers

A.   Incorrect. This paraphrase is far too informal and incomplete.

B   Incorrect. This paraphrase is actually a plagiarism of the quotation. There are too many words in the same progression and in the same syntax.

C   Incorrect. This paraphrase is far too informal and incomplete.

D   Correct. This paraphrase is a rewording and a syntactical alteration by the author of the paper; it is both accurate and academic.

SPEAKING AND LISTENING

Oral communication skills make up the second part of a student's mastery of the English language: along with writing and reading, speaking and listening are essential language skills for every student. Indeed, oral communication skills have a place in the classroom just as written communication skills do. An effective teacher must be able to apply various instructional strategies for testing and improving students' oral communication skills.

ORAL COMMUNICATION

Oral communication exercises in the classroom come in a variety of forms; they may be formal or informal and may occur one-on-one, in small groups, or as a whole class. In planning an oral communication exercise, an effective teacher makes a number of considerations in order to ensure that the work is productive and purposeful: he or she must know the objective of the lesson, choose an appropriate and relevant topic for discussion, decide on a format, define appropriate student behavior, and determine accountability measures.

The objectives of oral communication exercises are often twofold in an ELA classroom. First, these exercises are often conducted in the context of a broader unit; thus, they may be centered on a particular reading objective, for example, and may serve, in part, to assess a student's grasp of a particular reading assignment, chapter, or unit. Second, these exercises address oral communication objectives themselves such as fluency, coherence, and clarity.

The **topic** of an oral communication exercise must, first and foremost, stem from the lesson objective. Second, it must be student friendly. That is, it must be age appropriate and must have some relevance to students' lives or the world at large. In choosing a suitable topic, an effective teacher considers the emotional and intellectual development of his or her students, the required background knowledge for discussion of the topic, and the objectives that he or she hopes to see mastered.

After choosing a topic, the teacher should decide what **form** the exercise will take. Will students give a speech or presentation, participate in a debate or discussion? Will they interact with only one other student, a group of students, or the whole class? Will communication flow in all directions or just in one? How directly will the teacher be involved?

A teacher may assign a **debate** in order to test students' abilities to speak intelligently on topics they have researched and defend their positions with evidence; a debate will also test the students' ability to handle stress and respond to academic arguments with composure. A debate can take many specific forms in the classroom, but, in general terms, a debate requires students to take a side on a particular issue and provide evidence as to their reasoning. Debates can be one-on-one, small group, or whole class, depending on the teacher's objective.

A teacher may assign a **speech** in order to test students' formal public speaking abilities and to observe their fluency and their ability to communicate emotionally with an audience. A speech requires students, usually one at a time, to stand in front of a group and speak on a particular topic. The speech format is fairly versatile: speeches can range in length and formality depending on purpose, audience, and topic—all of which can vary widely. More information on delivery of speeches is provided below.

A teacher may assign a **discussion** in order to assess students' informal speaking and listening abilities as well as their verbal reasoning skills. Discussions, in general, allow participants to gain a deeper understanding of a specific topic or text—but otherwise are varied in format. An effective teacher might consider the objective and the culture of his or her classroom in choosing between discussion formats.

For less complex topics, **one-on-one** discussions may be assigned in the form of **think-pair-shares**, in which students have the opportunity to first share briefly with a partner before sharing their responses with the whole class. Think-pair-shares are appropriate when everyone in the class can be expected to comment on the topic without much prompting, when every student can be expected to have a response; they are also helpful in new classes, when students are still getting to know their classmates and might feel safer if they have the chance to test their responses out on just one classmate first.

Small group discussions also allow for a level of safety, as students are asked to share on a smaller, more intimate scale. Thus, they are particularly helpful in classes where students may be unwilling to speak in front of a large group. On the other hand, in classes that are large or particularly vocal, small groups can be helpful for getting every student engaged and giving everyone the opportunity to share. However, teachers might also find that small group discussions can be difficult to manage, as the teacher must monitor many discussions at once. Accountability measures are especially important in small groups.

Whole class discussions, especially when conducted in classrooms that are safe and productive, can be especially useful for taking on broad, complex ideas that require many perspectives. Larger thematic questions related to the human condition, for example, can be explored in more dimensions when a larger number of perspectives and opinions comes together. Especially effective and engaging is the **Socratic seminar** format, in which a leader (the teacher or a student, depending on the classroom culture) prompts discussion solely by asking questions and allowing the class to share and then respond to and build upon one another's ideas.

Once the teacher has determined the objective, topic, and format of the oral exercise, he or she should consider and define **appropriate student behavior** for the exercise and then share this information with students. Some teachers may, instead, prefer to involve their students in the conversation: what is appropriate discussion or debate behavior? Some particulars to consider include the following: Are students required to participate? If so, when and how much? Is there a maximum that students can contribute? Will they be required to use academic language during the exercise? What is appropriate behavior in response to a disagreement? Can students talk over each other? If not, how will that be managed? What is an effective or meaningful contribution? How will the group respond to comments that are inappropriate, irrelevant, or distracting?

In addition to defining appropriate behavior for students, teachers should also be prepared to share with students how they will be held **accountable** for their contributions to a discussion or debate. Accountability may take the form of a rubric-based grade, a follow-up written assignment, or a related project that requires tangible output.

SAMPLE QUESTIONS

7) **Which of the following would be an appropriate assignment for assessing how well students can integrate evidence into an argument in order to prove a point?**

    A.   a speech

    B.   a debate

    C.   a think-pair-share

    D.   a Socratic seminar

Answers

    A.   Incorrect. While speeches may use evidence, they are not necessarily argumentative.

    B.   Correct. A debate requires students to research a particular topic and gather evidence to support their position on the topic.

    C.   Incorrect. While it is possible to use a think-pair-share to quiz students on appropriate evidence, it does not necessarily test their ability to prove a cohesive point.

    D.   Incorrect. Socratic seminars should be exploratory, not argumentative.

8) **Mr. Green's class will soon be completing a discussion on F. Scott Fitzgerald's use of figurative language in *The Great Gatsby*. Which of the following is NOT an effective way for Mr. Green to hold his students accountable for this activity?**

    A.   He can require students to participate a minimum number of times during the discussion and track the students' contributions.

    B.   He can have students complete a series of multiple choice questions covering figurative language in *The Great Gatsby*.

    C.   He can have students write an independent response after the debate to discuss any moments that stood out or changed their minds about something.

    D.   He can require students to complete a pre-discussion list of questions to turn in on discussion day.

Answers

A. Incorrect. This tactic would be effective because it would ensure that students participate effectively in the actual discussion.

B. **Correct.** This approach would **not** be effective because it would not necessitate participation in the discussion; that is, the students could likely answer these questions without engaging with the discussion.

C. Incorrect. Asking students to write an independent response to the discussion will not only allow them to reflect upon and synthesize the information they have just heard, but it will also allow Mr. Green to determine who was truly engaged and who was not.

D. Incorrect. If students are required to complete a pre-discussion list of questions, they will have to engage with the discussion questions and may even be more likely to participate in the in-class portion of the exercise.

TECHNOLOGY AND COMMUNICATION

Today's student is technologically savvy and socially connected. Many if not most students use technology to communicate with friends and family outside of school via text messages, emails, and social media. It follows, reasonably, that educators should seek to integrate this multipurpose tool, with which students are so readily familiar, into their lesson plans. Indeed, **technology** can be used in a variety of ways to enhance communication and learning in the ELA classroom.

Teachers should help students discover the unique applications of the various communication tools that are available to them as a result of technology, tools that are making communication possible in new and interesting ways. For example, when it comes to computer-based media for presentation support, the possibilities may as well be endless: using **presentation software** (like Microsoft PowerPoint or Prezi), a speaker may integrate into his or her presentation slides and images, videos and movie clips, charts and graphs, songs and sound clips, or any combination of these and other technologies to support and emphasize his or her main points. Teachers must understand these technologies not only so that they can apply them in their classrooms but also so that they can instruct students in the effective use of these types of technology—a skill that will continue to benefit them throughout their educational careers and into the workplace.

Other types of technology can also be employed in the classroom to enhance communication and prepare students for a technology-driven world. Web logs, more commonly known as **blogs**, have become popular communication tools in classrooms across the country, especially at the collegiate level. A blog is an online format that allows the owner of the webpage to share his or her thoughts and ideas in the form of journal-type entries; they can rely primarily on words, or they can enhance their posts using images, videos, sound clips, and hyperlinks. Readers can read and, usually, provide feedback in the form of comments, allowing for an exchange of ideas between the blogger and the reader and between the readers themselves. Most of the time, blogs have themes and are aimed at appealing to a specific audience; thus, any given blog's readership is likely composed of like-minded individuals—or at least individuals who have some interest or quality in common.

Like blogs, **wikis** provide an avenue for groups of people with similar interests to exchange ideas and information in an online forum. However, unlike blogs, wikis usually are not controlled by one or two individuals; rather, wikis are intended to be collaborative communities, in which all participants can contribute to the group's collective knowledge or understanding. *Wikipedia*, a popular example of the power of wikis, exists to provide information to the general public, and with thousands upon thousands of entries, it is a testament to the power of wikis and of online collaboration. Students should understand, however, that the collaborative nature of wikis can also make them less reliable in terms of accuracy; they should be instructed in effective research practices as well as in the appropriate application of online technologies.

SAMPLE QUESTION

9) **Which medium would best suit a teacher who wanted to put out regular materials and announcements to his or her class and allow students to respond with questions?**

   A.   a blog

   B.   a wiki

   C.   an infographic

   D.   a PowerPoint presentation

Answers

   A.   **Correct.** Today's teachers use blogs to disseminate information—both subject matter information and logistics information—to their classes.

   B.   Incorrect. A wiki will not give the teacher full control over the site, as wikis are intended to be collaborative.

   C.   Incorrect. While infographics may be useful to impart some kinds of information, the format is limited. Additionally, infographics only allow communication to flow in one direction.

   D.   Incorrect. PowerPoint may enhance classroom presentations, but it is not the most user-friendly software for disseminating information across distances.

EFFECTIVE SPEECHES AND PRESENTATIONS

In preparation for the professional world, today's students must know not only how to write a speech but also how to deliver a speech or presentation effectively. As with writing, purpose and audience are the two most important considerations in writing and giving a speech. Other elements of effective presentations include but are not limited to eye contact, body language, tone, bias, conciseness, clarity, and visuals.

Eye contact and body language are integral in effective speech delivery. A speaker who makes **eye contact** with the audience, for example, will likely be perceived as more honest, genuine, and accessible than a speaker who looks above the audience or does not meet the eyes of the general audience at all. Effective speakers make an emotional connection with their audiences by meeting the gaze of as many members as possible throughout the course of a speech. Additionally, effective speakers consider **body language** and seek to present themselves as calm and confident in their gestures and posture.

Audiences pick up on nuances of **tone** almost as quickly as they recognize a lack of eye contact or the use of unusual body language. Indeed, *how* the speaker delivers the message of a speech may be just as, if not far more, important than *what* is said. A speaker should rehearse extensively leading up to the delivery of a speech in order to ensure that he or she is employing the appropriate gradations of emotional tone: genuine or sarcastic, casual or formal, cold or warm, sincere or insincere, familiar or distant, kind or harsh, judgmental or nonjudgmental, passionate or disinterested.

> QUICK REVIEW
>
> Make the following statements more concise: *during the time that, for the purpose of, in the near future, in spite of the fact that, on the local scene, proceeded to walk, in this day and age, for the simple reason that, at this point in time, day by day, as a matter of fact, in a very real sense, in a manner of speaking.*

Conciseness in writing and speech delivery means much more than shortness. Conciseness involves the conscious ridding of superfluous wording including clichés, fillers, and verbose sentence structure. A speech writer who is editing for conciseness cuts words not purely for the sake of shortening a speech but for the sake of choosing language that is clear and simple and that the audience will easily be able to understand.

> *I went to college in the city I was living in, so I was able to take the subway and didn't have to worry about putting gas in my car or paying tolls.*

The word choices are not necessarily the problem. Clarity is the problem. The speaker must arrange the words to deliver clarity. Here is a revision of the sentence in the above example:

> *Subway travel to the college in my hometown saved gas and toll expenses.*

Sometimes writers must continuously play with words until conciseness and clarity result. They may move, replace, cut, and add words until their sentence says exactly—no more or less than—what they want it to say. While this practice can be tedious, the process of revising for clarity and conciseness allows a writer to apply his or her knowledge of word nuances to achieve a satisfying end.

When it comes to speeches and presentations, **visual aids** can be extremely helpful and can allow the writer or speaker to emphasize elements throughout his or her presentation. However, if used incorrectly, visual aids can be a detriment to a good presentation. Some recommendations about the use of visual aids follow:

Table 3.2. Visual Aids

Recommendation for Visual Aids	Explanation
Do not let the visual aid overpower the presenter.	The speaker should be the focus throughout most of a presentation, not the visual aid. A PowerPoint presentation, for example, can be distracting if too much detail or animation is included on the slides.
Do not stand in front of a visual aid.	Most importantly, the speaker must avoid blocking the visual aid for any portion of the audience. With a projection, standing in front of the visual aid creates a silhouette effect. Both are distracting and prevent the audience from experiencing the effect of the presentation as a whole.
Practicing with the visual is important.	Sometimes good intentions with a powerful visual aid go awry because the speaker has not sufficiently practiced with it or has not considered possible mishaps. Especially when using technology, speakers should know troubleshooting methods and have an alternative approach ready if and when their technology fails.
Look at the audience despite the visual aid.	Nervous speakers might depend on the visual aid for support and look more at the visual aid than at the audience. This signals a lack of confidence and prevents the speaker from fully connecting with his or her audience.
Make sure the room is appropriate for the visual aid.	Sometimes a visual aid will be too large or too small for the location or audience; either fault can be distracting. Thus, a speaker should be familiar with the presentation space and location of the audience.
Make sure the visual aid has a clear purpose.	A visual aid—especially a chart, graph, or image—will only be effective if the audience understands its purpose. If a visual aid is never explained or referred to throughout the course of a presentation, it can probably be cut.

Recommendation for Visual Aids	Explanation
Keep it simple.	When it comes to visual aids, in most cases, simpler is better. Endless bullet points, too many sensory images, or too much information can overwhelm an audience and cause viewers to lose interest in the visual, the speaker, or both.

The same considerations that speakers make about visual aids in a presentation should be made by teachers in the classroom. Teachers should not, by any means, shy away from visual aids; rather, they should embrace visual aids and learn to apply and execute them appropriately in the context of a lesson. A lesson, much like a presentation, can be derailed by a faulty, unnecessary, or otherwise distracting visual aid.

SAMPLE QUESTIONS

10) **Which of the answer choices is a concise, clear revision of the following sentence?**

Fred was still on the wrong track, and his friends told him he should stop barking up the wrong tree.

A.   Fred was still on the wrong track, so his friends told him he should stop barking up the wrong tree with his choices and decisions.

B.   Fred continued to make poor choices, so his friends encouraged him otherwise.

C.   Barking up the wrong tree caused Fred to be on the wrong track.

D.   Fred continued to make poor choices, and his friends told him to stop barking up the wrong tree so he could be on the right track.

Answers

A.   Incorrect. Though adding the phrase "with his choices and decisions" may help to clarify the meaning of the sentence a bit, it fails to be considered concise.

B.   **Correct.** This sentence clarifies the message of the sentence without using a cliché.

C.   Incorrect. Relying heavily on clichés clouds the meaning of the sentence.

D.   Incorrect. This revision is wordy and still somewhat unclear.

11) **What are some guidelines that a speaker should follow when using a PowerPoint for a speaking engagement regarding city planning?**

    A.   He or she should simply sit down by the PowerPoint with a clicker in hand, and let the slides speak for themselves.

    B.   He or she should fill the PowerPoint with graphics, animation, word art, music, and surprise sounds to entertain the audience; the message will be most effective with a flashy and exciting design.

    C.   He or she should use the PowerPoint as a visual tool with carefully chosen, dynamic images, incorporated at specifically chosen moments.

    D.   He or she should create several slides with bullet points and then add transitions that cause the words to bounce in and out of each slide to keep the attention of the audience.

Answers

    A.   Incorrect. Speakers should not rely solely on visuals like PowerPoint to make their presentations effective.

    B.   Incorrect. A busy PowerPoint can easily become a distraction for the audience, distracting viewers from the true purpose of the presentation.

    C.   **Correct.** Visuals should be used sparingly and purposefully.

    D.   Incorrect. Bullet points and busy transitions can easily distract the audience, making it difficult to understand and remember the key points.

TEACHING AND ASSESSING COMMUNICATION

Instructional and assessment strategies are some of the most vital tools for today's educator. Effective teachers rely on research-based techniques and strategies to teach and assess their students. Student performance on assessments allows teachers to constantly revise their lessons and reshape their instruction in order to continuously meet their students' needs, creating a classroom environment that is responsive, dynamic, and productive.

Responsive teaching also means recognizing the unique background, strengths, and needs of each student and being able to differentiate instruction and assessment in a way that allows each student to fulfill his or her potential.

RESEARCH–BASED STRATEGIES FOR WRITING INSTRUCTION

Research into writing instruction has resulted in a number of empirically-tested, outcome-driven strategies that ELA teachers employ to continuously teach and assess their students. Some of the most commonly practiced strategies are described below:

Writing workshop is an approach that integrates instruction, practice, and assessment in a consistent, daily schedule. Writing workshop time is first signaled by a particular sound, image, announcement, or environmental change. The teacher then teaches a mini-lesson on a particular skill or segment of the writing process (beginning with idea generation and ending with publication and celebration). Next, students have time to work on their writing independently or in small groups while the teacher circulates to do one-on-one and small group conferences. Finally, students share their work from the day, especially if they have applied knowledge from the mini-lesson.

A writing teacher might also employ models or modelling in his or her instruction. **Models** are exemplary examples of writing, which the teacher uses to highlight certain qualities or characteristics. Students view and discuss the model and then attempt to apply their knowledge to their own writing. The teacher may also **model** a particular skill by practicing the skill, along with the thought process, aloud in front of students.

Collaborative writing is especially useful when students are new to a particular skill or process or when all may not be entirely confident. Collaborative writing occurs when partners or small groups of students work together to complete segments of a writing process (or the full process) together. This strategy is useful not only for allowing students to share ideas and build confidence but also for providing an avenue by which students can practice reviewing writing and providing feedback.

Process writing involves instructing students in the use of a clear process for writing and in the use of techniques and strategies for completing each part of the process. The writing process typically includes planning (brainstorming, outlining, mapping); drafting (writing); revising (adding and deleting, rewriting, reorganizing); and editing (editing and proofreading).

SAMPLE QUESTION

12) **Ms. Johnson wants to teach a simple introduction to the process of revising for coherence by adding transitional words and phrases. What instructional method should she employ?**

    A. collaborative writing

    B. writing workshop

    C. process writing

    D. modelling

    Answers

    A. Incorrect. Collaborative practice is helpful later in the learning process as a method of reviewing and providing feedback.

B.   Incorrect. The writing workshop process is much more involved than a simple introduction and would require that a large amount of time be devoted to the process.

C.   Incorrect. Process writing, like the writing workshop method, is much broader in scope than an initial introduction would need to be.

D.   Correct. When first introducing a new skill, teachers should model that skill for students in order to illustrate confidence and eliminate confusion.

PURPOSES AND METHODS OF ASSESSMENT

Effective assessment is the cornerstone of good teaching. A teacher who cannot properly assess his or her students cannot meaningfully adjust instruction nor provide useful feedback to encourage student growth. Thus, knowledge of different kinds of assessments and their applications is necessary for any educator who aims to provide the best instruction possible for his or her students.

Different methods of assessment have different applications, and each method has unique strengths and flaws. Understanding these qualities will allow an educator to choose effective assessment techniques—techniques that are truly aligned with the objective he or she is hoping to assess.

In general, all assessments fall into one of two categories: formative or summative. **Summative assessments** are those assignments (tests and exams) that are most commonly thought of as assessments—tasks that are intended to assess a student's overall mastery of a long-term objective. **Formative assessments** (daily work, homework, quizzes) are those assignments that are given leading up to the summative assessments, which the teacher uses to evaluate student progress and adjust instruction. For example, a teacher who is teaching a unit on sentence construction might give formative assessments on parts of speech, phrases and clauses, and types of sentences before giving a final, summative assessment on the unit as a whole; if the instructor finds that all or most students failed the third formative assessment, he or she could plan to teach another lesson on types of sentences to ensure mastery across the board.

If a teacher is planning to provide a traditional, numbered score (usually zero to one hundred) on an assignment, he or she may want to include a **rubric.** Rubrics are assessment tools that teachers use to objectively assign scores to projects or assignments whose merits are difficult to quantify, especially writing assignments. Well-designed rubrics make grading guidelines clear for both the teacher and the student so that confusion and subjectivity are eliminated as much as possible. Some rubrics, called **holistic rubrics**, provide a grade based on the overall effectiveness of the product; **analytic rubrics**, on the other hand, break the product down so that points are assigned by component part. A holistic rubric, for example, might assign a score based on the overall effectiveness of an argumentative essay, while an analytic rubric for the same project would score separately the thesis, the evidence, the organization, and the grammar to produce an overall score. Thus, analytic rubrics are more useful than holistic rubrics when it comes to highlighting areas of improvement for students, but holistic rubrics are more efficient as grading tools and more reflective of how writing is assessed and evaluated in the real world.

Writing teachers employ a variety of other assessment techniques, in addition to rubrics, to provide students with useful, timely feedback. A skill in itself, providing feedback is a responsibility that can be shared between the teacher and students.

Effective teachers understand the value of constructive criticism and prioritize the need for regular writing feedback. Sometimes, they may hold **writing conferences**, either as needed or at particular times throughout the year, to provide the feedback themselves. The purpose of a writing conference is to help each student improve his or her writing skills by highlighting individual strengths and honing in on the areas most needing improvement. **Peer reviews** can also be used to make sure students are receiving frequent feedback on their work. Students exchange essays with classmates and, with the guidance of a checklist or rubric, provide each other with positive and constructive feedback. Students ultimately must develop the ability to review their own work; thus, **self-assessment** is a valuable practice. Furthermore, students benefit from the ability to track and observe their growth over time, so **portfolios** are a useful tool for self-assessment.

The goal in all of these assessment tools and response strategies is to provide students with useful feedback about their writing. Useful feedback neither consists of falsified praise nor crushing criticism; it is an authentic celebration of strengths and a suggested pathway for improvement in the future.

SAMPLE QUESTIONS

13) **What is your analysis of a paper that is returned to a student with a grade at the top yet no comments inside of the paper and no rubric along with the final grade?**

   A. The student must expect that an instructor is busy; the grade adequately assesses the paper.

   B. A grade at the top of a paper assumes that the instructor read the final project completely.

   C. Students should submit to authority and assume the best of a professional.

   D. The instructor did not assess the assignment objectively, providing a proper rubric with comments.

Answers

   A. Incorrect. No professional instructor should assess a paper in this way.

   B. Incorrect. Students will probably assume that the paper was not read thoroughly.

C. Incorrect. Students may assume the best, but they will also experience frustration.

D. Correct. A grade on a paper should be accompanied with comments and a rubric.

14) **Assess the following comment from an instructor on a literary analysis writing task:**

This paragraph in your paper is gobbledegook. Your logic is faulty, and your conclusions are ridiculous.

A. The writer needs to understand how worthless that particular paragraph was.

B. The instructor offered no useful feedback in those comments whatsoever.

C. Writers must be faced with their lack of critical thinking.

D. The instructor's comments reflect the frustration of reading multiple assignments from incompetent students.

Answers

A. Incorrect. The wording is offensive, and the emphatic statements are judgmental.

B. Correct. The object of comments is useful feedback. No part of these statements is useful.

C. Incorrect. Critical thinking does not come by way of shallow comments.

D. Incorrect. Even if an instructor is frustrated, useful feedback must overcome frustration.

CULTURAL CONSIDERATIONS

One of the biggest challenges a language arts teacher will face is making the knowledge and skills taught in their classroom relevant and accessible to all learners. To do so, teachers must make a number of considerations to ensure that the needs of each student are being met.

First, a teacher must create a safe learning environment. Students must be taught what is appropriate and inappropriate in an academic environment, especially with regard to academic risk-taking and personal identity. Students should never be shamed (by the teacher or by other students) for making mistakes or for sharing their opinions, lest they discontinue making an effort altogether. Further, teachers should create an inclusive environment by involving numerous, varied voices in classroom discussions, reading material by authors of different backgrounds, and having students write and speak about their own experiences: together, these tactics can breed acceptance in the classroom. Ultimately, all students need to feel that they, their perspectives, and their opinions and ideas are valuable in the classroom environment.

In addition to creating a safe classroom environment, teachers must understand the identities of their students—both as individuals and as a group—in order to practice instruction that is responsive to students' needs and circumstances. A class that consists of college-bound seniors, for example, may have a different set of needs than a class of seniors who plan to graduate and move immediately into the workforce. A classroom with a high immigrant population will have different needs than a classroom of students who speak English as their first language.

SAMPLE QUESTIONS

15) **A student may become emotional after receiving verbally aggressive yet objective comments from an instructor assessing his or her speech. Why?**

   A.   Whereas assertiveness may be typical in the United States, in some cultures people receive aggressive comments personally rather than objectively.

   B.   Parents in some cultures must simply instruct their children to grow up by being tough.

   C.   Young people today are coddled far too often, and instructors can help them to face criticism.

   D.   The student may be seeking sympathy from fellow students.

Answers

   A.   Correct. Probably A is the best answer when considering cultural variance and assessment.

   B.   Incorrect. Cultural variance does not change with an assessment.

   C.   Incorrect. This is a personal opinion; by its nature, an objective assessment should not reflect personal opinions.

   D.   Incorrect. While this statement may be somewhat true, it is more likely that cultural variance is the reason for the student's reaction.

16) **An argumentative paper may defend imperialism and colonization. Some students may become intensely defensive as they gather for group assessment. Why?**

   A.   The students do not care for the writer.

   B.   The students are over-reacting to imperialism.

   C.   Students may be culturally sensitive regarding the history of their countries and imperialism.

   D.   Some students do not like to work in groups, so they become defensive.

Answers

   A.   Incorrect. They may not like a fellow student, but the emotional intensity of their reaction probably stems from another source.

B.   Incorrect. This response does not address why the students are upset.

C.   **Correct.** Students from countries that have been affected by imperialism and colonialism may have strong opinions regarding those topics due to personal experience with their consequences.

D.   Incorrect. While some students do not like group work, this is unlikely to be the root of such an emotional reaction.

17) **How would an instructor encourage a safe learning environment when a student responds with an answer that is entirely incorrect in front of a large group of peers and adult learners?**

    A.   The instructor should laugh right along with the other students to acknowledge the incorrect response of a student.

    B.   The instructor should acknowledge some true aspect of the response in order to publicly support the student and clarify the correct response to the question.

    C.   The instructor should simply say, "That's incorrect" and move on.

    D.   The instructor should ask a fellow student, "Why is that response completely incorrect?"

Answers

    A.   Incorrect. Laughing at the student's expense does not foster a safe learning environment because students may fear ridicule.

    B.   **Correct.** Respecting the student who responds incorrectly fosters a safe and comfortable learning environment by allowing students to make mistakes.

    C.   Incorrect. While this response saves time, the intimidated student may never respond again to a question. The student's comfort level is compromised.

    D.   Incorrect. This response further embarrasses the student who answered incorrectly.

Practice Test

READING

Questions 1 – 3 refer to the speech "The Man with the Muckrake" by Theodore Roosevelt, delivered April 14, 1906.

Over a century ago Washington laid the corner stone of the Capitol in what was then little more than a tract of wooded wilderness here beside the Potomac. We now find it necessary to provide by great additional buildings for the business of the government.

This growth in the need for the housing of the government is but a proof and example of the way in which the nation has grown and the sphere of action of the national government has grown. We now administer the affairs of a nation in which the extraordinary growth of population has been outstripped by the growth of wealth in complex interests. The material problems that face us today are not such as they were in Washington's time, but the underlying facts of human nature are the same now as they were then. Under altered external form we war with the same tendencies toward evil that were evident in Washington's time, and are helped by the same tendencies for good. It is about some of these that I wish to say a word today.

1

If a teacher asks students to write notes about what they think Roosevelt will discuss in the rest of the speech, what reading strategy is he or she emphasizing?

A.   visualizing

B.   summarizing

C.   predicting

D.   clarifying

2

What is the central idea of Roosevelt's speech?

A.   The growth of the United States has resulted in a war between the conflicting interests of many groups in government.

B.   While the U.S. government and population have grown, the United States continues to deal with the basic characteristics of human nature, both positive and negative.

C.   Many Americans have gained great wealth and are now attempting to control the government.

D.   The country has grown so fast and has acquired so much wealth that the government is struggling to deal with rising inequality between the wealthy and the poor.

3

Roosevelt mentions construction of "great additional buildings for the business of government" to emphasize

A.   changes that have taken place in the type of government.

B.   the complexity of democratic principles.

C.   the power of the United States as a world leader.

D.   the growth of the United States.

4

What kind of writing is factual and verifiable, but written in an artistic way?

A.   fiction

B.   nonfiction articles

C.   creative nonfiction

D.   poetry

5

How are stanzas and paragraphs used in writing?

A.   Poetry is often divided into stanzas or groups of lines, and prose is divided into paragraphs or groups of related sentences.

B.   Poetry is sectioned into lines that form stanzas, and prose is sectioned into main points and details.

C.   A prose text includes paragraphs, headings, and stanzas that are unified by a central idea.

D.   A paragraph is carefully structured and developed using examples, but a stanza is creative, without specific form or structure.

Questions 6 – 8 refer to the introductory sentences of Louisa May Alcott's "Street Scenes in Washington" below.

The mules were my especial delight; and an hour's study of a constant succession of them introduced me to many of their characteristics; for six of these odd little beasts drew each army wagon and went hopping like frogs through the stream of mud that gently rolled along the street. The <u>coquettish</u> mule had small feet, a nicely trimmed tassel of a tail, perked-up ears, and seemed much given to little tosses of the head, affected skips and prances; and, if he wore the bells or were <u>bedizened</u> with a bit of finery, put on as many airs as any belle. The moral mule was a stout, hard-working creature, always tugging with all his might, often pulling away after the rest had stopped, laboring under the conscientious delusion that food for the entire army depended upon his private exertions. I respected this style of mule; and, had I possessed a juicy cabbage, would have pressed it upon him with thanks for his excellent example.

6

What is Alcott's purpose in the section of text from "Street Scenes in Washington"?

A. to inform readers about the activity on the streets of Washington

B. to persuade readers that life in the city is fascinating

C. to convince people to take the time to observe human activity

D. to express her thoughts as she observes mules on a street in Washington

7

How does Alcott organize the details in this section of text?

A. according to the chronology of events

B. from the general (a wagon pulled by mules, moving along the street) to the specific (each specific mule)

C. from the most important—the most attractive mule—to the least important mule

D. spatially, from the left side of the street to the right side

8

To determine the meanings of <u>coquettish</u> and <u>bedizened</u> in the passage, a lesson on _____ would be most helpful.

A. figurative language

B. context clues

C. connotation

D. denotation

9

A memoir written by a person about his/her life or about verifiable events he/she experienced, expressed in an artistic way, is an example of

A.   poetry.

B.   creative nonfiction.

C.   fiction.

D.   naturalistic fiction.

10

A creative text that is written about a realistic problem and that is relatable and relevant to readers, is an example of

A.   American literature.

B.   realistic nonfiction.

C.   young adult literature.

D.   constructivist writing.

11

Essays written by Jonathan Swift, John Locke, and Jean Jacques Rousseau express the ideas of

A.   the Enlightenment.

B.   the Renaissance Period.

C.   the Victorian Period.

D.   the Romantic Period.

12

Consider the first lines of "Autumn" from *The Belfry of Bruges and Other Poems* by Henry Wadsworth Longfellow (below). What sound device is used in the line "With banners, by great gales incessant fanned"?

Thou comest, Autumn, heralded by the rain,

With banners, by great gales incessant fanned,

Brighter than brightest silks of Samarcand,

And stately oxen harnessed to thy wain!

A.   assonance

B.   mood

C.   symbolism

D.   tone

13

One characteristic of metaphysical poetry is

A.   using a serious, stern tone.

B.   addressing the practical, everyday concerns of life.

C.   addressing the value of scientific discoveries.

D.   using paradoxes and puns as well as everyday language.

Questions 14 – 16 refer to the following stanzas from "The Haunted Oak" by Paul Laurence Dunbar.

Pray why are you so bare, so bare,
Oh bough of the old oak-tree;
And why, when I go through the shade you throw,
Runs a shudder over me?

My leaves were green as the best, I trow,
And sap ran free in my veins,
But I saw in the moonlight dim and weird
A guiltless victim's pains.

I bent me down to hear his sigh;
I shook with his gurgling moan,
And I trembled sore when they rode away,
And left him here alone.

...

I feel the rope against my bark,
And the weight of him in my grain,
I feel the throe of his final woe
The touch of my own last pain.

And never more shall leaves come forth
On a bough that bears the ban;
I am burned with dread, I am dried and dead,
From the curse of a guiltless man.

14

The initial speaker of the poem asks an old oak tree "why are you so bare, so bare…?" When a student explains she is convinced that the old oak tree is bare because an innocent man was hung on one of the tree's branches, she is

A.   making an inference.

B.   making a prediction.

C.   stating a theme of the poem.

D.   stating a pattern in the poem.

15

The student goes on to elaborate on her explanation by quoting the lines, "I feel the rope against my bark,/And the weight of him in my grain[.]" In doing so, she is

A.   analyzing the point of view.

B.   demonstrating the perspective of the author.

C.   showing the rhyme scheme.

D.   supporting her explanation with textual evidence.

16

When a teacher provides information about the context of Dunbar's poem, what is he or she doing?

A.   building students' background knowledge

B.   explaining the author's intentions

C.   analyzing the author's word choice

D.   providing opportunities for discussion

Questions 17 – 19 refer to the following excerpt from "The Whistle" by Benjamin Franklin.

When I was a child of seven years old, my friends on a holiday filled my pocket with coppers. I went directly to a shop where they sold toys for children; and, being charmed with the sound of a *whistle* that I met by the way in the hands of another boy, I voluntarily offered and gave all my money for one. I then came home, and went whistling all over the house, much pleased with my *whistle*, but disturbing all the family. My brothers and sisters and cousins, understanding the bargain I had made, told me I had given four times as much for it as it was worth; put me in mind what good things I might have bought with the rest of the money, and laughed at me so much for my folly, that I cried with vexation; and the reflection gave me more chagrin than the *whistle* gave me pleasure.

…

When I see a beautiful, sweet-tempered girl married to an ill-natured brute of a husband, *What a pity*, say I, *that she should pay so much for a whistle!*

In short, I conceive that great part of the miseries of mankind are brought upon them by the false estimates they have made of the value of things, and by their *giving too much for their whistles.*

17

Which of the following does the author use to engage the attention of the reader?

A.   sarcasm

B.   an implicit assertion

C.   an anecdote

D.   understatement

18

What can be inferred about the motives of the narrator's family?

A.   The family wanted to teach the narrator caution in spending his money.

B.   The family is simply teasing the narrator, who seems to take things too seriously.

C.   The family wanted to discourage the narrator from playing the whistle.

D.   The family wanted to make sure the narrator would not grow up to be easily influenced by others.

19

When the narrator asserts that people are *giving too much for their whistles*, he is speaking

A.   figuratively.

B.   literally.

C.   generally.

D.   paradoxically.

Questions 20 – 22 refer to the poem "The Scholar's Wife" by John Dryden, below.

To a deep scholar said his wife:
"Would that I were a book, my life!
On me then, you would sometimes look.
But I should wish to be the book
That you would mostly wish to see.
Then say, what volume should I be?"

"An Almanack," said he, "my dear;
You know we change them every year."

20

What is the tone of this poem?

A. irreverent

B. mean-spirited

C. scornful

D. satirical

21

The lines "An Almanack," said he, "my dear;/You know we change them every year" are an example of a(n)

A. heroic couplet

B. pun

C. truism

D. annotation

22

John Donne and John Milton are British writers of the

A. Romantic Period

B. Restoration Period

C. Elizabethan Age

D. Victorian Era

23

What is one main assertion of reader-response theory?

A. There is one correct interpretation of a literary text.

B. Readers do not interpret literary text; they simply experience it.

C. There is a simple process for understanding text that involves paying careful attention to the repeated elements of the text and the emotions elicited by those elements.

D. Readers participate in the creative process; the meaning of a literary text is found partially in the author's design and partially in the reader's experience of the text.

24

One literary device that enhances meaning is

A.   imagery.

B.   plot.

C.   setting.

D.   characterization.

Questions 25 – 27 refer to the following excerpt from the essay "Hints on Conversation" by Jonathan Swift.

Nothing is more generally exploded than the folly of talking too much; yet l rarely remember to have seen five people together, where someone among them has not been predominant in that kind, to the great constraint and disgust of all the rest.

...

Of such mighty importance every man is to himself, and ready to think he is so to others; without once making this easy and obvious reflection, that his affairs can have no more weight with other men than theirs have with him; and of how little that is, he is sensible enough.

...

I know a man of wit who is never easy but where he can be allowed to dictate and preside; he neither expects to be informed or entertained, but to display his own talents. His business is to be good company, and not good conversation; and therefore he chooses to frequent those who are content to listen and profess themselves his admirers. And indeed the worst conversation l ever remember to have heard in my life was that at Will's coffee-house, where the wits (as they were called) used formerly to assemble: that is to say, five or six men who had writ plays, or at least prologues, or had share in a miscellany, came thither, and entertained one another with their trifling compositions, in so important an air as if they had been the noblest efforts of human nature, or that the fate of kingdoms depended on them; and they were usually attended with a humble audience of young students from the inns of court or the universities; who, at due distance, listened to these oracles, and returned home with great contempt for their law and philosophy, their heads filled with trash under the name of politeness, criticism, and *belles lettres*.

25

This passage is primarily concerned with

A.   people who dominate conversations.

B.   the wits.

C.   poor manners.

D.   people who admire writers.

26

What literary device does Swift use to emphasize his point?

A.   ambiguity

B.   personification

C.   simile

D.   archetype

27

Which of the following pieces of textual evidence best supports the interpretation that Swift has contempt for people who talk too much?

A.   "Nothing is more generally exploded than the folly of talking too much; yet I rarely remember to have seen five people together, where someone among them has not been predominant in that kind…"

B.   "Of such mighty importance every man is to himself, and ready to think he is so to others; without once making this easy and obvious reflection, that his affairs can have no more weight with other men than theirs have with him; and of how little that is, he is sensible enough."

C.   "I know a man of wit who is never easy but where he can be allowed to dictate and preside; he neither expects to be informed or entertained, but to display his own talents."

D.   "His business is to be good company, and not good conversation; and therefore he chooses to frequent those who are content to listen…"

28

To be designated as literary text—literature—a text must

A.   use literary devices.

B.   have an effect on the reader.

C.   advance a belief system.

D.   reflect some universal aspect of life.

29

When readers are involved with what they are reading, making connections with the text, and making sure they understand the ideas being communicated, they are

A.   making predictions.

B.   reading actively.

C.   using their imaginations.

D.   reflecting on their emotional responses.

30

Poetry that conforms to a specific shape or form in terms of the number of lines, meter, and rhyme scheme is

A. closed form poetry.

B. open form poetry.

C. blank verse.

D. traditional poetry.

31

What is one way authors develop their characters?

A. through the literary context

B. by assigning roles

C. with verifiable facts

D. directly

Questions 32 – 34 refer to the following sections from the essay "On Lying News-Writers," from *The Idler* by Samuel Johnson.

No species of literary men has lately been so much multiplied as the writers of news. Not many years ago the nation was content with one gazette; but now we have not only in the metropolis papers for every morning and every evening, but almost every large town has its weekly historian, who regularly circulates his periodical intelligence, and fills the villages of his district with conjectures on the events of war, and with debates on the true interest of Europe.

To write news in its perfection requires such a combination of qualities, that a man completely fitted for the task is not always to be found. In Sir Henry Wotton's jocular definition, "An ambassador is said to be a man of virtue sent abroad to tell lies for the advantage of his country; a news writer is a man without virtue, who writes lies at home for his own profit." To these compositions is required neither genius nor knowledge, neither industry nor sprightliness; but contempt of shame and indifference to truth are absolutely necessary. He who by a long familiarity with infamy has obtained these qualities, may confidently tell to-day what he intends to contradict to-morrow; he may affirm fearlessly what he knows that he shall be obliged to recant, and may write letters from Amsterdam or Dresden to himself.

In a time of war the nation is always of one mind, eager to hear something good of themselves and ill of the enemy. At this time the task of news-writers is easy; they have nothing to do but to tell that a battle is expected, and afterward that a battle has been fought, in which we and our friends, whether conquering or conquered, did all, and our enemies did nothing.

Among the calamities of war may be justly numbered the diminution of the love of truth, by the falsehoods which interest dictates and credulity encourages. A peace will equally leave the warrior and relater of wars destitute of employment; and I know not whether more is to be dreaded from the streets filled with soldiers accustomed to plunder, or from garrets filled with scribblers accustomed to lie.

32

The author's view of news writers is

A. stated explicitly.

B. implicit.

C. revealed by the point of view.

D. indicated by the matter-of-fact tone.

33

What kind of appeal does Johnson use to support his perspective?

A. ethical appeal

B. logical appeal

C. emotional appeal

D. evidential appeal

34

A teacher asks his students to rewrite this passage about news writers, changing the position on the veracity of reporters, using more current language, and incorporating evidence from current news stories about a war going on today. What sort of activity did this teacher assign?

A. a jigsaw activity

B. a Socratic seminar

C. a research project

D. a role playing activity

35

When do English teachers require students to provide textual evidence?

A. to make a reasoned argument about a social issue

B. during a quick write

C. during creative writing

D. to support an interpretation of a text

36

What is an example of fallacious reasoning?

A.   using a red herring

B.   using emotional language

C.   including facts

D.   including syllogisms

37

In a persuasive text, when one of the main arguments is based on the premise that if one thing happens, a series of other things will automatically happen, the reasoning may be referred to as

A.   a hasty generalization.

B.   dichotomous thinking.

C.   a slippery slope.

D.   an emotional appeal.

Questions 38 – 40 refer to the poem "The Lake Isle of Innisfree" by William Butler Yeats.

I will arise and go now, and go to Innisfree,

And a small cabin build there, of clay and wattles made:

Nine bean-rows will I have there, a hive for the honeybee,

And live alone in the bee-loud glade.

And I shall have some peace there, for peace comes dropping slow,

Dropping from the veils of the morning to where the cricket sings;

There midnight's all a glimmer, and noon a purple glow,

And evening full of the linnet's wings.

I will arise and go now, for always night and day

I hear lake water lapping with low sounds by the shore;

While I stand on the roadway, or on the pavements grey,

I hear it in the deep heart's core.

38

What is one poetic device Yeats uses to develop his theme?

A.   extended metaphor

B.   imagery

C.   simile

D.   irony

39

What is the speaker's perspective?

A.   The speaker believes the country is a peaceful place.

B.   The speaker considers the country to be as noisy as the city.

C.   The speaker realizes that his trips to the country are a thing of the past.

D.   The speaker is standing on the road feeling gloomy.

40

Which line from the poem is the best example of precise word choice?

A.   "I will arise and go now, and go to Innisfree"

B.   "There midnight's all a glimmer, and noon a purple glow"

C.   "Nine bean-rows will I have there, a hive for the honeybee"

D.   "While I stand on the roadway, or on the pavements grey"

41

Which of the following terms describes those primary source documents that include magazine and newspaper articles, interviews, photographs, TV or radio broadcasts?

A.   testimonials

B.   literary nonfiction

C.   visual aids

D.   media sources

42

What is an inference based on?

A.   facts and specific examples in the text

B.   details of the text and the reader's knowledge of the topic of the text

C.   understanding the author's purpose

D.   recognizing the author's tone

43

What is one effective way to activate students' prior knowledge?

A.   silent sustained reading

B.   quick writes

C.   rigor

D.   reciprocal teaching

44

When a teacher includes pictures and graphics as part of instruction in order to support learning, she is using

A.   metacognitive practices.

B.   prior knowledge.

C.   visual aids.

D.   a research application.

Questions 45 – 47 refer to the following excerpt from *Anecdotes of the Late Samuel Johnson* by Samuel Johnson.

There is no private house in which people can enjoy themselves so well as at a capital tavern. Let there be ever so great plenty of good things, ever so much grandeur, ever so much elegance, ever so much desire that everybody should be easy, in the nature of things it cannot be: there must always be some degree of care and anxiety. The master of the house is anxious to entertain his guests—the guests are anxious to be agreeable to him; and no man, but a very impudent dog indeed, can as freely command what is in another man's house as if it was his own. Whereas, at a tavern, there is a general freedom from anxiety. You are sure you are welcome; and the more noise you make, the more trouble you give, the more good things you call for, the welcomer you are. No servants will attend you with the alacrity which waiters do, who are incited by the prospect of an immediate reward in proportion as they please. No, sir, there is nothing which has yet been contrived by man, by which so much happiness is produced as by a good tavern or inn.

45

What is the author implying about taverns in this passage?

A.   People enjoy themselves in taverns because they are relaxed and not worried about pleasing anyone.

B.   People want to behave rudely, like impudent dogs, at house parties, but do not because they will be thrown out.

C.   People who give house parties make their guests uncomfortable by hovering over them.

D.   People are only happy in taverns because they can boss around the waiters, who will listen because they want tips.

Go on

46

The author's statement that in a tavern, "the more noise you make, the more trouble you give, the more good things you call for, the welcomer you are" is an example of

A. symbolism
B. hyperbole
C. evidence
D. analysis

47

What organizational pattern is Johnson using in this section of text?

A. sequential
B. compare and contrast
C. cause and effect
D. chronological

Questions 48 – 50 refer to "A Scholar's Proposal of Marriage" from *Middlemarch* by George Eliot (Mary Ann Cross).

My dear Miss Brooke: I have your guardian's permission to address you on a subject than which I have none more at heart. I am not, I trust, mistaken in the recognition of some deeper correspondence than that of date in the fact that a consciousness of need in my own life had arisen contemporaneously with the possibility of my becoming acquainted with you. For in the first hour of meeting you, I had an impression of your eminent and perhaps exclusive fitness to supply that need (connected, I may say, with such activity of the affections as even the preoccupations of a work too special to be abdicated could not uninterruptedly dissimulate); and each succeeding opportunity for observation has given the impression an added depth by convincing me more emphatically of that fitness which I had preconceived, and thus evoking more decisively those affections to which I have but now referred. Our conversations have, I think, made sufficiently clear to you the tenor of my life and purposes: a tenor unsuited, I am aware, to the commoner order of minds. But I have discerned in you an elevation of thought and a capability of devotedness which I had hitherto not conceived to be compatible either with the early bloom of youth or with those graces of sex that may be said at once to win and to confer distinction when combined, as they notably are in you, with the mental qualities above indicated. It was, I confess, beyond my hope to meet with this rare combination of elements both solid and attractive, adapted to supply aid in graver labours and to cast a charm over vacant hours; and but for the event of my introduction to you (which, let me again say, I trust to be superficially coincident with foreshadowing needs, but providentially related thereto as stages toward the completion of a life's plan), I should presumably have gone on to the last without any attempt to lighten my solitariness by a matrimonial union.

Such, my dear Miss Brooke, is the accurate statement of my feelings; and I rely on your kind indulgence in venturing now to ask you how far your own are of a nature to confirm my happy presentiment. To be accepted by you as your husband and the earthly guardian of your welfare, I should regard as the highest of providential gifts. In return I can at least offer you an affection hitherto unwasted, and the faithful consecration of a life which, however short in the sequel, has no backward pages whereon, if you choose to turn them, you will find records such as might justly cause you either bitterness or shame. I wait the expression of your sentiments with an anxiety which it would be the part of wisdom (were it possible) to divert by a more arduous labour than usual. But in this order of experience I am still young, and in looking forward to an unfavourable possibility I cannot but feel that resignation to solitude will be more difficult after the temporary illumination of hope. In any case, I shall remain, yours with sincere devotion,

EDWARD CASAUBON

48

What is the point of view of the section of text?

A. first person, subjective

B. first person, objective

C. third person, omniscient

D. third person, limited

49

The proposal letter is most likely taken from which of the following?

A. a young adult novel

B. a nonfiction text

C. a magazine

D. a fictional prose narrative

50

If a critic indicates that Edward Casaubon demeans Miss Brooke by focusing on the ways she would enhance his life, and the fact that he would be "the earthly guardian" of her welfare, as if she was a child; what might be the theoretical perspective or field of this critic?

A. New Criticism

B. structuralism

C. queer theory

D. feminist theory

LANGUAGE USE AND VOCABULARY

Read the following prompts and select the best answer.

1

Identify the part of speech for the underlined word in the following sentence:

Several administrators <u>did</u> understand the proposal, but most of them voted against it.

A.   conjunction

B.   pronoun

C.   verb

D.   adverb

2

The underlined phrase in the sentence below functions as which of the following parts of speech?

<u>Writing letters to editors</u> remains a favorite pastime for the elderly neighbor.

A.   noun

B.   pronoun

C.   adjective

D.   adverb

3

The underlined phrase in the sentence below functions as which of the following parts of speech?

<u>To save lots of money,</u> the young family shopped for clothing at the local thrift store.

A.   noun

B.   pronoun

C.   adjective

D.   adverb

4

Identify the part of speech for the underlined word in the following sentence:

We will move to Arizona <u>if</u> Dave continues to struggle with asthma.

A.   preposition

B.   adverb

C.   conjunction

D.   interjection

5

Identify the part of speech for the underlined word in the following sentence.

The <u>wood</u> stove overheated in the little cabin, so the smoke filled the main room.

A.   noun

B.   pronoun

C.   adjective

D.   adverb

6

Identify the sentence error in the following example:

Statistics do not reflect high graduation rates from doctoral programs but perseverance and encouragement help increase the percentage of successful graduates.

A.   fragment

B.   lack of parallelism

C.   fused/run-on

D.   comma splice

7

Identify the error in the following example:

The representative's example of humility and integrity make him a popular incumbent.

A.   lack of parallel structure

B.   punctuation error

C.   subject and verb disagreement

D.   pronoun and antecedent disagreement

8

Identify the error in the following example:

Neither Venezuela nor Saudi Arabia may be expected to lower their oil prices in the coming days.

A.   lack of parallel structure

B.   punctuation error

C.   subject and verb disagreement

D.   pronoun and antecedent disagreement

9

Identify the error in the following example:

The daughters decided to make a calendar of events for Christmas; the choices included either going bowling or to play games.

A.   lack of parallel structure

B.   punctuation error

C.   subject and verb disagreement

D.   pronoun and antecedent disagreement

10

Identify the error in the following example:

Watching birds in flight and photographing birds in flight occupies the bulk of his work.

A.   lack of parallel structure

B.   punctuation error

C.   subject and verb disagreement

D.   pronoun and antecedent disagreement

11

Adding the prefix *anti-* to a root word means what?

A.   in favor of

B.   against

C.   before

D.   around

12

Adding the prefix *ex-* to a root word means what?

A.   without

B.   off

C.   former

D.   more

13

What type of phrase is underlined in the following sentence?

Mark, <u>a native of Massachusetts</u>, worked one summer at the Boston Globe.

A.   appositive

B.   absolute

C.   prepositional

D.   gerund

14

What type of clause is underlined in the following sentence?

Alice missed the most exciting part of the game; <u>consequently, she returned to the car disappointed</u>.

A.   noun clause

B.   adverb clause

C.   adjective clause

D.   independent clause

15

Which type of sentence is the following?

Although the politician denied that he intended to run for the presidency, he behaved as if he might.

A.   simple

B.   complex

C.   compound

D.   compound-complex

16

What type of phrase is underlined in the following sentence?

<u>Writing a children's story</u> challenged the creative writers.

A.   appositive

B.   absolute

C.   prepositional

D.   gerund

17

What type of clause is underlined in the following sentence?

Occasionally, dancers discover <u>that the stage is not their only love</u>.

A.   noun clause

B.   adverb clause

C.   adjective clause

D.   independent clause

Go on

18

Which type of sentence is the following?

The carpet's coloring was rich, and its pattern was complex.

A. simple

B. complex

C. compound

D. compound-complex

19

Which of the following describes narrative prose or verse that is a symbolic representation imparting a deeper meaning?

A. alliteration

B. caesura

C. allusion

D. allegory

20

Which of the following describes a contrast in parallel phrases or clauses?

A. ambiguity

B. anecdote

C. antithesis

D. archetype

21

Which of the following describes the driving tension throughout a literary work?

A. ambiguity

B. cacophony

C. *carpe diem*

D. conflict

22

Which of the following describes a striking revelation during the course of a story?

A. catharsis

B. epiphany

C. euphemism

D. crisis

23

Which of the following describes the unraveling or completion of the plot of a story?

A.   ambiguity

B.   blank verse

C.   denouement

D.   climax

24

Which style manual is preferred in education, psychology, and the social sciences?

A.   APA

B.   MLA

C.   Chicago

D.   Turabian

25

Which style manual is preferable in humanities and the arts?

A.   APA

B.   MLA

C.   Chicago

D.   Turabian

26

Which writing style manual is preferred in history and theological studies?

A.   APA

B.   MLA

C.   Chicago

D.   Turabian

27

Which statement is true of a spell-checker?

A.   Because a spell-checker is part of a computer program, it is always reliable.

B.   The spell-checker can tell what the word should be according to the context.

C.   Writers should edit the entire paper even if using a spell-checker.

D.   Spell-checkers can distinguish between words like *form* and *from* due to their placement in a sentence.

28

Which sentence is correct?

A. After the car accident, the musician was hearing bad and could not play for several months.

B. Irregardless, she should not have been with that questionable crowd.

C. Complaining about the boss did not help the kitchen team's moral.

D. The student had twenty-three quotations in a short paper.

29

Which sentence is correct?

A. The principal of the school spoke about the school's principal mission: to educate children.

B. The police should of investigated the house further for hidden compartments.

C. To try and survive a gorilla attack, the zookeeper wore protective gear.

D. The neighbors had very unique decorations on their lawn.

30

Which statement reveals an understanding of cultural variance?

A. The students should have a basic understanding of a learning management system.

B. The word *syllabus* may have to be defined carefully on the first day.

C. Students who look down have no interest in the class.

D. Students do not laugh at a teacher's jokes on the first day because they do not like the instructor.

31

Which statement reveals an understanding of cultural variance?

A. Agreeing with the instructor constantly by nodding up and down reveals a wide range of knowledge on the part of the student.

B. Family needs should not conflict with educational goals.

C. An instructor's understanding of promptness may not be the same as some students' understanding of it.

D. When students help each other too much, they are displaying a tendency to cheat.

32

What is the act of shared creation and/or discovery as a tool in learning diversification?

A. collaborative learning

B. appropriation

C. distance education

D. constructivism

33

Which of the following terms describes the virtual and shared universe comprised of the world's computer network, which is used as a tool in learning diversification?

A. artificial intelligence

B. distance education

C. cyberspace

D. fiber optics

34

What is the active monitoring of one's own thinking as a tool in learning diversification?

A. just-in-time learning

B. experiential learning

C. metacognition

D. local knowledge systems

35

What is an instructional system in which most of the process is controlled by the learner as a tool in learning diversification?

A. server

B. metacognition

C. surfing the net

D. open learning

WRITING, SPEAKING, AND LISTENING

Read the following prompts and select the best answer.

1

Identify the writing strategy wherein writers list ideas related to a specific topic.

A. focused freewriting
B. brainstorming
C. mapping/clustering
D. incubation

2

Identify the writing strategy wherein writers write non-stop for a designated period of time about anything that comes to mind.

A. focused freewriting
B. journaling
C. mapping/clustering
D. freewriting

3

Identify the writing strategy wherein writers consult with others during the writing process.

A. collaborative
B. clustering
C. incubation
D. journaling

4

Identify the writing strategy wherein writers record ideas, observations, and opinions on a regular basis.

A. maintaining a diary
B. maintaining an idea book
C. journaling
D. focused freewriting

5

Which writing element/strategy directs the entire research process for a writer?

A. the research question

B. the outline

C. the drafting stage

D. searching the Internet

6

Which of the following elements shapes each paragraph in a writing task?

A. the thesis

B. the topic sentence

C. the drafting stage

D. the outline

7

Inserting necessary words, phrases, and sentences, and substituting words, phrases, and sentences are two major activities that take place during which stage of the writing process?

A. editing

B. planning

C. proofreading

D. revising

8

The final review of a document to check for errors is which stage of the writing process?

A. editing

B. planning

C. proofreading

D. revising

9

Checking for grammatical accuracy and punctuation placement accuracy is which stage of the writing process?

A. editing

B. planning

C. proofreading

D. revising

10

Which of the following results when a writer focuses the content of each paragraph on a single idea?

A. coherence

B. development

C. unity

D. mapping

11

Writers would consider website creation to be what mode of writing?

A. critical

B. journalistic

C. academic

D. technical

12

Writers would consider a reasoned response to an article to be what mode of writing?

A. critical

B. creative

C. literary journalism

D. technical

13

Writers would consider an argumentative research paper to be what mode of writing?

A. creative

B. academic

C. journalistic

D. technical

14

Which of the following defines the term *writing task*?

A. categorizing a piece of writing

B. an individual writing assignment

C. specifically listing writing requirements

D. the writing process

15

Which of the following correctly lists, in order, the elements of a formal outline for a written assignment?

A. thesis statement, phrases for main points, restatement of thesis

B. thesis statement, independent clauses articulating main points, restatement of thesis

C. introductory paragraph, thesis statement, topics, restatement of thesis, concluding paragraph

D. introductory paragraph, thesis statement, independent clauses for main points, restatement of thesis, concluding paragraph

16

A formal outline ought to have which of the following?

A. passive voice

B. specific content details

C. first and second person pronouns

D. either all clauses or all phrases

17

Which sentence best demonstrates parallelism?

A. To see is to really believe.

B. The scientist's goal was eventually both teaching and to travel.

C. The Bronze Star and the Silver Star are awarded for heroism.

D. Trisha always has and always will enjoy studying literature.

18

Which of the following would NOT be considered a credible digital source?

A. *msmith.ENG101.suchandsuchuniversity.edu*

B. *departmentofeducation.gov*

C. *article from JSTOR*

D. *commondisordersinchildren.apa*

19

Which of the following would indicate that a digital source is reliable?

A. The source appears first at the top of the page in a general search.

B. Its bibliography included peer reviewed articles.

C. Its date of publication is extremely recent.

D. Its web address ends with *.org*.

20

Which of the following would NOT be a credible print source?

A. *Foreign Affairs*

B. *Encyclopedia Britannica*

C. *People* Magazine

D. *Biology: The Uniqueness of Life*

21

Which of the following would NOT be a credible print source?

A. *The Journal of the American Medical Association*

B. a PETA brochure

C. *Across Five Aprils* by Irene Hunt

D. *MLA Style Manual and Guide to Scholarly Publishing*

22

Citing outside sources in any writing style involves what three elements?

A. In-text introductions of the outside source; in-text citations; and a reference page, bibliography, or works cited page listing the sources.

B. Introductions through the use of footnotes; in-text citations; and a reference page, bibliography, or works cited page listing the sources.

C. In-text introductions of the outside source; listing authors and dates separately in the text for clarity; and a reference page, bibliography, or works cited page listing the sources.

D. Superscript numbers that correspond with footnotes; footnotes that include authors and dates; and a reference page, bibliography, or works cited page listing the sources.

23

Which of the following represents common knowledge that would NOT need documentation in a research paper?

A. the fact that the U.S. Civil War lasted from 1861 to 1865

B. metadata from a study on the effects of sleep deprivation on driving

C. the results of a survey on a major university campus regarding the subject of free speech

D. a police report summarizing the murder rates from the top ten most populous cities in the United States

24

Which of the following would be the most egregious consequence of plagiarism?

A.   destroyed student reputation

B.   destroyed academic reputation

C.   destroyed lives from medical research

D.   destroyed finances from being sued

25

Which of the following is NOT an effective method in speech preparation?

A.   Skip the outline, and express your thoughts from the heart.

B.   Know your motive for speaking.

C.   Use a visual map to create the speech.

D.   Practice with a live audience.

26

Which is the best technique for eye contact while giving a speech or presentation?

A.   Look just above the crowd.

B.   Focus on the back wall as a relaxation technique.

C.   Make contact with the eyes of those in the audience.

D.   Rotate looking at the outer walls.

27

Which of the following best defines being concise in academic writing?

A.   being succinct

B.   the fewest words

C.   being clear

D.   using clichés

28

Flaws in reasoning that lead to questionable assumptions are

A.   redundancies.

B.   fallacies.

C.   emphases.

D.   patterns.

Go on

29

The following statement reflects the usage of what logical fallacy?

The corruption of the leadership is inevitable because a fish rots from the head down.

A.   hasty generalization

B.   false analogy

C.   irrelevant argument (*non-sequitur*)

D.   false cause (*post hoc ergo propter hoc*)

30

The following statement reflects the usage of what logical fallacy?

Why should I care about the corruption on the school board? The property taxes are of far greater concern.

A.   bandwagon

B.   card-stacking

C.   red herring

D.   false dilemma (either-or fallacy)

31

What would be the best summative assessment for a secondary education drama student?

A.   a lengthy test that covers all of the terminology and techniques for effective drama

B.   a PowerPoint presentation that analyzes the best drama techniques

C.   a critical analysis paper arguing the merits of a drama program in secondary schools

D.   writing, directing, and performing a play

32

Which tool for learning modes of speaking does not offer direct experience?

A.   language modelling

B.   speaking workshops

C.   using public speaking blogs

D.   university writing centers

33

Which tool would most effectively use pictures to enhance communication?

A. wikis

B. a visual thinking map

C. a PowerPoint presentation

D. a digital publication

34

Assessing writing, speaking, and listening involves which of the following specific tasks?

A. choosing a matching assessment for the writing, speaking, or listening tasks

B. choosing the best learning management system for digital assessments

C. designing a rubric for the assessment

D. designing a test to be administered on a learning management system

35

What would be the best summative assessment for a history student returning from a study tour in Europe?

A. a written test on an LMS that makes the student accountable for places and dates

B. a collaborative Wiki from fellow study tour members summarizing the trip

C. a portfolio that journals each day of the tour along with several famous readings from each stop on the tour

D. a speech that recounts all of the places seen on the study tour

36

What would be the best summative assessment for a secondary AP class in speech?

A. a written test that requires the student to define all public speaking techniques

B. a twenty-minute presentation using two visual aids on an argumentative topic

C. to collaborate with others in developing a list of the most important elements of speech

D. to play a learning game like Jeopardy that covers all of the public speaking techniques

⟶

Go on

37

Which statement is NOT true regarding rubrics?

A.   Rubrics represent objective assessment.

B.   Rubrics reduce disputes over final grades.

C.   Rubrics may be downloaded easily from the Internet.

D.   Rubrics are not necessary if assessment comes in the form of personal comments.

38

Which statement is NOT true regarding rubrics?

A.   Mathematically, the lowest grade a student could receive on a rubric would be zero.

B.   Mathematically, the students should receive credit for effort.

C.   Mathematically, certain sections should be weighted more heavily than others.

D.   Mathematically, the deductions should be clear for each item.

39

What is the best example of useful feedback?

A.   an objective rubric

B.   an encouraging paragraph in the comment section of a rubric

C.   a rubric with a comment section that provides commendation and suggestions

D.   a personal conversation with a student to suggest areas of improvement

40

What is the downside of asking students to give useful feedback regarding the course itself?

A.   Constructive criticism may come across negatively.

B.   Outlier statements may not express useful feedback.

C.   The suggestions may reveal a misunderstanding on the part of many students.

D.   Useful feedback done frequently exposes a potential catastrophe at the end of the course.

41

Which of the following would NOT be a specific requirement for a writing task?

A. to use active voice

B. a clear informative or argumentative purpose

C. to consider the reception of the audience

D. the length of the paper

42

Which statement is NOT true of writing conclusions?

A. Leaving a reader with a sense of completion wraps up the plots and sub-plots.

B. Recalling the main points for a lengthy thesis would be wise in the conclusion.

C. Leaving a reader with a sense of the absurd makes the reader thirst for more.

D. Leaving a reader with a manipulative device might be unsatisfying for the reader.

43

Which of the following is true when using PowerPoint in a presentation?

A. The speaker should fill the slides with transitions.

B. Slides should include graphics like bar charts.

C. The presentation should include plenty of photos.

D. The PowerPoint presentation itself should remain simple.

44

In writing and speaking tasks, what does the word *explain* mean in the instructions?

A. to comment on various elements

B. to interpret a complex process

C. to arrange into groups

D. to give reasons in defense

45

Writers would consider a laboratory report to be which mode of writing?

A. creative

B. academic

C. journalistic

D. argumentative

→ Go on

46

Writers would consider creating speaking points for an introduction to a poet at a poetry slam to be what mode of writing?

A.   creative

B.   academic

C.   argumentative

D.   informative

47

A teenager's journal is best defined as which mode of writing?

A.   narrative

B.   journalism

C.   critical

D.   nonfiction

48

Which of the following best explains how details can support the writing task?

A.   Details provide support for the writer's argument.

B.   Details make writing more interesting.

C.   Details add credibility to the writing task.

D.   By varying the types of details they use, writers can make their writing more interesting and convincing.

Answer Key

READING

1)

    A.   Incorrect. Visualizing asks students to form mental images of descriptions in text.

    B.   Incorrect. Summarizing asks students to state the main points of the text in their own words.

    C.   **Correct.** Predicting asks students to infer the next point to be made or addressed in the text, based on what has been read so far.

    D.   Incorrect. Clarifying involves students looking up unfamiliar vocabulary or allusions or re-reading complicated sentences in order to understand the thoughts expressed by the writer (or, in this case, the speaker).

2)

    A.   Incorrect. While Roosevelt does say that the nation has seen "growth of wealth in complex issues," conflict of interest is not his main point.

    B.   **Correct.** Roosevelt states his purpose when he says, "…we war with the same tendencies toward evil that were evident in Washington's time, and are helped by the same tendencies for good. It is about some of these that I wish to say a word today."

    C.   Incorrect. There is mention of wealth but not of the activities of wealthy people.

    D.   Incorrect. There is no mention of the inequalities that resulted from national growth.

3)

    A.   Incorrect. Government activity has increased as a result of the growing population and varying interests, but the type of government has not changed.

    B.   Incorrect. Roosevelt does say there is "growth of wealth in complex interests," but he does not suggest that there is complexity of democratic principles themselves.

    C.   Incorrect. Roosevelt does not discuss the global power of the United States here.

    D.   **Correct.** According to the text, additional government buildings have been necessary to accommodate the growth in government activity that has accompanied the corresponding growth of the country.

4)

    A.   Incorrect. Fiction is an imaginative form; stories are not based in fact.

    B.   Incorrect. Nonfiction articles do report observable facts and details, but they are not written artistically.

    C.   **Correct.** As long as a text is a factual presentation of real people or events, it is considered nonfiction.

    D.   Incorrect. The imaginative, forceful language of poetry is artistic, but not factual.

5)

    A.   **Correct.** Stanzas in poetry are groups of lines that are arranged in a pattern, while the paragraphs of a prose piece each develop a main point.

    B.   Incorrect. Poetry does have lines, but the lines are not sections. Prose does have main points and details, but they are not necessarily sectioned as such.

    C.   Incorrect. A prose text is unified by a central idea, has paragraphs, and might have headings, but it does not include stanzas.

    D.   Incorrect. A paragraph may or may not be developed and structured using examples. A stanza may or may not be written using a formal structure.

6)

    A.   Incorrect. The mules are the author's focus, not the activities on the street.

    B.   Incorrect. The author is fascinated by the mules but says nothing about life in the city.

    C.   Incorrect. The author is not observing human activity.

    D.   **Correct.** The author says that she is delighted by the mules and shares what she notices.

7)

A.   Incorrect. There is no passing of time or sequence of events.

B.   Correct. The author begins by saying that she studied the mules that are pulling a wagon; then she discusses each mule.

C.   Incorrect. The author identifies the characteristics of each mule, but does not indicate that the attractive mule is more important than the others.

D.   Incorrect. There is no indication which mule was first or on the right or left.

8)

A.   Incorrect. Neither word is used figuratively.

B.   Correct. The student could use the description of the mule's behavior, "much given to little tosses of the head, affected skips and prances" as a clue for *coquettish* and the phrases "if he wore the bells" or "a bit of finery" to determine what the word *bedizened* means.

C.   Incorrect. The connotation of a word is its implied associations; while this may help students to determine the charge (positive or negative) of the word, it likely will not lead them to a definition.

D.   Incorrect. A lesson on denotation will not equip students to define words based on context.

9)

A.   Incorrect. Memoirs can be written in a poetic style, but they are classified as nonfiction.

B.   Correct. Creative nonfiction is based in truth and is expressed in a compelling, artistic way.

C.   Incorrect. Fiction is an imaginary story or stories, not verifiable accounts of actual events.

D.   Incorrect. Naturalistic fiction tells a story about an imaginary event in an objective and realistic way.

10)

A.   Incorrect. American literature is not exclusively realistic.

B.   Incorrect. The story in question may be realistic, but it is invented, not based on verifiable events.

C.   Correct. Young adult literature is inventive, realistic, and relevant to young readers.

D.   Incorrect. There is no category called *constructivist writing*.

11)

    A.   **Correct.** The writers Jonathan Swift, John Locke, and Jean Jacques Rousseau expressed the belief that social problems can be solved by the use of reason.

    B.   Incorrect. The Renaissance Period was a time of rebirth and interest in Classical ideas; some representative writers are Francis Bacon, William Shakespeare, and Edmund Spencer.

    C.   Incorrect. The Victorian Period was a time of scientific discovery and industrial advancement; some Victorian writers are Jane Austin, the Bronte sisters, and William Blake.

    D.   Incorrect. The Romantic Period poets include William Wordsworth, John Keats, Lord Byron, and Percy Bysshe Shelley; Romantic writers revolted against the use of reason, preferring to use their imagination and intuition to understand truth.

12)

    A.   **Correct.** The assonance is the repetition of the /an/ sound in the words *banners, incessant, fanned.*

    B.   Incorrect. Mood is not a sound device; it is a literary element. However, sound devices emphasize certain words, which can contribute to mood.

    C.   Incorrect. Although the banners could be symbols, symbolism is not a sound device.

    D.   Incorrect. Tone, like mood and symbolism, is not a sound device.

13)

    A.   Incorrect. Though its subject matter is serious and philosophical, metaphysical poetry uses a witty and sometimes sarcastic tone.

    B.   Incorrect. Metaphysical poetry addresses spiritual concerns, not practical ones.

    C.   Incorrect. Metaphysical poetry does not address physical realities like scientific discoveries.

    D.   **Correct.** Metaphysical poetry is noted for plays on words and complex ideas about the contradictions of life.

14)

    A.   **Correct.** The poet does not state that a person was hung on a bough of the oak tree. The reader is using her knowledge of hangings as well as details revealed in subsequent stanzas to infer this.

    B.   Incorrect. The reader is explaining her interpretation of the text, not using details from the text to predict what will happen next.

    C.   Incorrect. The student's explanation does not communicate an idea about life or human nature as suggested by the poem.

D.   Incorrect. A pattern relates to the structure and repeating elements of the poem, which the student does not address in her explanation.

15)

A.   Incorrect. The student is not analyzing point of view, as she does not address the identity of the narrator.

B.   Incorrect. The lines quoted are from the perspective of the tree, not necessarily the author.

C.   Incorrect. The rhyme scheme (*abab*) is not addressed in the student's response.

D.   Correct. A quotation from the text that supports a particular interpretation is textual evidence.

16)

A.   Correct. The context of a text includes information about what was occurring when the text was written.

B.   Incorrect. While context may influence the author's purpose, the concept itself is much more inclusive, as it includes the social and historical situations related to the text.

C.   Incorrect. Word choice is a literary element, related to the meaning, and unrelated to the teaching of a work's context.

D.   Incorrect. While engaging students may be a positive side effect of introducing context, discussion alone is not the goal of a context lesson.

17)

A.   Incorrect. The tone of the passage is sincere; the author is sharing a practical life lesson.

B.   Incorrect. The assertions of this passage are stated in a straightforward, explicit manner.

C.   Correct. The author tells the short story of overpaying for an appealing toy, which illustrates his main point.

D.   Incorrect. No understatement is used. The author emphasizes the importance of his early lesson; he summarizes this importance when he says, "I conceive that great part of the miseries of mankind are brought upon them by the false estimates they have made of the value of things."

18)

A.   Incorrect. The fact that the family was disturbed by the narrator's constant whistling is the more likely explanation.

B.   Incorrect. The narrator does take things seriously, but laughing at him for making a bad deal is not teasing—it is shaming.

C. **Correct.** The narrator did play the whistle less because he was upset about spending too much for it.

D. Incorrect. No evidence for this general concern on the part of the family exists.

19)

A. **Correct.** Speaking figuratively is speaking metaphorically, using something concrete to make an idea clear. Paying too much for a whistle is a concrete example that illustrates placing too much value on something.

B. Incorrect. Speaking literally means stating actual facts. He is not literally suggesting that all people have purchased a whistle for an unfair price.

C. Incorrect. Though the tendency the author is describing may be a general tendency, the language is, first and foremost, figurative.

D. Incorrect. Speaking paradoxically means juxtaposing two ideas that seem contradictory, but are actually not. There is no contradiction about the fact that sometimes people find something attractive and pay too much for it.

20)

A. Incorrect. The husband is teasing his wife but is not doing so in a disrespectful way.

B. Incorrect. The sound of the rhyming couplet, the husband's response, is playful; his teasing is not mean-spirited.

C. Incorrect. The husband does not express any contempt toward his wife.

D. **Correct.** The husband is using humor and exaggeration to ridicule his wife for seeking attention.

21)

A. **Correct.** A heroic couplet is a pair of rhyming lines written in iambic pentameter.

B. Incorrect. A pun is a type of word play that uses multiple meanings of words to create a humorous effect.

C. Incorrect. A truism states the obvious.

D. Incorrect. An annotation is a note or comment on a text that adds explanation.

22)

A. Incorrect. The Romantic Period began at the end of the eighteenth century and continued into the early nineteenth century. Wordsworth, Coleridge, Byron, Shelley, and Keats are a few Romantic poets.

B. Incorrect. The Restoration Period followed after the writings of Donne and Milton.

C. **Correct.** Donne and Milton both wrote during the Elizabethan Age.

D. Incorrect. The nineteenth century Victorian Era includes the novels of Charles Dickens and Jane Austen.

23)

A. Incorrect. Many possible interpretations can be considered correct because each reader brings different experiences to and interacts differently with the text.

B. Incorrect. Although reader-response theory does place great importance on the imaginative and aesthetic experience of reading a literary text, the theory also recognizes that readers come away from their experiences with new or deeper understandings of some aspect of life.

C. Incorrect. Reader-response theory does view reading as a process and addresses the way elements of the text elicit emotion in the reader; however, the theory explores all elements, not just repeated ones.

D. **Correct.** Some of the ways readers participate in the creative process are by imagining, remembering, and feeling what the text reminds them about in their own experiences. The artistic choices of the author inspire the reader's reflections.

24)

A. **Correct.** Imagery uses sensory detail to create an experience within the reader's imagination and to contribute to the suggested meanings by evoking emotions, memories, and thoughts.

B. Incorrect. *Plot* refers to the events of the story. It is the foundation of a narrative, whose meaning can then be enhanced by using literary devices.

C. Incorrect. The setting is the time and place of the story and, like plot, is an integral part of its meaning.

D. Incorrect. Characterization also plays a significant role in communicating the meaning of a text; like plot and setting, it does more than just enhance meaning.

25)

A. **Correct.** Swift describes such people as presenting "the folly of talking too much…"

B. Incorrect. The wits are writers who seek an audience; here, they provide an example of people who dominate conversations.

C. Incorrect. Having bad manners is the general topic, but this text is focused specifically on the offensiveness of dominating a conversation.

D. Incorrect. The people who admire writers also tend to listen to those who talk too much, but these listeners are not Swift's primary concern.

26)

    A.   Incorrect. Ambiguity is a device that involves being deliberately unclear, in that more than one interpretation is possible. Swift clearly criticizes people who dominate conversations.

    B.   Incorrect. Personification is a literary device by which animals, objects, and ideas are given human characteristics. Swift is speaking of an offensive human characteristic but does not ascribe it to a nonhuman entity.

    C.   **Correct.** Swift uses a simile to emphasize his point that the wits overestimate their own importance. He writes that they share their works "as if they had been the noblest efforts of human nature, or that the fate of kingdoms depended on them."

    D.   Incorrect. An archetype is a character that represents a universal idea in literature across time and cultures. An archetype does not exist to describe the individual who talks too much.

27)

    A.   Incorrect. This sentence identifies people who talk too much, but does not reveal Swift's contempt for those specific people.

    B.   **Correct.** In this sentence Swift expresses contempt for people who dominate conversations because they see themselves as superior.

    C.   Incorrect. This description of a self-indulgent individual does not reflect Swift's general contempt for these types of people.

    D.   Incorrect. This sentence expresses Swift's general understanding of why wits behave as they do, but it does not reflect his contempt for them.

28)

    A.   Incorrect. A text can use literary devices without suggesting anything fundamental about the human experience.

    B.   Incorrect. Many texts make an impression or have an effect on the reader, but that effect may not be recognized by all readers as familiar or representative of the human experience.

    C.   Incorrect. Any text can promote a belief system; to be a literary text, however, the belief system must be expressed representing a universal human experience in some way.

    D.   **Correct.** Literary texts (literature) are those texts to which people can universally relate or recognize as a reflection of some aspect of human nature.

29)

    A.   Incorrect. Making predictions is a reading strategy that involves anticipating or inferring what is to come in a text.

B. **Correct.** Active reading is being engaged with the text and the process of understanding a text.

C. Incorrect. Imagining scenes and events in a text is only part of active reading. Active reading also involves using reading strategies and making text-to-self, text-to text, and text-to-world connections.

D. Incorrect. When readers are aware of how a text makes them feel, they are reading actively. However, emotional responses are unrelated to other kinds of connections and the monitoring of one's understanding; reflecting on them is only one element of active reading.

30)

A. **Correct.** Examples of closed forms include villanelles, sonnets, ballads, and haikus.

B. Incorrect. Open form poetry has no restrictions; the poets are free to create unique arrangements of lines and stanzas.

C. Incorrect. Blank verse poetry has meter, but no rhyme scheme or specific form. Shakespeare's plays are written in blank verse.

D. Incorrect. Traditional poetry can be any poetry that reflects the customs of the time and culture in which it is written.

31)

A. Incorrect. The literary context includes the genre of the text, other texts that influenced the writer, and allusions in the text. These qualities are typically unrelated to character.

B. Incorrect. In drama, actors play roles, becoming the characters they play, but character development occurs in the script or text itself, long before actors are cast.

C. Incorrect. Verifiable facts may be part of realistic literature or historical nonfiction, but usually characters are inventions of the author's mind and, thus, are not based on fact.

D. **Correct.** Using the direct method of characterization, the narrator explicitly describes the character's traits to the reader.

32)

A. **Correct.** The author directly states, "Among the calamities of war may be justly numbered the diminution of the love of truth, by the falsehoods which interest dictates and credulity encourages... I know not whether more is to be dreaded from the streets filled with soldiers accustomed to plunder, or from garrets filled with scribblers accustomed to lie."

B. Incorrect. Samuel Johnson does not imply his opinion; he tells the reader directly how he views news writers.

C.   Incorrect. Samuel Johnson's text is expository, not narrative, so he states his point of view directly.

D.   Incorrect. The author is adamant about his view; he is appalled by the lies that he believes news writers tell. His tone is forceful and filled with contempt, not matter-of-fact.

33)

A.   Correct. Johnson quotes someone who was apparently a respected, credible figure in his time. The quote is as follows: "In Sir Henry Wotton's jocular definition, 'An ambassador is said to be a man of virtue sent abroad to tell lies for the advantage of his country; a news writer is a man without virtue, who writes lies at home for his own profit.'"

B.   Incorrect. A logical appeal draws conclusions from a set of premises or a body of evidence. Johnson is just expressing his conclusion without showing how he arrived at it.

C.   Incorrect. Johnson is elaborating on his response to news writers; he is expressing his views without attempting to elicit an emotional response from readers.

D.   Incorrect. An evidential appeal shows a logical connection between a set of evidence and a result. This passage does not include evidence of news reporters lying.

34)

A.   Incorrect. A jigsaw activity is a cooperative group activity. Each group completes a different part of the assignment, and all groups share their part with the class, creating a composite understanding analogous to solving a puzzle.

B.   Incorrect. A Socratic seminar is a discussion based on a text, using open-ended questions, with students explaining their own thoughts and their responses to the thoughts of others. It is not a writing activity.

C.   Correct. Students will have to identify one event that occurred in a current war; locate several news stories about the event, making sure the stories are written by different writers/news organizations; compare the information in each, as well as how it is presented; evaluate the truthfulness of the accounts; make a judgment about news reporters today; and use their research to rewrite Johnson's text.

D.   Incorrect. Role playing is a creative dramatization of a text, not a writing activity.

35)

A.   Incorrect. If the argument is about a social issue and not a text, textual evidence may not be required.

B.   Incorrect. A quick write is a strategy used to inspire students to think and to bring ideas to a conscious level. Usually, students are responding freely to an open-ended prompt, so no textual evidence is required.

C.   Incorrect. Creative writing is imaginative, not analytical, and thus involves ideas that do not need to be supported.

D.   Correct. Although teachers encourage original thought, an individual's interpretation must be rooted in the details of the text.

36)

A.   Correct. Using a red herring means introducing distracting information that does not contribute to the argument and, instead, takes attention away from the main points.

B.   Incorrect. Using emotional language is not flawed reasoning.

C.   Incorrect. A persuasive text has a position or central idea that is supported by main arguments and facts; the incorporation of these details is not fallacious reasoning.

D.   Incorrect. Including the logical structures of a text is effective reasoning.

37)

A.   Incorrect. A hasty generalization is coming to a conclusion without enough evidence.

B.   Incorrect. Dichotomous thinking is thinking in terms of two extremes and overlooking all of the possibilities in between the extremes.

C.   Correct. A slippery slope argument occurs when one assumes that a series of occurrences will happen as a result of a particular action or event.

D.   Incorrect. An emotional appeal speaks to the feelings of the audience and is unrelated to a series of events being set in motion.

38)

A.   Incorrect. In using extended metaphors, poets continuously demonstrate similarities between the metaphor and its correlating topic throughout several lines in the poem rather than simply using the device one time. This poem has a metaphoric description of peace ("dropping slowly"), but it is not extended.

B.   Correct. The poem provides sensory descriptions of his cabin, garden, "the bee-loud glade," the crickets singing, the night's "glimmer, and noon a purple glow," the "lake water lapping," and the speaker standing "on the roadway, or on the pavements grey."

C.   Incorrect. There is no simile in this poem.

D.   Incorrect. There are no contradictory meanings in the poem.

39)

A. **Correct.** The speaker says, "And I shall have some peace there, for peace comes dropping slow…"

B. Incorrect. The speaker yearns to go to the country because it is peaceful, unlike the city; indeed he dreams of it while standing "on the roadway, or on the pavements grey" in an urban area.

C. Incorrect. The speaker says, "I will arise and go now, and go to Innisfree."

D. Incorrect. The speaker yearns for the country but is not sad; he says he hears his country home "in the deep heart's core."

40)

A. Incorrect. The line has a nice cadence, with the word *go* repeated for emphasis, but the word choice itself is not precise.

B. **Correct.** The words "glimmer" and "purple glow" are precisely intended and specifically chosen to give the reader a specific image of the peace the speaker finds in the country sky.

C. Incorrect. Although there is a precise detail about the number of bean-rows, the words do not generate a specific description or image.

D. Incorrect. There are no evocative words to create a sense of uniqueness.

41)

A. Incorrect. Testimonials are formal accounts of someone's qualifications or character. Sometimes a documentary about a noteworthy person includes testimonials.

B. Incorrect. Magazine and newspaper articles, interviews, photographs, TV or radio broadcasts are nonfiction, but they must have artistic or creative qualities to be considered literary.

C. Incorrect. Visual aids are pictures and graphics used as part of instruction; they can be found in media sources.

D. **Correct.** Media sources record events and reactions to events, often while the events are occurring, giving them great value as primary sources.

42)

A. Incorrect. It is true that readers use details of the text to infer meaning. However, an inference is made when certain information is not explicitly stated and readers have to fill in the blank.

B. **Correct.** In order to read between the lines, readers must use their own knowledge as well as draw on the information provided.

C. Incorrect. Understanding the author's purpose may help a reader to draw an inference, but it is not necessarily essential to the process.

D.   Incorrect. Readers can infer an author's tone, but tone itself does not necessarily provide enough information for one to make an inference.

43)

A.   Incorrect. Silent sustained reading involves having students read a text of their choice for a short time each day. Unless the text is about something they already know, they are not activating prior knowledge.

B.   Correct. With a quick write prompt, students are to write for three to five minutes on a topic, in continuous sentences, without pausing to plan or to edit. Afterward, they can share their thoughts in a discussion.

C.   Incorrect. Emphasizing rigor means teachers provide challenging content, use engaging activities, and teach cognitive strategies; it is generally unrelated to the concept of prior knowledge.

D.   Incorrect. With reciprocal teaching, through explicit modelling, teachers show students how to guide group discussions using strategies; then, students become discussion leaders. In this case, students are developing skills, not activating prior knowledge.

44)

A.   Incorrect. Metacognitive practices require students to think about their thinking.

B.   Incorrect. Prior knowledge is what students already know. While pictures and graphics might be useful for activating it, prior knowledge is not, in itself, a tool that teachers use.

C.   Correct. Visual aids support learning by attracting and holding students' attention and focus, helping students process and retain information.

D.   Incorrect. A research activity involves using both primary and secondary sources to answer a research question or solve a problem.

45)

A.   Correct. The text says that at house parties, "there must always be some degree of care and anxiety… [w]hereas, at a tavern, there is a general freedom from anxiety. You are sure you are welcome…"

B.   Incorrect. People try to be agreeable at someone's house. "…the guests are anxious to be agreeable …and no man, but a very impudent dog indeed, can as freely command what is in another man's house as if it was his own."

C.   Incorrect. Both the host and the guest work hard to be agreeable.

D.   Incorrect. There are other reasons people are happy in taverns, including feeling welcome and free to be noisy.

46)

A. Incorrect. Symbolism involves using objects or people to represent ideas. The statement is simply a reason the author likes taverns.

B. Correct. The reader knows that if a person is combative or too disruptive in a tavern, he or she would actually not be more welcome ("welcomer"). However, the hyperbole does emphasize the point that people can be more relaxed, loud, argumentative, and demanding in a tavern than they can be in someone's home.

C. Incorrect. Here, evidence would include specific descriptions of behavior and examples of "giving trouble" in a tavern.

D. Incorrect. Analysis is examination of the parts of something and how one part is connected to another and to the whole. In this text, the author is making a general observation about how relaxed he is in a tavern as opposed to a house party, not analyzing the specific components of either option.

47)

A. Incorrect. The author does not provide a sequence or hierarchy of occurrences dependent on one another.

B. Correct. Socializing at a tavern is contrasted with the practice of socializing at someone's house during a house party.

C. Incorrect. The text does give reasons as to why one might prefer a tavern, but he does not structure the text by giving the cause of something followed by the effect.

D. Incorrect. The author does not provide a timeline of events.

48)

A. Correct. The narrator is Edward Casaubon speaking to Miss Brooke, who is the woman he wants to marry.

B. Incorrect. The narrator is intensely motivated to convince Miss Brooke that she is perfect for him; he expresses his feelings freely.

C. Incorrect. The narrator is a character in the text, not a voice outside the action of the narrative.

D. Incorrect. The narrator uses first person pronouns.

49)

A. Incorrect. Young adult literature is realistic and relevant to young readers; the language and content of this text are antiquated and not relevant to young people today.

B. Incorrect. Nonfiction texts present verifiable facts and details; they are not written subjectively.

    C.   Incorrect. A proposal letter might be published in a magazine, but this letter refers to meetings the narrator had with the woman and the woman's guardian, indicating that it is part of a much larger narrative.

    D.   **Correct.** A long fictional prose narrative is a novel.

50)

    A.   Incorrect. The New Critics analyze how literary elements work together to create meaning in a text; this critic says nothing about the elements of the text.

    B.   Incorrect. Structuralism examines how a text is structured; this critic does not mention anything about the structure of the letter.

    C.   Incorrect. Queer analysis is concerned with traditional ideas of gender identity. The proposal letter does present the traditional views of the male and female in marriage; however, the critic is focused on how the female is demeaned.

    D.   **Correct.** Feminists would likely contest the idea that marriage is the best option for a woman and that women have to be cared for, as dependents.

LANGUAGE USE AND VOCABULARY

1)

    A.   Incorrect. The word *did* is not joining words within the sentence.

    B.   Incorrect. The word *did* is not taking the place of a noun.

    C.   **Correct.** The word *did* is helping the main verb *understand* and expresses emphatic tense.

    D.   Incorrect. The word *did* is not modifying the main verb *understand*; *did* is part of the verb phrase.

2)

    A.   **Correct.** The phrase *writing letters to editors* is the subject of the sentence in the form of a gerund phrase. Subjects can be nouns or pronouns only.

    B.   Incorrect. The phrase *writing letters to editors* is not taking the place of another noun.

    C.   Incorrect. The phrase *writing letters to editors* is not modifying a noun or pronoun.

    D.   Incorrect. The phrase *writing letters to editors* is not modifying a verb, adjective, adverb, or entire sentence.

3)

    A.   Incorrect. The phrase *to save lots of money* is acting as a modifier, not as a noun.

    B.   Incorrect. The phrase *to save lots of money* is not taking the place of a noun.

    C.   Incorrect. The phrase *to save lots of money* is modifying the verb *shopped* and not modifying a noun or pronoun.

    D.   **Correct.** The phrase *to save lots of money* is modifying the verb *shopped*— why did the young family shop at the local thrift store. (Note—all introductory infinitive phrases are adverbial.)

4)

    A.   Incorrect. Here, *if* does not come before an object and is not used as a preposition.

    B.   Incorrect. The word *if* does not modify a verb, adjective, adverb, or entire sentence.

    C.   **Correct.** The word *if* introduces an adverb clause, a dependent clause. Subordinating conjunctions introduce adverb clauses.

    D.   Incorrect. The word *if* does not express strong emotion and *does* have a grammatical role.

5)

A.   Incorrect. In this sentence, *wood* is a modifying noun, which becomes an adjective in usage.

B.   Incorrect. Here, *wood* does not take the place of a noun.

C.   Correct. In this sentence, *wood* describes the type of stove (wood stove, electric stove, gas stove).

D.   Incorrect. The word *wood* is modifying a noun, not a verb, adjective, adverb, or entire sentence.

6)

A.   Incorrect. Two independent clauses comprise this sentence.

B.   Incorrect. Parallel structure is not a problem in this sentence.

C.   Correct. Because no punctuation precedes the coordinating conjunction *but* that divides the two independent clauses, the example is fused/run-on (*programs, but perseverance*).

D.   Incorrect. There are no commas in the sentence at all.

7)

A.   Incorrect. Parallel structure is not a problem in this sentence.

B.   Incorrect. No punctuation errors occur in the example sentence.

C.   Correct. Even though the nouns *humility* and *integrity* appear before the verb *make*, they are not the subjects of the verb, but actually the objects of the preposition *of*. As such, they comprise a prepositional phrase describing *example*, which itself is the subject of the verb. Therefore, since the verb has a singular subject, it should be conjugated appropriately (*makes*).

D.   Incorrect. No pronoun and antecedent disagreement occurs in the example sentence.

8)

A.   Incorrect. Parallel structure is not a problem in this sentence.

B.   Incorrect. No punctuation errors occur in the sentence.

C.   Incorrect. No subject and verb disagreement occurs in the sentence.

D.   Correct. When subjects are joined by *neither/nor*, the antecedent agrees with the nearer subject.

Neither Venezuela nor Saudi Arabia may be expected to lower its oil prices in the coming days.

9)

A.   Correct. The choices included either going bowling or playing games.

B.   Incorrect. No punctuation errors occur in the sentence.

    C.   Incorrect. The subjects and verbs agree.

    D.   Incorrect. The example sentence does not contain any pronouns.

10)

    A.   Incorrect. The sentence is written with parallel structure.

    B.   Incorrect. No punctuation errors occur in the example sentence.

    C.   **Correct.** *Watching* and *photographing* are two distinct subjects. Plural subjects take plural verbs. The verb should be conjugated accordingly (*occupy*).

    D.   Incorrect. No pronoun and antecedent disagreements occur in the example sentence.

11)

    A.   Incorrect. The prefix meaning *in favor of* is *pro-* (*proactive*).

    B.   **Correct.** *Antilock brakes*, for example, means brakes that will not lock, a safety feature on many cars.

    C.   Incorrect. The prefix meaning *before* is *pre-* (*predetermine*, or even *prefix*).

    D.   Incorrect. The prefix meaning *around* is *circum-* (*circumvent*).

12)

    A.   Incorrect. The prefix meaning *without* is *a-* (*amoral*).

    B.   Incorrect. The prefix meaning *off* is *de-* (*devalue*).

    C.   **Correct.** *Ex-governor*, for example, means *former governor*.

    D.   Incorrect. The prefix meaning *more* is *hyper-* (*hyperactive*).

13)

    A.   **Correct.** The phrase *a native of Massachusetts* renames the noun *Mark*.

    B.   Incorrect. Absolute phrases have a noun and a participial modifier within the phrase itself.

    C.   Incorrect. This phrase contains a prepositional phrase, but the entire phrase is an appositive.

    D.   Incorrect. There is no verbal in this phrase.

14)

    A.   Incorrect. The clause is not functioning as a noun in the sentence.

    B.   Incorrect. The clause is not modifying the main verb of the sentence.

    C.   Incorrect. The clause is not describing a noun or pronoun that precedes it.

    D.   **Correct.** The underlined clause is independent. Remember, a semi-colon must be preceded AND followed by an independent clause.

15)

    A.   Incorrect. This sentence has one independent clause, but it also contains three dependent clauses.

    B.   **Correct.** This sentence has one independent clause and three dependent clauses, so it is a complex sentence.

    C.   Incorrect. This sentence contains only one independent clause (*he behaved*).

    D.   Incorrect. This sentence has only one independent clause, so it cannot be a compound sentence.

16)

    A.   Incorrect. The phrase *writing a children's story* does not rename a noun.

    B.   Incorrect. Absolute phrases have a noun and a participial modifier within the phrase itself.

    C.   Incorrect. This phrase does not begin with a preposition.

    D.   **Correct.** This phrase begins with a verbal ending in *-ing*, the phrase is acting in a noun function (subject), and its verb is *challenged*.

17)

    A.   **Correct.** The entire clause is the direct object of the verb *discover*. (Discover what?)

    B.   Incorrect. The clause is not modifying the verb; the clause is the direct object.

    C.   Incorrect. The clause is not describing a noun or pronoun that precedes it.

    D.   Incorrect. The underlined clause is not independent.

18)

    A.   Incorrect. This sentence has more than one independent clause.

    B.   Incorrect. This sentence does not have any dependent clauses.

    C.   **Correct.** Two independent clauses are divided properly with the coordinating conjunction *and*.

    D.   Incorrect. This sentence does have two independent clauses, but it does not have any dependent clauses.

19)

    A.   Incorrect. *Alliteration* is the repetition of the same vowel sound (usually the initial letter).

    B.   Incorrect. A *caesura* is a break or interruption.

    C.   Incorrect. An *allusion* is usually a reference to a historical person, place, or event.

D. **Correct.** An *allegory* is a narrative symbolic of a broader meaning. For example, George Orwell's *Animal Farm* is an allegory about communism in the Soviet Union.

20)

A. Incorrect. *Ambiguity* is using vague terms to achieve multiple meanings.

B. Incorrect. An *anecdote* is a short story summarizing an interesting or entertaining event.

C. **Correct.** The opposite or contrast of a phrase, clause (or even idea) is its *antithesis*.

D. Incorrect. An *archetype* is an overarching, easily identifiable symbol.

21)

A. Incorrect. *Ambiguity* is the use of vague terms to achieve multiple meanings.

B. Incorrect. *Cacophony* is language considered harsh in its sound.

C. Incorrect. *Carpe diem* means "seize the day"; it emphasizes the brevity of life.

D. **Correct.** *Conflict* is the driving tension throughout a work such as *humanity versus nature*.

22)

A. Incorrect. *Catharsis* is the purging of emotions.

B. **Correct.** *Epiphany* is a striking revelation or lesson learned during the course of a story.

C. Incorrect. *Euphemism* is a pleasant-sounding expression for a harsh reality.

D. Incorrect. *Crisis* is a reversal or climax of events in the common plot structure.

23)

A. Incorrect. *Ambiguity* is the use of vague terms to achieve multiple meanings.

B. Incorrect. *Blank verse* is the use of unrhymed iambic pentameter.

C. **Correct.** The *denouement* is the unraveling and/or completion of plots and sub-plots in a narrative.

D. Incorrect. *Climax* refers to the pinnacle moment of the rising action in a story.

24)

A. **Correct.** APA is generally used in education, psychology, and the social sciences.

B. Incorrect. MLA is preferred for the humanities and the arts.

C. Incorrect. Chicago is used in social sciences and history.

D. Incorrect. Turabian is used in history and theological studies.

25)

    A.   Incorrect. APA is preferable for education, psychology, and the social sciences.

    B.   **Correct.** MLA is preferred in the humanities and the arts.

    C.   Incorrect. Chicago is preferred in the social sciences and history.

    D.   Incorrect. Turabian is used in history and theological studies.

26)

    A.   Incorrect. APA is preferable for education, psychology, and the social sciences.

    B.   Incorrect. MLA is preferred in the humanities and the arts.

    C.   Incorrect. Chicago is preferred in the social sciences and history.

    D.   **Correct.** Turabian is used in history and theological studies.

27)

    A.   Incorrect. Computer programs are constantly evolving.

    B.   Incorrect. Spell-checker cannot always detect context.

    C.   **Correct.** Spell-checkers are helpful tools, but writers should edit their papers in addition to using any tools.

    D.   Incorrect. Spell-checkers cannot always distinguish proper context.

28)

    A.   Incorrect. If an accident caused hearing trouble, the musician who suffered from it was hearing *badly*. The adverbial form is required to describe the verb phrase *was hearing*, meaning that he or she was temporarily poorly skilled in the art of hearing.

    B.   Incorrect. *Irregardless* is non-standard; the sentence should begin with the word *regardless*.

    C.   Incorrect. A *moral* is a lesson; *morale* is a general mood or attitude.

    D.   **Correct.** *Quotations* is a noun acting as the direct object of *had*. *Quotes* is a verb.

29)

    A.   **Correct.** As a noun, *principal* means *the head of a school*; as an adjective, *principal* means *main* or *most important*.

    B.   Incorrect. *Should of* is incorrect. The correct wording is *should have*.

    C.   Incorrect. Both verbs must appear in the infinitive form; one (*to survive*) is acting as a prepositional phrase modifying the other (*to try*).

    D.   Incorrect. *Very unique* is redundant. *Unique* should be used alone here: if something is unique, it is automatically superlative.

30)

    A.   Incorrect. Instructors should never make an assumption that all students who come from a variety of backgrounds will share an understanding of any issue.

    B.   **Correct.** Some students may come from backgrounds or cultures where syllabi are not used and will thus be unfamiliar with them.

    C.   Incorrect. In some cultures, making eye contact with an authority figure is not respectful.

    D.   Incorrect. Not all cultures may find the same references humorous.

31)

    A.   Incorrect. Some cultures encourage conformity even if a student does not fully understand a situation or concept; agreeing with the instructor does not necessarily mean a student understands the instructor.

    B.   Incorrect. Some cultures place a higher priority on family than education.

    C.   **Correct.** This statement is true; in some cultures, a student may not be considered late even if he or she arrives ten minutes after class is scheduled to begin.

    D.   Incorrect. Students from some backgrounds may regard helping each other as practicing academic integrity.

32)

    A.   **Correct.** *Collaborative learning* is shared creation and/or learning discovery. Collaborative learning may take place online or in person.

    B.   Incorrect. *Appropriation* in learning diversification means that individuals and groups acquire knowledge from the world around them.

    C.   Incorrect. In *distance education*, students learn online processes through structured instruction, not in a physical classroom.

    D.   Incorrect. *Constructivism* implies that students do not simply absorb knowledge but that they construct knowledge based on present and past knowledge and experience.

33)

    A.   Incorrect. *Artificial intelligence* refers to tools that exhibit human intelligence and behavior (like robots).

    B.   Incorrect. In distance education, students learn online processes through structured instruction, not in a physical classroom.

    C.   **Correct.** *Cyberspace* describes the virtually shared universe of the world's computer network where learning takes place in a global space.

    D.   Incorrect. *Fiber optics* are simply a vehicle for the transmission of data more efficiently and rapidly.

34)

A. Incorrect. *Just-in-time learning* is immediately providing information to people in language that they understand.

B. Incorrect. *Experiential learning* is learning by doing.

C. Correct. *Metacognition* is thinking about one's own thinking.

D. Incorrect. *Local knowledge systems* refers to the framework for interpreting and constructing meaning from one's own local surroundings and oral tradition.

35)

A. Incorrect. A *server* is a computer that provides a service across a network from login to file access.

B. Incorrect. *Metacognition* is thinking about one's own thinking.

C. Incorrect. *Surfing the net* describes scanning anything on the Internet (like news, forums, or blogs).

D. Correct. *Open learning* describes instructional systems that are under the control of the learner.

WRITING, SPEAKING, AND LISTENING

1)

    A.   Incorrect. Focused freewriting may involve writing across many topics.

    B.   **Correct.** The key to success in brainstorming is the listing of related ideas.

    C.   Incorrect. Mapping/clustering involves visually illustrating a number of topics related to a main idea.

    D.   Incorrect. No writing takes place during the incubation process.

2)

    A.   Incorrect. Focused freewriting helps the writer concentrate more on a particular topic or idea.

    B.   Incorrect. Journaling emphasizes documenting ideas, dreams, thoughts, opinions, and experiences.

    C.   Incorrect. Mapping/clustering involves visually illustrating a number of topics related to a main idea.

    D.   **Correct.** Freewriting engages a writer non-stop for a designated period of time, during which he or she transcribes anything that comes to mind.

3)

    A.   **Correct.** Collaborative writing strategies include peer review and peer writing.

    B.   Incorrect. Clustering visually illustrates a number of topics related to a main idea.

    C.   Incorrect. No writing takes place during the incubation process.

    D.   Incorrect. Journaling emphasizes documenting ideas, dreams, thoughts, opinions, and experiences on an ongoing basis.

4)

    A.   Incorrect. Writers use diaries to record daily and current events.

    B.   Incorrect. Writers use idea books to jot down specific writing ideas as they come to mind.

    C.   **Correct.** Journaling is for more in-depth writing about ideas, dreams, thoughts, opinions, and experiences.

    D.   Incorrect. Focused freewriting occurs in a limited amount of time.

5)

    A.   **Correct.** Once the research question is defined, it will drive the entire research project.

B.   Incorrect. The outline will direct the drafting stage of writing.

C.   Incorrect. By the drafting stage, the writer is more concerned with writing than research.

D.   Incorrect. Searching the Internet may be part of the research process, but it should not be the driving factor.

6)

A.   Incorrect. The thesis drives the entire essay.

B.   Correct. The topic sentence for each paragraph introduces the idea that the paragraph will discuss.

C.   Incorrect. The drafting stage addresses writing the entire document; it does not unify the content within each paragraph.

D.   Incorrect. The outline drives the overall direction of the essay.

7)

A.   Incorrect. Editing does not necessarily involve rewriting.

B.   Incorrect. Planning takes place before writing begins.

C.   Incorrect. Proofreading addresses final errors and is the last stage of the writing process.

D.   Correct. Revising includes cutting, adding, deleting, and moving words and sentences to enhance the quality of the document.

8)

A.   Incorrect. Editing involves more than just a final read; editing involves a grammar and punctuation check.

B.   Incorrect. Planning takes place before writing begins.

C.   Correct. Proofreading addresses final errors and is the last stage of the writing process.

D.   Incorrect. Revising includes cutting, adding, deleting, and moving words and sentences to enhance the quality of the document.

9)

A.   Correct. Editing usually involves a grammar and punctuation checklist.

B.   Incorrect. Planning takes place before writing begins.

C.   Incorrect. Proofreading addresses final errors and is the last stage of the writing process.

D.   Incorrect. Revising includes cutting, adding, deleting, and moving words and sentences to enhance the quality of the document.

10)

A. Incorrect. Coherence is the smooth flow of words and ideas throughout a writing task.

B. Incorrect. Development is the way a writer arranges the details in a writing task.

C. Correct. Unity results when one main idea shapes and controls the content of each paragraph.

D. Incorrect. Mapping is a visual aid in pre-writing.

11)

A. Incorrect. In critical writing, writers form arguments to respond to debatable topics.

B. Incorrect. Journalism relates the news, current events, or some types of personal narratives.

C. Incorrect. Academic writing is most appropriate for research, critical analyses, and providing educational information.

D. Correct. Technical writers train to create websites; many technical writers begin small companies to help individuals launch their websites.

12)

A. Correct. In critical writing, writers form arguments to respond to debatable topics.

B. Incorrect. Creative writing usually involves working on a literary piece like a script, a poem, a short story, or a novel.

C. Incorrect. Literary journalism (or creative nonfiction) records the facts of a particular situation while employing literary story-telling devices.

D. Incorrect. Technical writing focuses on manuals, computer terminology, website design, and instructional intent.

13)

A. Incorrect. Creative writing usually involves working on a literary piece like a script, a poem, a short story, or a novel.

B. Correct. Academic writing is most appropriate for research, critical analyses, and providing educational information.

C. Incorrect. Journalism relates the news, current events, or some types of personal narratives.

D. Incorrect. Technical writing focuses on manuals, computer terminology, website design, and instructional intent.

14)

A.   Incorrect. Categorizing a piece of writing determines what type of text it is; the writing task is the assignment itself, not its characterization.

B.   Correct. The individual assignments are the individual writing tasks.

C.   Incorrect. Writing tasks require much more than a list of specific requirements: they are slotted into categories, audiences, and specific purposes.

D.   Incorrect. Writing tasks are the assignments themselves; the writing process is the framework for accomplishing the task.

15)

A.   Incorrect. In preparation for the drafting process, independent clauses are more helpful in describing the main points in the essay than phrases are.

B.   Correct. The thesis statement, main points, and restatement of thesis in the outline along with sub-points should be consistent in their clausal construction.

C.   Incorrect. Outlines do not include introductory or concluding paragraphs; constructing paragraphs is part of the drafting process. Furthermore, topics are not main points.

D.   Incorrect. Outlines do not include introductory or concluding paragraphs; constructing paragraphs is part of the drafting process.

16)

A.   Incorrect. Active voice is preferable.

B.   Incorrect. Outlines are maps of content; they should not contain specific details.

C.   Incorrect. Third person pronouns are preferable.

D.   Correct. Consistency is key.

17)

A.   Incorrect. To see is to believe.

B.   Incorrect. The scientist's goal was both teaching and traveling.

C.   Correct. The two introductory noun phrases are strictly parallel in their wording and are joined by *and*.

D.   Incorrect. Trisha always has enjoyed and always will enjoy studying literature.

18)

A.   Correct. This digital source is likely a student's paper.

B.   Incorrect. This *.gov* digital source is from the Department of Education; thus it is reliable.

C. Incorrect. An article from the data base *JSTOR* would be reliable as it has undergone peer review.

D. Incorrect. The American Psychological Association would provide reliable digital sources.

19)

A. Incorrect. A general search will not yield a reliable digital source simply by popularity.

B. **Correct.** A bibliography that includes peer reviewed articles would make a digital source more credible.

C. Incorrect. A recent date does not necessarily mean a source is reliable.

D. Incorrect. A website that ends with *.org* may or may not be reliable.

20)

A. Incorrect. A well-known periodical is a credible source.

B. Incorrect. An established encyclopedia set is a credible source.

C. **Correct.** A gossip magazine like *People* Magazine would not be considered a credible source.

D. Incorrect. An informative textbook is a credible source.

21)

A. Incorrect. A well-known periodical is a credible print source.

B. **Correct.** A well-known advocacy group for animals with a possible bias is not a credible print source.

C. Incorrect. A well-known novel may be a credible print source for a literary paper.

D. Incorrect. A style guide is a credible print source.

22)

A. **Correct.** Introductions within the text lend credibility to the author(s) or the source's origins; the in-text citations are crucial to identify and to connect the source to a reference page or works cited page; and the listing of sources correlates all of the sources used or consulted within a text.

B. Incorrect. Not all writing styles use footnotes.

C. Incorrect. Authors and dates are in the in-text citation.

D. Incorrect. Again, not all styles use footnotes.

23)

A. **Correct.** The dates of the Civil War are widely known and do not need documentation.

B. Incorrect. This type of study requires documentation.

C. Incorrect. Survey results require documentation.

D. Incorrect. A police report of this nature would need documentation.

24)

A. Incorrect. Plagiarism can indeed destroy a student's reputation; however, there is a worse consequence listed among these answer choices.

B. Incorrect. Plagiarism can and does ruin academic careers, but a worse consequence is listed among these answer choices.

C. **Correct.** Poor quality medical research, including plagiarism, could result in consequences as severe as loss of life.

D. Incorrect. Lawsuits and other severe consequences result from plagiarism; however, worse consequences are possible.

25)

A. **Correct.** A speaker may be charismatic and sincere, but at minimum, an outline is necessary to ensure that all details are addressed. Listeners may become irritated if they sense that a speaker is disorganized.

B. Incorrect. Clarity of motive will drive the speech emotionally.

C. Incorrect. When developing a speech, using a visual map will help ensure that pertinent information is not missing or otherwise ignored.

D. Incorrect. Practicing with a live audience is invaluable in speech preparation, providing an opportunity for constructive criticism.

26)

A. Incorrect. Looking just above the crowd will not help the speaker to connect with the audience. After a while, listeners may wonder what is in the back of the room.

B. Incorrect. Like looking just above the crowd, listeners may wonder what is in the back of the room. An audience is very perceptive and aware of a speaker's eyes.

C. **Correct.** Whenever a speaker faces an audience, he or she should make direct eye contact with its members. Eye contact is not synonymous with staring, but scanning the faces of an audience captures listeners' attention.

D. Incorrect. This is distracting to an audience.

27)

A. **Correct.** Conciseness does not necessarily refer to length; rather, it refers to the most succinct expression of ideas.

B. Incorrect. Being concise means being succinct. The most succinct phrasing may not be the shortest (although it frequently is).

C. Incorrect. Concise wording should be clear, but redundancy is not necessarily unclear.

D. Incorrect. Clichés tend to complicate things and are never preferable in academic writing.

28)

A. Incorrect. Redundancies are not necessarily fallacious.

B. **Correct.** Logical fallacies result when reasoning is based on questionable assumptions.

C. Incorrect. Emphases can add variety to writing.

D. Incorrect. Sentence patterns do not typically relate to questionable assumptions.

29)

A. Incorrect. Hasty generalizations are based on insufficient evidence.

B. **Correct.** A rotting fish is not analogous to a position of leadership.

C. Incorrect. There is no real conclusion here, only a reason.

D. Incorrect. This statement does not involve two events happening at the same time.

30)

A. Incorrect. This statement does not build an argument based on its popularity.

B. Incorrect. This statement does not emphasize one side of an argument and suppress the other.

C. Incorrect. The speaker has not introduced an unrelated topic to distract the listener.

D. **Correct.** The speaker has introduced a false dilemma: he can care about corruption or taxes, but not both.

31)

A. Incorrect. A written test would not adequately assess a student's learning acquisition in a genre like drama, which involves physical and oral activity.

B. Incorrect. An oral presentation would not adequately assess a student's learning acquisition in a genre like drama, which involves physical activity and some literary knowledge.

C.   Incorrect. A critical analysis paper would not adequately assess a student's learning acquisition in a genre like drama, which involves physical and oral activity.

D.   Correct. This choice would adequately assess a student's learning acquisition in a genre like drama; it addresses both physical and oral activity and literary dexterity.

32)

A.   Incorrect. Language modelling naturally provides students with direct exposure to speaking techniques.

B.   Incorrect. Speaking workshops allow students to personally and immediately improve their public speaking skills.

C.   Correct. Blogs offer many resources for public speaking tools, but do not provide the opportunities for hands-on practice in public speaking that other teaching strategies do.

D.   Incorrect. University writing centers offer peer support in speech writing and practice, giving students direct, hands-on experience in the process.

33)

A.   Incorrect. Wikis may have pictures, but they rely primarily on text.

B.   Correct. Visual thinking maps are terrific for communicating a message in pictures.

C.   Incorrect. PowerPoint slides may use pictures, but visual thinking maps provide more information about the relationships between images.

D.   Incorrect. Digital publications have pictures, but they require additional media to maximize communication.

34)

A.   Correct. To assess students accurately, it is most important to utilize an assessment aligned with whatever objective was assigned.

B.   Incorrect. Assessing may not involve a learning management system at all.

C.   Incorrect. Assessing may not always involve a rubric.

D.   Incorrect. Assessing may not involve a test.

35)

A.   Incorrect. A test would assess only a narrow segment of what may have been learned on the tour.

B.   Incorrect. The bulk of the input might come from other collaborators, making it difficult to assess the individual student's experience.

C.   Correct. The student could create a portfolio not only for the assessment, but also to use in future job applications or to present in job interviews.

D.   Incorrect. This assessment would only require a rudimentary recollection of the events of the tour.

36)

A.   Incorrect. A written test will not address all elements of speech and thus will not properly assess the student.

B.   Correct. This task would provide an excellent summative assessment for this AP class because it requires sustained speaking, the formation of an argument, and the effective use of visual aids.

C.   Incorrect. Collaborative efforts may be effective learning strategies, but they are not useful for summative assessments of individual students.

D.   Incorrect. A learning game is likely too casual a format for a summative assessment.

37)

A.   Incorrect. Objective assessment helps both the student and the teacher understand and administer grades.

B.   Incorrect. Comprehensive rubrics reduce misunderstandings and questions about final grades.

C.   Incorrect. If teachers find it difficult to create various rubrics, they can often be downloaded for free from the Internet.

D.   Correct. Personal comments may be ambiguous and subjective. Rubrics provide objectivity.

38)

A.   Correct. A rubric should be designed so that the students receive credit for what they did correctly and for the effort demonstrated in the assignment.

B.   Incorrect. The rubric must address the effort of the student in some way.

C.   Incorrect. Content must not be weighted the same as a comma error, for example. So a rubric should be designed in such a way that skills are weighted by their importance.

D.   Incorrect. Along with weighted sections, the mathematical deductions should be clear for each item.

39)

A.   Incorrect. A student may need dialogue in addition to the rubric.

B.   Incorrect. A student needs encouragement and suggestions for growth.

C.   Correct. This combination provides useful feedback.

D.   Incorrect. An instructor may be hesitant or overbearing in a personal conversation alone; a rubric supplies the student with supplementary objective data.

40)

    A.   Incorrect. Even though constructive criticism may come across negatively, it may help the teacher improve the course.

    B.   **Correct.** Outlier statements are not useful.

    C.   Incorrect. Revealing misunderstandings early in a course helps improve it for the remainder of the semester.

    D.   Incorrect. Feedback every week or two may expose a misunderstanding that could avert a catastrophe close to the end of the course. Periodic feedback is a good thing for both educators and learners.

41)

    A.   Incorrect. Active voice is usually a specific requirement.

    B.   Incorrect. The purpose of a writing task is an overarching requirement.

    C.   **Correct.** The writer should consider the reception of the audience, but it is not usually a specific requirement.

    D.   Incorrect. The length of the paper is definitely a specific requirement.

42)

    A.   Incorrect. This is true; generally, a sense of completion characterizes a good conclusion.

    B.   Incorrect. Again, this is true. A lengthy thesis may require that the main points be reiterated.

    C.   **Correct.** Generally, audiences desire a sense of completion.

    D.   Incorrect. This is true of a conclusion. If writers try to manipulate readers with strong emotion, for example, the readers may be turned off.

43)

    A.   Incorrect. Transitions can become irritating and distracting for an audience.

    B.   Incorrect. Providing the audience with handouts depicting detailed graphics like bar graphs would be more beneficial than placing the graph up on the screen.

    C.   Incorrect. Like transitions, too many photos can overwhelm an audience.

    D.   **Correct.** Presentation software like PowerPoint should support the speaker, not replace him or her.

44)

    A.   Incorrect. To comment on various elements is to discuss.

    B.   **Correct.** *To explain* means to interpret complexities.

    C.   Incorrect. Arranging into groups is classification.

    D.   Incorrect. *To defend* is to provide reasons supporting one side of an issue.

45)

A.   Incorrect. A lab report is factual, not creative.

B.   Correct. Academic writing refers to research, education, and criticism, not basic information.

C.   Incorrect. Journalism uses factual sources and generally includes interviews, reviews, and updates to provide information. On the other hand, a lab report describes the hypothesis, procedure, and conclusion of a laboratory experiment.

D.   Incorrect. A lab report is not intended to persuade the reader; it is the presentation of an experiment and its results.

46)

A.   Incorrect. While the poet would be presenting creative work, an introduction to the poet and his or her work would not be creative.

B.   Incorrect. Academic writing refers to research, education, and criticism, not basic information.

C.   Incorrect. Argumentative writing aims to persuade the reader of a position or perspective. An introduction provides expository information about its subject.

D.   Correct. Introductions provide expository information to the audience, giving listeners more information about the subject (here, the poet and his or her background and work).

47)

A.   Incorrect. A journal may provide a narrative of an experience, but it would also likely contain factual information such as ideas and feelings. Journals offer more than just recounting of experiences.

B.   Incorrect. Journalism uses factual sources and generally includes interviews, reviews, and updates. A personal journal is a record of ideas, experiences, and emotions.

C.   Incorrect. In critical writing, writers form arguments to respond to debatable topics. Such writing may appear in personal journals as ideas, but journals are not purely critical responses to topics or events and are not for public consumption.

D.   Correct. A journal provides a place for a writer to informally record his or her own thoughts, experiences, emotions, and ideas, without regard for an audience or readership. It is nonfiction, albeit informal. While the writer may choose to be creative, the purpose of a journal is not to write fiction.

48)

    A.   Incorrect. Details can provide logical reasoning supporting an argument; however, this answer choice does not explain how details can benefit all writing tasks—it only addresses argumentative writing.

    B.   Incorrect. Again, while providing details makes writing more engaging for the reader, details and examples are not necessarily only used to generate interest in the text.

    C.   Incorrect. While details may provide credibility by providing examples or references, making it more convincing, they serve other purposes as well. There is a better answer choice here.

    D.   **Correct.** Details add depth to writing, making it interesting, convincing, *and* credible. RENNS (Reasons, Examples, Names, Numbers, and Senses) is a helpful acronym for writers to remember useful types of details.

Follow the link below to take your second Praxis English Language Arts: Content Knowledge (5038) practice test and to access other online study resources:

www.cirrustestprep.com/praxis-5038-online-resources

Made in the USA
Coppell, TX
19 September 2021